Farm Recipes
and
Food Secrets
from the
Norske Nook

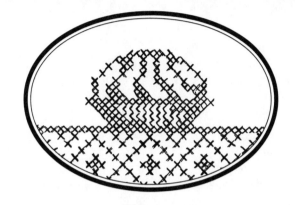

Farm Recipes

and

Food Secrets

from the

Norske Nook

 The Midwest's #1 Roadside Cafe

Helen Myhre with Mona Vold

Crown Publishers, Inc.
New York

Published by Crown Publishers, Inc.
201 East 50th Street
New York, New York 10022
Member of the Crown Publishing Group

Random House, Inc., New York, Toronto, London,
Sydney, Auckland

CROWN is a trademark of Crown Publishers, Inc.

Manufactured in the United States of America

Design by Nancy Kenmore

Instructional illustrations by J. Runions and
decorative drawings by Joy Sikorski

Library of Congress Cataloging-in-Publication Data
Myhre, Helen.
Farm recipes and food secrets from the Norske Nook :
the Midwest's #1 roadside cafe / by Helen Myhre with
Mona Vold.—1st ed.
Includes index.
1. Cookery. 2. Norske Nook (Restaurant) I. Vold,
Mona.
TX714.M94 1992
641.5′09775′49—dc20   92-12628   CIP
ISBN 0-517-58550-2

10 9 8 7 6 5 4 3 2 1

First Edition

To those farm women who
still know how to serve up
a good roast dinner
on Sunday

CONTENTS

Contents

ACKNOWLEDGMENTS

From HELEN MYHRE

Over the years farm women have been the able cooks, bakers, and waitresses that I employed in the Norske Nook. Without them I couldn't have kept the Nook going, and it wouldn't have the same flavor and feel that it continues to have today. There is such a thing as real home cooking that has been the Nook tradition, and with help from farm and hometown women, I worked to keep that tradition alive. I extend my thanks to them. I also want to recognize Jerry Berchard, my new colleague who I know I can count on to carry on as I would.

Special thank-yous to Lorraine Eide; my daughters Beverly, Nancy, and Ellen; my sons, Dennis, Larry, and Craig; my mother, Golga Lundberg; Marion Chappelle; and my husband, Ernie.

And of course, thank you to our agent Malaga Baldi, and to our editor Joyce Engelson, and to Mona Vold, a farm girl who came home to help me write this.

From MONA VOLD

Without Joyce Engelson, this book would not be what it is. I was told I would find it a blessing to have her as an editor. I learned well why, and I'm forever grateful.

Our agent, Malaga Baldi, handled this project with great energy and grace from the beginning, and I thank her.

I also want to thank at Crown production editor Andrea Connolly and designer Nancy Kenmore for their great efforts on our behalf.

Helen, in addition to her good humor and cooking secrets, gives the best lesson in being no one but herself, always.

Lorraine Eide, like Helen, is someone everyone should meet. Her long hours of help on this project made not only this book but also my life better.

The following people also helped with this work in their many different ways, and I thank them: Rita Speicher; Sharon Lehtinen; Evelyn C. White; Laurie Blakeney; Jane Miller; Beth Woods; Irene Myers; Alice Ruckert; Chet Maug; Selma, Leonard, Jane, and Merlin Brown; Tammy Smith-Schroeder; David Ernat; Norm Bunderson; Adeline Nelson; Arlie Schwoch; Diane Weber and Nancy Coffee at the Extension office; Vold's Inc.; Earl, Chuck, and Dennis at the post office; Jerry Berchard and the Norske Nook; EDP Computers; and Pat and his sons at Pat's Country Meat Market. Thanks also to Helen's children, especially her daughter Bev; and, of course, her husband, Ernie, and her mother, Golga; my family, Steven, Scott, Kelly, Trevor, Cheryl, Aaron, Lynn, Kay, and the lights of our lives, Stephen Luke and Matthew Aaron. Also, Marlin, Henry, Hodd, and John Lester.

I'm grateful for and to my parents, Lester and Ester, true farm people who give me all they have in life and are always steadfast and willing.

Finally, I want to thank Peter Manso—my challenge and comfort.

ME *and the* NORSKE NOOK,
the Restaurant in Osseo, Wisconsin

If folks had told me years ago that I'd own a restaurant and then that *Esquire* magazine would call it "one of the USA's ten best," that it'd be featured on "NBC Nightly News" and in the *New York Times,* and that I'd have to teach that crazy David Letterman how to make a pie, I'd have done nothing but run around in circles wondering how I'd ever make that come about!

I was a farm wife. And for years, I lived the life of most farm wives. I cooked and canned and baked, cared for the house and kids, sewed, fed the pigs, tended a garden, milked the cows, drove a tractor for haying and harvest. I'd been a farm daughter, and at thirteen, I hired out as a kitchen hand to other farm women. Then at sixteen, I cooked for a country minister and his wife until I married a farmer three years later. Not until 1967, when I was nearing forty, and four of my six children were grown, did I take work off the farm, at a drive-in root-beer stand.

Five P.M., after all the day chores were done, I'd drive to work and work until four in the morning as a waitress, dishwasher, and cook—every week I peeled six hundred pounds of potatoes. Then in 1973, although I was denied a bank loan, I found enough backing to buy one of Osseo, Wisconsin's, three restaurants. Because I, like most of the rest of the town, was Norwegian or some kind of Scandinavian, I renamed the small cafe the Norske Nook ("Norwegian Corner") for the lively little group of retired Norwegian farmers who came in at the same time every day and sat in the same corner for their morning coffee (I've included a few of my Scandinavian recipes in the book for you, too). Anyway, I took over and soon became the target of gossip: "Who does she think she is?" "She won't last six months." "She knows nothing about business."

Today some of those same townspeople complain and fuss: "There's never nowhere to park," "There're strangers standin' all the way to Buster's Barber Shop," "Helicopters are landin' in the church parking lot." But most in Osseo are happy for the cars from Texas, New York, Idaho, Louisiana, Florida, Maine, California. Those strangers help us keep alive what would otherwise be just another dying Midwest farm town.

People sometimes say it's a phenomenon, all this traffic and success here in the heart of cow country, but for me, I just took what I knew best—plain farm cooking. My husband, Ernie, was milking cows and wanted nothing to do with a restaurant so I was on my own, and the first two years, believe me, I barely made it because I hated to charge people. I never charged sales tax, I absorbed those costs, trying to make up to people because when you're in the country, and you're cooking for everybody, you just say "help yourself," and I thought, Terrible to cook and have somebody pay for it.

Even today, after all the attention, it's hard for me to think there's anything great about this. It's just working every day, it's just what you do. Only when I stop a minute, then it can seem unreal—Jane and Michael Stern, Willard Scott, Charles Kuralt, the publicity, the people, and this tiny town. I start to wonder to myself, Are my pies and cooking really that good? Sometimes I still think, They're just saying that to be nice.

But, of course, luck too had a hand in it. I thank my lucky stars we had a few pieces of Sour Cream Raisin Pie and Carrot Cake left the evening the Sterns happened by back in 1976. I'd never heard of them so their names meant nothing to me when one of my waitresses came back to the kitchen and said, "Some people out there want to know if they can put a writeup in their book." "Couldn't hurt," I said, and I didn't think any more of it. But some months later, the writeup of the Norske Nook came out in the Sterns' *Roadfood*, and it was shortly after that that *Esquire* picked up on us as having "some of the best pies and cakes in the world." That's when, as my assistant Lorraine Eide says, "all hell broke loose."

Besides meats and gravies, soups, sandwiches, vegetables, cakes, tortes, cookies, doughnuts, and seasonal specials, we were quickly up to baking 75, then 100, then more than 150 pies a day in the summer and 75 a day from December to March, the off-season. My fingers have flown over pie dough while Lorraine's stirred up enough meringue to clothe a mountain. Her whisk is getting pretty worn, and the rolling pin I use isn't completely level anymore. Even the pie table we stand over has a visible dip where the crusts have been rolled.

But through it all, I've had something steadier than luck—good help. Like Lorraine, my other three main cooks are farm women with decades of practical experience. One is seventy-seven; the others are sixty-six and fifty-five years old. Though we laugh and joke about such foolishness as fishing for North Sea lutefisk in Lake Martha, we all grew up with the old farm ethic "You work hard, then you work harder."

In the seventeen years before I started this book, I never had a vacation until Lorraine and I went out to be on the David Letterman show. We left the restaurant at four thirty in the afternoon, got our hair done, and drove two hours to the airport in Minneapolis. At two A.M., like two lost lambs, we checked into one of those tall Manhattan hotels, filmed the show later that afternoon, and were back in the restaurant by eight the next morning stirring up meringue and rolling crusts. I never felt I should be away, because I've always sampled all of what's served, day in and day out. I've thought of it as farming: If the same person doesn't milk the cows, the cows don't produce.

That's one thing that crossed my mind when I was riding down those big streets in New York in that limo. It's sure a good thing no one there gets it in their head to start a fad and raise their own cows. All that noise and soot, the poor things would never give milk; they'd have a nervous breakdown. And something else Lorraine and I couldn't get over—all those people and they never say hi or even bother to wave to each other. But the studio people for Letterman were as good as gold. A couple of 'em called me aside afterward and said I stole the show the way people were laughing at how I ordered Mr. Letterman around.

But then I got back home, and Hilda Fuller said to me, "Twenty million people watching, why didn't you think to mention Osseo?" And Ester Johnson wondered if I hadn't maybe been just a little too much of a boss for such a popular show. But I had a job to do. I had six minutes to teach that character how to make a pie, and the stage director told me, "Watch out, David'll do anything to distract you." So when he started asking me about this and that and the Green Bay Packers, I put the rolling pin right to him and said, "Come on now, we're out here to make pie."

Most folks said it was good I was just my everyday self, but that's how it is with anything, you can't get too nervous or too confident. You just do what you do because you like it no matter who believes in you or doubts you, and that's got to be enough.

That's just how I am about cholesterol. I know I use enough butter and sugar to make a cardiologist swoon, but I figure my customers, like the rest of us, have heard a two-ton-truck's load of warnings about the stuff. And whether they've changed their daily habits or not, when they come into the restaurant I figure they've thrown cholesterol to the wind, for that day anyway, and have decided they're going to enjoy a piece of pie or some other farm food, so if I'm going to serve it to 'em, it's going to be the best I can make it. And for me that means lots of butter. Besides, as far as I can see, the verdict's still out on cholesterol. It's not unusual for people around here to be active through their eighties and into their nineties. To die in your seventies is young. On the farm, if we're busy, we eat these butter-filled recipes, not once, but six times a day, and we're still standin' where the sun shines. Of course, maybe it's because we are so active!

(Only once, when I catered a meal for a terminally ill man on a very restricted diet, has a stick of margarine been in the restaurant.) If you want anything to taste good, you have to use butter. And fresh, quality ingredients.

The salesmen call me a bitcher sometimes. I won't change, and I never go for bargains. I want first-rate stuff, and if I don't get it, I call 'em up. The salesmen say, "Helen, why don't you save yourself some labor and buy this frozen stuff, it's just as good, you just pop it in the oven."

I say, "Nah, I've always done it this way, and they're eating it."

One even wanted me to buy pies. He said, "You need a vacation."

I said, "Nah, I don't go anyplace anyway."

As my grandma liked to say, "Unless you're the queen, you don't get somethin' for nothin' when it comes to effort." So you won't find too many modern-day shortcuts here, just good old reliable country recipes.

Like my cooks, I grew up in an era when

women gathered in neighbors' kitchens to cook and bake for threshing crews or in church basements to prepare a supper in honor of the harvest or to raise money for a family whose barn burned down. We all learned to cook from women who could judge a perfectly seasoned roast by the smell in the kitchen, folks who knew the "feel" of a tender crust and the "look" of quality ingredients. Their eggs were fresh from the henhouse; their cream, thick and still warm. Their meat, a pig, chicken, or cow butchered out back; their fruit, fresh from a berry patch or orchard just up the road.

Daughters learned from mothers, aunts, grandmas, greatgrandmas, and godmothers. Recipes weren't so much on paper as in your head—a handful of this, throw in some of that—or maybe you had a few notes scribbled on the back of a Ladies' Aid bulletin, a funeral remembrance, or high-school band program as a reminder. That's what this book is. I spent a year putting down what was in my head, perusing grease- and coffee-stained jottings, deciphering how many cups of sugar or flour had been scrawled over "The Lord is my shepherd . . ."

I don't know who through the years made me an expert, but there're days I've had to go to the phone five, six times with doughy hands. People even from Hawaii call for recipes and tips, and I think to myself, Good Gosh! I can only say to them as I do to the salesmen, "Well, this is what I do, and they're eatin' it." But it got to be so many calls and letters, and you hate to say no, I started to think it'd be easier if it were all in a book. But I never got to it, I just kept cooking and rolling crusts. Then after the *New York Times* piece, and David Letter-

man, Mona Vold called. She's a writer but she grew up as a farm girl herself, just north of town. She said, "Helen, it's time now." And I knew she was right. I was no spring chicken, I wouldn't be gettin' any younger; so I agreed, if she would help me.

And anyway, I'd started to see some things out here that were grabbing at my heart. Even if you're in the city, you've read it in the paper for years: "One family farm lost every ten minutes." "Landless farmers stand in line for government cheese, dried milk, and butter." It's no longer news, just old hat. But valley to valley we still hear the auctioneers' voices; we see the boarded-up store windows, deserted farmhouses, back roads gone to dirt.

Oh, there've always been hard times on the farm, what with the weather and giant machines. A husband's leg is mangled in the power take-off, a child wanders into the high corn and hides in the path of a combine, ceaseless rain drowns budding fields, drought cracks the soil so deep it turns to dust and blows off to Ohio. Because we're poised for such punishing blows, we've been awful good at taking the small ones. A crop fails—"we'll raise more next year." Market prices fall—"we'll work harder, we'll ride it out." That's farm people.

But the 1980s, and these first years of the '90s, have been a holy fright. Many good folks just haven't been able to hold on. Oh, we still have more cows than people here in most rural areas. Our corn still grows right up side the churchyard, and our oats border the school and Little League fields. We still visit with our neighbors, wave even to strangers, and sleep with our doors unlocked. True to tradition, those who remain work hard, then harder, believing things will turn around. Only in quiet moments do we stop to wonder, with more of our neighbors gone and other states now with new "factory farms" that milk two thousand cows three times a day, if maybe our age-old way of life might disappear.

That's why I got to thinking. The farm and its lessons have made me a good living these years in the restaurant. Like you do to the land in spring, I wanted to give something back.

Years ago on wash days, town ladies used to really fuss with how they hung their clothes on the clothesline. "You can always tell a woman by her line," they'd say. But us farm women, we were usually in such a hurry we strung 'em up every which way. Instead, we were judged by our food. That's how I hope it is with these pages: That with my recipes and old-fashioned, sometimes wacky, hints not only will you be able to make the pie or cake or roast and gravy you ate in the restaurant but you might also get a sense of the women, the land, and way of life that have taught me.

But now just one more thing before you charge off to preheat the oven. Some people think if you can follow a recipe, you can cook. But for heaven's sakes, you gotta have some sense. Recipes aren't just formulas. You have to get to know how things should look and feel. You have to dig in. You use your hands. Hands were made before anything else, and as long as they're washed and clean, they're as important as butter to good food.

FARM RECIPES

and

FOOD SECRETS

from the

NORSKE NOOK

BREADS, ROLLS,

and

SWEET DOUGH
TREATS

My grandmother would talk about what a rough time some of the immigrants had when they first came to these parts. Before they got their crops going, they were lucky if they had milk instead of water for their porridge, and there was hardly ever any butter or lard to waste on the bread. Many times the only furniture was a bench set beside a wood-burning stove. But no matter how little those women had, or how awfully barren their kitchens, there was usually a wooden bowl or heavy crock with yeast working—a treasured, cloudy concoction set aside for when there'd be grain, and they could bake bread.

I remember my grandmother making bread from "everlasting yeast." It was kept in a fruit jar in the basement. It would work and work, then when she would bake, she'd measure out a certain amount for the batch, leave a little in the jar for seed, and add lukewarm potato water and a scant bit of sugar. If the precious stuff stopped working for some reason—if it got too hot or one of the kids broke the jar—she was in a pickle. She'd have to hike to the neighbor's and borrow.

Bread and yeast were so central to our lives, even in my day, I don't think there was a farm woman around who didn't bake ten to twenty loaves a week, depending on the size of her family. In summer, with extra field hands to feed, we'd bake even more.

When I think back, it seems it must have been a lot with all our other work, but we didn't pay it much mind, it was just what we did. That's why you won't find much that's fancy here. I've experimented now and then through the years, but I've found nothing that beats these good old-fashioned, simple country breads.

Hints

• Today, there are two kinds of yeast: the active dry yeast that comes in small packages and the baker's yeast, which is a compressed, moist cake. Either type will work for these recipes, but I prefer the compressed cake. I don't feel dry yeast works as well, and I think it also tends to give too strong a yeast flavor.

• If you're buying caked yeast at the store, get an eight-ounce package, slice it up into six pieces, use what you need for the recipe, wrap the unused pieces individually in plastic wrap, and put them in the freezer. In these recipes, one and one-third ounces of caked yeast means one of these six pieces. One of these pieces equals one package of dry yeast.

• When dissolving yeast, always remember to put about one teaspoon of sugar into the lukewarm water or milk. It helps to get the yeast working so the dough will raise. If you forget, you'll be singing "Pass the biscuits, Mirandy," or something like it, to ease your mind because you'll have one heavy clump if the yeast doesn't work.

• Be sure when soaking the yeast and the sugar in a little dish or cup that the water or milk is only lukewarm, not too hot. Test it on your wrist as you would baby's milk. If the liquid is too hot, it will kill the yeast, and the bread won't raise.

• The yeast will form a foam on top when it's ready to use (usually five minutes). When mixing together all the liquid, the yeast, sugar, salt, and eggs (if the recipe calls for eggs), at first add only one-quarter of the amount of flour called for, then mix everything well with a spoon. The batter should be stringy like thick elastic (so elastic that it wants to slide off the spoon). At that point, add more flour until it's too thick to stir. Remove the dough from the bowl, lay it on a floured board or table, and knead it by pushing it with the palms of your hands. After every push, bring the dough back toward you, gather up the sides, and push again. (If you don't know how to knead, watch a kitten nursing.) Keep kneading until the dough talks. It will sort of snap and crackle. The more you knead, the finer the texture. Don't use too much flour on the board or the dough will get too stiff, and try not to poke holes in the dough with your fingers. Knead it until it has a silky smoothness and doesn't stick to your hands. And don't forget to give it a spanking (a friendly gesture of mine) before you put it into its greased bowl to raise.

• Some women like to let the dough set ten minutes or so before kneading—they say it lets the ingredients all work together and gives the dough a chance to firm up. But both on the farm and at the restaurant, we're usually in a hurry so we have to plow ahead, and still our bread always turns out okay.

• Flours are goofy today. There are so many different kinds, and they vary so much from brand to brand, it takes more of some and less of others. In these recipes, unless it says otherwise, use all-purpose flour, and kind of watch as you go. Add the flour gradually; you can always add more if you need to; you don't want the dough so sticky you can't handle it.

• Some recipes say to scald the milk. On the farm, we used raw milk so we had to get it so hot it formed a skin. If you are using store-bought milk and don't want to boil it that hard and fast, just heat it well. However, if you do scald it, don't let it scorch and do be sure to remove the skin.

• When you put the dough into the greased bowl to raise, brush the top with soft butter. Treat your dough the way we used to treat our babies. Room temperature for raising should be about 75° F. Cover the dough with a clean cloth or towel and place it on a counter or table away from the drafts of a door or window. If the room is not warm enough, lightly cover the dough with plastic wrap and a cloth and wrap the whole bowl in a large bath towel (but not too tightly, the dough has to have room to raise). Be sure, though, that the warm place you choose isn't stifling hot or the dough will either fall or you'll have a coarse-textured bread from the dough raising too fast.

• Dough can be warmed by the sun as it's raising, if it's not more than 80° F. Use your sense.

• Let dough raise until double in size, then knead down, and let it raise again until double. (My recipes will say "until double in size," but this doesn't have to be *exactly* double; it's not that fussy. But if you've had to wait more than three hours for the dough to double, you've got a flop.) Then divide the dough into sections according to the recipe and put into greased pans to raise again to about one inch above the pan, then bake.

• If the dough seems to take too long to raise, maybe your liquid was too warm or too cold, or your room temperature was too cold. If it fails to raise the amount called for, bake it anyway. Use it for bread pudding or dry it and use it for breadings, stuffings, or croutons. Or feed it to the squirrels and birds. (If it fails to raise at all, forget it.)

• Always brush the tops of your yeast breads and rolls with melted butter when you put the dough into the pans, but do it *before* it raises a final time. Use just enough butter to glaze the top. This adds so much flavor and a golden brown color. Then just as you take it from the oven, brush the tops again with soft butter.

• Remove your bread from the tin to cool. If you leave it in the tin, the bottom will get too moist.

• Remember, homemade bread contains no preservatives, so if you're keeping it for more than a few days, it must be refrigerated.

• All breads freeze well. Just place the individual loaf in a plastic bag, tie it really tight, and throw it into the freezer. When ready to use, let it thaw out in its bag. Unwrapping a cold bag in a warm room will draw moisture and the bread will get wet.

Breads

COMPANY BREAD

In those early days on the farm, my family, like most, didn't get into town much, and it cost money to buy white, refined flour. Farm women usually used flour from their own grain, which they took to the local mill to have ground. It was coarse and unbleached and still contained the wheat germ. But whenever the women got a chance, they'd go into the store and buy a few pounds of white flour. They'd hoard this until a special time—when they knew company was coming, or for a birthday or holiday, then they'd bake a few loaves of white "company" bread.

When we were kids, whenever my mother made this bread, we hung around and begged for a little hunk of dough so we could put it on the top of the wood stove, fry it, and grab it still hot. Sometimes we would beg for brown sugar, but mostly we'd eat it dripping with butter.

MAKES 4 LOAVES
(TO MAKE 2 LOAVES,
CUT BY HALF)

4 cups milk

1/2 cup (1 stick) butter

1 1/3 ounces caked yeast or 1 package dry yeast

1/2 cup lukewarm water

1/4 cup sugar

4 teaspoons salt or a little in hand to scatter
in (depending on taste)

12 cups white flour (or more)

Enough butter to brush tops of loaves

1. Scald the milk (so hot it can burn your finger). Add ½ cup butter and set aside to cool.

2. In a cup or small bowl, mix the yeast with the water and sugar. The yeast will dissolve and form sort of a little foam. (Do not use hot water or it'll burn the yeast, and the bread won't raise.)

3. Pour the milk and butter mixture into a large bowl, and add the salt. Then add the dissolved yeast and 4 cups of the flour. Beat thoroughly until sort of elastic. Add the rest of the flour (8 or 10 cups), whatever it takes for you to knead it on a floured board or table. Knead until it's smooth and spongy.

4. Place the dough in a large greased bowl, brush the top with soft butter, cover with a cloth, and let raise until doubled. Knead down and let raise a second time until double in size.

5. Divide the dough into 4 loaves. Knead each loaf and plop into a greased bread pan. Brush the tops of the loaves with butter. Cover with a cloth, and let the dough raise until it gets about 1 inch over the top of the pans. Meanwhile, preheat the oven to 375° F.

6. Bake 30 to 45 minutes, until golden brown. Remove from the oven, and brush the tops with butter while still warm.

NOTE: For this and all of the yeast breads, check the hints at the beginning of the chapter if you aren't sure you know what you are doing. Or maybe even if you are.

QUICK OATMEAL BREAD

MAKES 2 LOAVES

2⅔ ounces caked yeast or 2 packages dry yeast

2 tablespoons sugar

½ cup lukewarm water

½ cup boiling water

1 cup Quaker oats

⅓ cup butter

½ cup molasses

3 teaspoons salt

2 eggs, beaten

5½ cups flour

Enough butter to brush tops of loaves

1. In a small bowl, dissolve the yeast and sugar in the lukewarm water, and set aside.

2. In a large bowl, pour boiling water over the oats; add the butter, molasses, and salt. Stir together and allow to cool. Then add the yeast mixture, and blend well using a wooden spoon. Add the eggs and 4 cups of the flour. Mix well until the dough is soft. Add the rest of the flour. Knead on a floured board or table until it's soft and spongy, and then pat into a large greased bowl. Brush the top with soft butter.

3. Cover the bowl with a cloth, and let the dough raise 2 hours, until double in size. Shape it into 2 loaves, and put into greased loaf pans. Brush with butter. Let the dough raise until 1 inch above the pans. Preheat oven to 350° F.

4. Bake 45 to 50 minutes, until golden brown. Remove from the oven, and brush tops with butter while still warm.

DARK BREAD

Although years ago, dark bread was thought of by townspeople as poor man's, or farmer's bread, that pure, unprocessed graham, barley, rye, or whole wheat flour we toted home from the feed mill would be a health-conscious person's dream today. The ingredients were so fresh it seemed you could taste the good earth.

This recipe can be made with any one or any combination of those flours, and you need not use any white. (Although the white flour may make it easier if this is your first try, because it tends not to make as heavy a bread. But with the amount of yeast and shortening in this recipe, you should have no trouble.)

MAKES 4 LOAVES

2 cups milk (see Note)

3 tablespoons Home-Rendered Lard (page 257) or butter

2 tablespoons sugar

2²/₃ ounces caked yeast or 2 packages dry yeast

¹/₂ cup lukewarm water

4 teaspoons salt

6 tablespoons molasses

6 handfuls (about 3 cups) dark flour (rye or whole wheat)

8 handfuls (about 4 cups) white flour

Enough butter to brush tops of loaves

1. Scald the milk, remove it from the heat, and add the shortening while the milk is still hot so the shortening melts as it stands.

2. Take a small cup or saucer and dissolve the sugar and yeast in the water and let it stand.

3. Pour the milk mixture into a large bowl, and add the salt and molasses. Mix well, then stir in the dissolved yeast.

4. Add the dark flour and a couple of cups of the white, and beat well. Mix in more flour until the dough is quite thick to stir. Knead on a floured board or table until it's soft and spongy.

5. Place the dough in a large greased bowl. Brush the top with soft butter, cover with a cloth, and let it raise until double in size.

6. Divide the dough into 4 pieces, and shape into loaves. Put into buttered loaf pans. Brush the tops of the loaves with butter. Cover with a cloth and let raise until the dough is 1 inch above the tins. Meanwhile, preheat the oven to 350° F.

7. Bake 40 to 45 minutes, until brown on top. Remove from the oven, and brush the tops with butter while still warm.

NOTE: There is a traditional Swedish bread called Limpa that's made from this recipe. Use buttermilk instead of milk; rye, and white flour but no whole wheat flour; a little fennel and anise to taste; and ¹/₄ cup brown sugar. We never fussed much with those spices on the farm, but you might want to try it. If you do, and want to be traditional, forget the bread pans; form the loaves by hand and bake on greased baking sheets.

Rolls

LORRAINE'S REFRIGERATOR BUNS

An advantage to these buns is that you can make them the night before, leave the dough in the refrigerator, and take them out and finish them when you want to.

MAKES 3 DOZEN

1 tablespoon butter

1 tablespoon Butter Flavor Crisco

1/2 cup sugar

1 teaspoon salt

2 cups boiling water

1 1/3 ounces caked yeast or 1 package dry yeast

1 teaspoon sugar

1/2 cup lukewarm water

2 eggs, well beaten

5 1/2 cups flour

Enough butter to brush tops of dough and buns

1. In a heavy saucepan, melt 1 tablespoon butter, the shortening, 1/2 cup sugar, and the salt in 1/2 cup boiling water; cool until lukewarm.

2. In a small bowl, dissolve the yeast and 1 teaspoon sugar in 1/2 cup lukewarm water. Let set until foaming. Add the yeast mixture and the eggs to the shortening mixture in a large bowl, and stir all together. Add the flour, and mix thoroughly (this is too moist to knead; see Note).

3. Put the dough into a large greased bowl. Grease the top of the dough, and cover the bowl with plastic wrap. Place in the refrigerator overnight.

4. The next morning, form the dough into biscuits (about the size of golf balls), put them on a greased cookie sheet, and, using your fingers, flatten the balls. Brush the tops with melted butter. Let raise for 3 hours, until triple in size. Meanwhile, preheat the oven to 400° F.

5. Bake 20 minutes, until golden. Brush the tops of the warm buns with melted butter.

NOTE: Because the dough will be sticky, it will be easier to form into balls if you wet your hands slightly when working with it.

No Fuss Hamburger Buns

MAKES 4 DOZEN

1 cup milk

1/2 cup water

1/4 cup butter

4 teaspoons salt

2 2/3 ounces caked yeast or 2 packages dry yeast

1/2 cup sugar

1/2 cup lukewarm water

2 eggs

8 cups flour

Enough butter to brush tops of dough and buns

1. In a heavy saucepan, mix the milk with 1/2 cup water, the butter, and salt. Bring to a boil, and remove from heat. Let it cool.

2. In a small bowl, dissolve the yeast and sugar in 1/2 cup lukewarm water. When dissolved, add it to the cooled milk mixture in a large bowl. Add the eggs and the flour. Beat together until smooth.

3. Knead on a floured board or table until soft and spongy. Put the dough in a large greased bowl, brush the top with soft butter, cover with a cloth, and let it raise until doubled. Knead down, and let it raise again until doubled.

4. Shape the dough into about golf ball–size balls. Flatten slightly, and place in greased cake pans or on greased cookie sheets 1 inch apart. Brush with butter. Let the dough raise again. Meanwhile, preheat oven to 375° F.

5. Bake for 25 minutes, until golden. Remove from the oven, and brush the tops of the buns with butter while still warm.

Country Rolls

MAKES ABOUT 3 DOZEN CLOVERLEAF ROLLS

1 1/3 ounces caked yeast or 1 package dry yeast

1 1/2 cups lukewarm water

5 tablespoons plus 1 teaspoon sugar

1 cup scalded milk

1 tablespoon salt

6 tablespoons shortening

6 cups flour

Enough butter to brush tops of rolls

1. In a small bowl, dissolve the yeast in 1/2 cup of the lukewarm water and 1 teaspoon of the sugar, and let it stand.

2. In a large bowl, mix together the scalded milk, remaining 1 cup lukewarm water, remaining 5 tablespoons sugar, the salt, and the shortening. Add enough flour (about 3 cups) until pasty. Then add the yeast and water mixture, and blend together well.

3. Add the rest of the flour. Knead on a floured board or table until soft and spongy. Put the dough into a large greased bowl, brush the top with soft butter, cover with a cloth, and let it raise until double in bulk.

4. For cloverleaf rolls, make small balls the size of shooter marbles, and place 3 in each cup of a *well*-greased cupcake tin. Let the dough raise a second time. Meanwhile, preheat the oven to 375°F. Bake for 20 minutes, until golden.

HOT CROSS BUNS

MAKES 32 BUNS

½ cup lukewarm water

½ cup plus 2 teaspoons sugar

2⅔ ounces caked yeast or 2 packages dry yeast

½ cup lukewarm milk

¾ cup mashed potatoes

1¼ teaspoons salt

2 eggs, slightly beaten

1 cup raisins

1 teaspoon cinnamon

¼ teaspoon nutmeg

4 cups flour

Enough butter to brush tops of buns

Basic Powdered Sugar Frosting (page 193)

1. Grease two cookie sheets or 9 × 13-inch pans.

2. In a large bowl, place the lukewarm water, the 2 teaspoons of the sugar, and the yeast, and stir until dissolved.

3. Add remaining ingredients and mix well.

4. Turn the dough onto a floured board and knead until smooth. Place in a large greased bowl, brush the top with soft butter, cover with a cloth, and let raise until double in size (about 1½ hours). Punch down and divide in half. Shape each part into 16 buns and place on the prepared sheets or pans about 2 inches apart. Let the dough raise until double. Preheat the oven to 350°F, and bake the buns for about 30 minutes, until golden brown. Cool slightly, and make a cross on top with the frosting.

SWEET BUNS

These are great for sandwich or hamburger buns.

MAKES 4 DOZEN

1 cup milk

1½ cups water

¼ cup shortening

4 teaspoons salt

2⅔ ounces caked yeast or 2 packages dry yeast

½ cup sugar

½ cup lukewarm water

2 eggs

8 cups flour

Enough butter to brush tops of dough and buns

1. In a heavy saucepan, mix the milk, 1½ cups water, shortening, and salt, and bring to a boil.

2. Meanwhile, in a small bowl, place the yeast and sugar in the lukewarm water. Let sit until the yeast is dissolved, then add to the milk and water mixture.

3. When cool, add the eggs and flour, and beat until smooth.

4. Knead on a floured board until smooth. Put in a large greased bowl, brush top with soft butter, cover with a cloth, and let raise until doubled. Knead the dough and let raise again.

5. Shape the dough into golf ball–sized balls. Flatten slightly, and place on greased cookie sheets. Brush tops with butter. Let the dough raise again. Meanwhile, preheat the oven to 375°F. Bake for 25 minutes, or until golden. Brush the tops with butter while still warm.

GOLDEN BUTTER ROLLS

MAKES 30 ROLLS

1 cup milk

½ cup (1 stick) butter

1⅓ ounces caked yeast or 1 package dry yeast

1 teaspoon sugar

½ cup lukewarm water

½ cup sugar

1 teaspoon salt

3 eggs, beaten

4½ to 5 cups flour

Enough butter to brush tops of loaves

1. In a heavy saucepan, scald the milk and add ½ cup butter. Remove from heat, and cool.

2. In a small bowl, dissolve the yeast and 1 teaspoon sugar in the water. When foamy, put this in a large bowl along with ½ cup sugar, the salt, eggs, and flour. Add the cooled scalded milk mixture. Using a wooden spoon, mix until smooth.

3. Knead on a floured board or table until soft and spongy, then put into a large greased bowl and brush the top with soft butter. Cover the bowl with a cloth and let the dough raise until double in size.

4. Divide the dough into 3 portions. Using a rolling pin, roll each chunk out into a circle about ½ inch thick. Cut each circle into 10 to 12 wedges as you would a pie. Roll each slice up from the large end to the center point, and place 1 inch apart on all sides on a greased cookie sheet (pointed end on the bottom). Brush the tops of the rolls with butter. Let the dough raise again. Meanwhile, preheat the oven to 375° F.

5. Bake for 15 to 20 minutes, until golden. (They're done when a finger touch doesn't leave a dent.) Remove from the oven, and brush the tops with butter while still warm.

*Sweet
Dough
Treats*

BASIC
SWEET DOUGH

As I mentioned, out here in farm country, we older cooks go a lot by common sense and "feel." But the "feel" can be learned, and I hope my recipes and hints will help. You can make so many good things from sweet dough.

3½ DOZEN ROLLS OR 2 COFFEE CAKES

> *2⅔ ounces caked yeast or 2 packages dry
> yeast*
> *1 teaspoon sugar*
> *½ cup lukewarm water*
> *1 cup milk*
> *¼ cup butter*
> *½ cup sugar*
> *1 teaspoon salt*
> *4½ to 5 cups flour*
> *2 eggs, beaten*

1. In a small bowl, dissolve the yeast and 1 teaspoon sugar in the water.

2. In a heavy saucepan, scald the milk; add the butter, ½ cup sugar, and the salt. Cool to lukewarm and pour into a large bowl.

3. Add enough flour to make the batter thick (about 2 cups). Pour in the yeast mixture and the eggs, and beat well.

4. Add more flour (about 2½ cups) to make a soft dough. Turn the dough out on a floured board or table, and knead until glossy.

5. Place the dough in a large greased bowl, cover with a cloth, and let it raise until double in size. Knead it down, and let it raise again until about double in size (it's not that fussy).

RAISED DOUGHNUTS

MAKES 2 DOZEN

> *1 recipe Basic Sweet Dough (at left)*
> *Lard or oil for frying*
> *1 cup granulated sugar or 1½ cups powdered
> sugar plus ¼ cup cold water*

1. Divide Basic Sweet Dough in half. Flatten each half to ½ inch thick on a floured board or table. Cut the dough with a large water glass or round cookie cutter. Make the doughnut hole with a thimble. Stretch the hole with your finger and place on a floured board.

2. Cover the dough with a cloth, and let raise until puffy (not quite double in size, because they will puff up when you fry them).

3. Place the lard or oil in a large cast-iron skillet, and fry as you would fry cakes (page 213).

4. Roll the fried doughnuts in granulated sugar or make a glaze with the powdered sugar and cold water when still quite warm.

VARIATION: For jelly rolls, do not cut out the center hole. After frying the rolls, use a pastry-filling tube to fill with any flavor homemade jelly or frosting when still warm.

CARAMEL ROLLS

MAKES 3½ DOZEN

1 recipe Basic Sweet Dough (page 11)
¾ cup (1½ sticks) softened butter
2 cups brown sugar
¾ teaspoon ground cinnamon

FOR BOTTOM
OF PAN

2 cups brown sugar
1 cup melted butter
2 tablespoons light or dark corn syrup

1. Divide the Basic Sweet Dough in half. On a floured surface, roll each half of the dough into an oblong about ¾ inch thick. Spread each half of the dough with one-half of the softened butter and sprinkle each with one-half of the brown sugar and one-half of the cinnamon. Roll up each half like a jelly roll.

2. Grease two 9 × 13-inch cake pans. Sprinkle each with 1 cup brown sugar, and pour ½ cup melted butter over the sugar in each pan. Pour 1 tablespoon of syrup over the butter in each pan.

3. Cut the rolled-up dough into 1-inch slices, and place them, 1 inch apart, in the pans on top of the brown sugar mixture. Cover with a cloth and let the rolls raise until double in size. Meanwhile, preheat the oven to 375° F.

4. Bake 20 to 25 minutes, until golden brown. Remove pans from the oven and invert on trays, letting the caramel run over the rolls.

VARIATION: For Cinnamon Rolls: Omit the brown sugar mixture on the bottom of the pans. Instead, bake the dough slices on a greased baking sheet. After removing the rolls from the oven, frost with Basic Powdered Sugar Frosting (page 193).

COFFEE RING

MAKES 2 RINGS

1 recipe Basic Sweet Dough (page 11)
¾ cup (1½ sticks) melted butter
2 cups brown sugar
¾ teaspoon ground cinnamon
Nuts or dates (if desired)

1. Divide the Basic Sweet Dough in half. On a floured surface, roll each half into a ¾-inch-thick oblong, and brush each with melted butter. Sprinkle each half with brown sugar and cinnamon, and roll up like a jelly roll.

2. Form each roll into a ring, put on a greased cookie sheet, and pinch the ends together. Decorate with nuts or dates, if you want. Cover with a cloth, and let raise until almost double in size. Meanwhile, preheat the oven to 375° F.

3. Bake 20 to 25 minutes, until golden brown and your finger doesn't leave a dent.

COFFEE CAKE

MAKES 2 CAKES

2 cups dates, cut fine
1/2 cup sugar
1 cup water
1 recipe Basic Sweet Dough (page 11)
Nuts (if desired)

1. Place dates, sugar, and water in a medium saucepan and bring to a boil. Let it boil, and stir until thick. (If too thick, it can be thinned with water.) Let the filling cool (see Note).

2. Divide the Basic Sweet Dough in half. Roll each half into a 10 × 14-inch oblong directly onto a greased, 10 × 15-inch rimless cookie sheet.

3. Spread cooled filling down the center of the dough, about 5 inches wide. Sprinkle with nuts (if using).

4. Cut 1-inch strips from the edge of the dough to the filling (see top-right illustration). Now take the first strip and fold over the filling at a 20° angle (see illustration at right). Do the same on the other side. Continue folding strips until the end; the dough will look like a French braid. Tuck the ends of the last strips under and press gently. Cover with a cloth, and let raise for 1 hour, until light and fluffy. Meanwhile, preheat the oven to 375° F.

5. Bake 20 to 25 minutes, until golden brown, and your finger does not leave a dent.

NOTE: Any homemade filling, such as thickened blueberry, raspberry, apple, or apricot, can be used. Don't use store-bought filling, because it is so goopy the cake will get doughy on the bottom and will not bake through.

FINGER LICKIN' COFFEE CAKE

Oh my, this is good! I wouldn't ordinarily recommend what I'm going to say now, but if you're in the city and working night and day and are pressed for time, or you just don't have the knack for baking bread, go to the grocery and get some frozen dough and make this recipe starting with step 4. It won't be as good as homemade, but I'd hate to have you miss out completely just because your life's a hurry or you can't get the hang of baking bread.

To serve this, let your company pick pieces from the cake shape.

MAKES 1 CAKE

1/2 cup (1 stick) butter, melted

1/2 cup boiling water

1/3 cup sugar

3/4 teaspoon salt

1 1/3 ounces caked yeast or 1 package dry yeast

1 teaspoon sugar

1 cup lukewarm water

1 egg, beaten

3 cups flour

1 (16-ounce) package caramels

3/4 cup butter

1/2 cup evaporated milk

1 cup whole or chopped pecans

1. Mix the melted butter, boiling water, 1/3 cup sugar, and the salt together in a small bowl, and let it cool.

2. Dissolve the yeast and 1 teaspoon sugar in lukewarm water; let it get foamy, then pour it into a large bowl. Add the egg to the yeast mixture.

3. Pour the butter and water mixture into the yeast mixture, and add the flour. Beat well using a mixing spoon; put into a large greased bowl. Cover with a cloth, and let the dough raise for about 1 hour, until double in size.

4. Meanwhile, place the caramels in a heavy saucepan, and melt over low heat. Remove from heat, add the butter, milk, and pecans; mix well.

5. Generously grease an angel food tin. Take the dough, and form it into balls the size of whole, unshelled walnuts. Take a dough ball, dip it in the caramel mixture, and drop it into the cake pan. Repeat until the pan is three-quarters full. If any caramel mixture is left, pour it over the top of the dough balls in the pan. Cover the pan with a cloth and let the dough raise until 1 inch from the top of the pan. Meanwhile, preheat the oven to 375° F.

6. Bake 30 to 40 minutes, until a toothpick inserted in the center comes out dry (don't underbake). Remove the tin from the oven, and flop it upside down on a plate.

*Biscuits,
Quick
Breads,*

and Muffins

FAIR'S CHOICE BAKING POWDER BISCUITS

There are a lot of baking powder biscuit recipes in the world, but I am fond of this one. On the farm, baking powder biscuits are as handy as wheels on a wagon.

MAKES 1 DOZEN

2 heaping cups flour
1/2 teaspoon salt
1 tablespoon sugar
4 teaspoons baking powder
1/4 teaspoon cream of tartar
1/2 cup (1 stick) butter
1 egg
3/4 cup milk (approximately)

1. Preheat the oven to 350° F. In a large bowl, combine the flour, salt, sugar, baking powder, and cream of tartar. Add the butter, and using your fingers, mix until crumbly.

2. Put the egg into a 1-cup measuring cup; beat a little with a fork. Fill the cup with milk. Pour into the dry ingredients, and mix until the dry ingredients are just moistened (not too hard). The dough will be coarse and lumpy.

3. Pat the dough out on a floured board or table, and cut with a water glass or old sharp-edged Calumet baking powder can. Place biscuits on an ungreased cookie sheet.

4. Bake 15 to 20 minutes, until the biscuits begin to get golden.

GRAPE-NUT BREAD

Grape-Nuts was one of the first cereals groceries here carried, and women tried to think of every which way to use it. I don't know if people in the city make this, but on the farm this recipe was passed on from neighbor to neighbor. It has a rich, nutty taste.

MAKES 2 LOAVES

2 cups buttermilk or sour milk (page 157)
1 cup Grape-Nuts cereal
2 cups sugar
2 eggs
1/4 teaspoon salt
4 cups flour
1 teaspoon baking soda
2 teaspoons baking powder

1. Pour the sour milk over the Grape-Nuts in a medium bowl, and soak for about 1 hour.

2. Preheat the oven to 350° F. Add the sugar, eggs, and salt to the Grape-Nuts mixture; mix well using a wooden spoon.

3. Stir in the flour, baking soda, and baking powder. Mix thoroughly, and pour into 2 greased loaf pans.

4. Bake for 45 to 60 minutes, until a toothpick inserted in the center comes out dry.

BOSTON BROWN BREAD

I don't know if this is the Norwegian version of Boston Brown Bread or what, but unlike most, it doesn't call for molasses and cornmeal, and it isn't steamed all day long. Years ago, women here didn't always have molasses or cornmeal on hand and couldn't wait that long for bread to cook. Plain as it is, and traditional or not, this is Boston Brown Bread as I know it. We always serve it when we make baked beans or have pork on the table.

We like to bake this bread in 1-pound cans instead of loaf pans—pea and corn cans work well.

MAKES 5 SMALL LOAVES

2 cups pitted whole dates

2 cups cold water

1/4 cup butter, melted

2 eggs, slightly beaten

2 cups flour

1 teaspoon vanilla extract

2 teaspoons baking soda

Nutmeats (optional)

1. Cut up the dates and place in a medium saucepan with the water. Cook over medium heat until thick. Cool, and pour into a large bowl.

2. Preheat the oven to 350° F. Add the butter, eggs, flour, vanilla, baking soda, and nuts (if using) to the dates. Mix well.

3. Spoon the dough into 5 greased cans, filling one-half full.

4. Bake about 45 minutes, until a toothpick comes out clean. Remove the cans from the oven, and lay them on their sides on a cooling rack or breadboard. (When cool, the bread will come loose from the tins easily.)

FARMER'S BREAD

Citron mix is available in the stores during the holiday season because it's so popular in holiday breads. But it's also good in this bread, so if you have some on hand, throw it in.

MAKES 2 LOAVES

2 cups flour

1/2 teaspoon baking powder

1 teaspoon baking soda

1 cup sugar

1 teaspoon salt

2 cups graham flour

1/2 cup citron mix

1 cup nutmeats

1 egg, beaten

1 1/2 cups sour milk (page 157)

3/4 cup pitted, stewed prunes

2 tablespoons butter, melted

1. Preheat the oven to 350° F. Sift the flour, baking powder, baking soda, sugar, and salt together in a large bowl. Add the graham flour and citron mix, and stir well.

2. Add the nuts, egg, milk, prunes, and butter, mixing just enough to moisten. Pour into 2 greased loaf pans. Bake for 45 to 55 minutes, until a toothpick inserted in the center comes out dry.

JOHNNY CAKE CORN BREAD

Women used to get up and bake this long before the rooster crowed. They'd fry up some Side Pork (page 45) and serve this bread steaming warm out of the oven with the meat, butter, and Homemade Syrup (page 97). Johnny Cake Corn Bread without Side Pork was unthinkable—except during the drought years and the worst of the Great Depression, when we were glad for a little of nothing. We serve this at the restaurant in January on what we call Hard Times Day, when the waitresses dress up in rags and old clothes in mind of the Depression. Coffee is five cents that day.

This is also very good served with fish.

FOR A 9 × 13-INCH CAKE PAN

$1^{1}/_{2}$ *cups cornmeal*

2 *cups flour*

1 *teaspoon baking soda*

$^{1}/_{4}$ *cup sugar*

1 *teaspoon salt*

$1^{1}/_{2}$ *cups buttermilk*

2 *tablespoons butter, melted*

3 *tablespoons molasses*

2 *eggs, beaten*

1. Preheat the oven to 350° F. Mix the cornmeal, flour, baking soda, sugar, and salt together in a large bowl.

2. Add the buttermilk, butter, molasses, and eggs. Stir all together, then beat well using a wooden spoon. Pour into a greased 9 × 13-inch pan (see Note).

3. Bake for 35 minutes, until a toothpick inserted in the center comes out dry.

4. Cut into squares, and serve hot with lots of butter.

NOTE: For corn muffins, if you'd like, you can put these in a greased muffin tin, and bake 25 to 30 minutes, until lightly brown in the same oven as for bread.

CRANBERRY BREAD

MAKES 1 LOAF

2 *cups flour*

$^{1}/_{2}$ *teaspoon baking soda*

$^{1}/_{4}$ *teaspoon salt*

$1^{1}/_{2}$ *teaspoons baking powder*

1 *cup sugar*

Grated rind and juice of 2 oranges

$^{1}/_{2}$ *cup hot water*

2 *tablespoons butter, melted*

1 *egg, beaten*

1 *cup cranberries that have been cut in half*

1 *cup chopped nuts*

1. Preheat the oven to 350° F. In a large bowl, mix together the flour, baking soda, salt, baking powder, and sugar.

2. Combine the rind, juice, water, and butter in a medium bowl. Stir in the egg, and blend this into the dry ingredients. Add the cranberries and nuts. Pour into a greased loaf pan.

3. Bake 50 to 60 minutes, until a toothpick inserted in the center comes out dry.

BLUEBERRY MUFFINS

Muffin recipes are a dime a dozen, but these are a favorite at the restaurant. There's not much that's better when you make these with glistening berries fresh from the bluff and spread them with sweet butter.

MAKES 1 DOZEN LARGE MUFFINS

2 cups flour

1/2 cup sugar plus a little more to sprinkle on top of batter (if desired)

3 teaspoons baking powder

1/2 teaspoon salt

1 cup fresh blueberries

1 cup milk

1/3 cup vegetable oil

1 egg, slightly beaten

1. Preheat the oven to 400° F. In a large bowl, combine the flour, sugar, baking powder, and salt. Stir in the blueberries.

2. In a small bowl, combine the milk, oil, and egg, using a fork to mix well.

3. Make a well in the center of the flour mixture, pour in the liquid all at once, stir quickly with a fork, just until the dry ingredients are moistened (do not overmix or the batter will be lumpy).

4. Spoon the batter into a buttered muffin tin, and sprinkle the tops with a little sugar if you want.

5. Bake 20 to 25 minutes, until golden brown.

PUMPKIN BREAD

MAKES 1 LARGE LOAF

1 3/4 cups flour

1/4 teaspoon baking powder

1 teaspoon baking soda

1 teaspoon salt

1/2 teaspoon ground cinnamon

1/4 teaspoon ground cloves

1 cup sugar

1/3 cup soft butter

1 cup pumpkin puree

2 eggs, slightly beaten

1/3 cup milk

1/2 teaspoon vanilla extract

1/2 cup chopped pecans or walnuts

1/3 cup raisins (if desired)

1. Preheat the oven to 350° F. Mix the flour, baking powder, baking soda, salt, cinnamon, and cloves together in a medium bowl, and set aside.

2. In a large bowl, using a wooden spoon, beat the sugar and butter together until light and fluffy. Beat in the pumpkin, and add the eggs.

3. In a small bowl, mix together the milk and vanilla. Add the flour mixture alternately with the milk mixture into the pumpkin mixture. Fold in the nuts and raisins (if using). Pour into a greased loaf pan.

4. Bake 1 hour, until a toothpick inserted in the center comes out dry.

MAD ZUCCHINI BREAD

Every harvest, every farm woman I know says the same thing: "Next year, I'm not planting so gosh darn much zucchini!" But spring comes; the garden gets plowed; the warm, black soil is sprawled out under the sunshine; and sure enough—in goes the same amount of zucchini. Then when harvest comes, recipe after recipe is dragged out and tried; neighbors are busy on the phone giving zucchini away to neighbors. (This bread is a good one to freeze.)

MAKES 2 LARGE LOAVES

3 cups flour

1 teaspoon baking soda

1 teaspoon baking powder

1 teaspoon salt

3 teaspoons ground cinnamon

2 cups sugar

3 eggs, beaten

3 teaspoons vanilla extract

2 cups grated, unpeeled zucchini

1 cup chopped walnuts

1 cup peanut oil

1. Preheat the oven to 350° F. In a large bowl, mix together the flour, baking soda, baking powder, salt, cinnamon, and sugar.

2. Add the eggs, vanilla, zucchini, nuts, and oil. Mix well using a wooden spoon. Pour into 2 generously buttered and floured loaf pans.

3. Bake for 50 minutes, until a toothpick inserted in the center comes out dry.

ORANGE NUT BREAD

MAKES 1 LOAF

1 medium orange

Boiling water

2 tablespoons butter, melted

1 egg, beaten

1 teaspoon vanilla extract

2 cups flour

1/2 teaspoon salt

1 teaspoon baking powder

1 teaspoon baking soda

1 cup sugar

1/2 cup chopped nuts

1. Preheat the oven to 350° F. Squeeze the juice from the orange into a 1-cup measure. Fill the measuring cup with boiling water.

2. Grind (see Note) what remains of the orange, including the rind, into a large bowl. Add the diluted juice.

3. Stir in the butter, egg, and vanilla. Add the flour, salt, baking powder, baking soda, and sugar. Stir in the nuts. Pour into a greased loaf pan.

4. Bake 1 hour, until a toothpick comes out clean. Cool before cutting.

NOTE: To grind the remains of the orange and rind, you can use an old-fashioned grinder, a food processor, or a food chopper, whatever you have that will grind the rind very fine.

SOUPS

You can't hurry and rush a pig or a cow; if you do, they get riled and leave you flat. It's the same for soups. You have to take time and make a good slow-cooked broth with good seasonings. The old-timers around here like to say to young brides, *Koke med hete som er i hjerte* ("Cook by the warmth that's in your heart"), and corny as you might think that sounds, it's especially true for soups.

I've been places and ordered "home-made soup" that's nothing more than a packaged base of artificial colors and flavors used to season the water. The vegetables are dumped in and heated, and there it is—something no one's given a hoot about, and it tastes like it.

Here on the farm it's different. We dig in the dirt to plant the vegetables; we hoe between the rows and worry whether there'll be a drought or too much rain or deer or bugs or hail or an early or late killing frost. We run to see the first tiny green as it finally pokes through the thick soil; we scatter feed to the chickens, slop the hogs, and fence for the cows. That is our soup—real ingredients we've cared for and harvested and given much to.

I know you can't be that close to the earth in the city, but you can take time at the store and have patience at the stove. Feel the vegetables, consider their color, be fussy about the meat you bring home.

My soup recipes are simple. There's nothing here fancy or cold. To me (and I think most farm women will tell you this), soup means basic and hot.

Note that serving sizes are for medium to large bowls. For a Scandinavian soup, see page 249.

Hints

• I believe in cooking beef shanks for good broth. There's enough bone and meat on 'em to make a thick, flavorful stock that's not greasy. Neck bones tend to give more grease and less meat. Beef shanks are more tender, and the meat is plentiful enough that you don't think you're eating an old bull. But when cooking a soup bone, no matter how good the meat, be sure to season it with plenty of onion and salt and pepper so you get a tasty stock.

• Chicken backs and bones—seasoned properly and cooked slowly in a cast-iron kettle—also make a hearty broth. But stay away from skinny, pale-skinned chickens. And again, don't be tempted to take a shortcut; never substitute with the packaged or canned stuff. Real, quality ingredients, slowly cooked, is the only way to good soup. (Beats having the chicken scoot through the water and calling it broth.)

• Always use pressure cookers according to the manufacturer's instructions, and read the instructions carefully first before using. I like to use the cooker without the pressure because the broth doesn't cook away, and it holds flavor, but if using the cooker without the pressure and the pressure regulator, don't use the cooker's own cover; use a cookie sheet because if the cover should seal, it'll blow up and, at the very least, scare the daylights out of you.

• You have to have a little fat for flavor, but if it's too much, skim it off. (I skim the fat from the chicken broth and use it for Sandbakkels, page 252.)

• All cream soups have to be heated slowly in a heavy kettle because the creams have a tendency to scorch, and *uff da* (an everyday Nordic expression of dismay) if they do.

• I cook all my soups but the split pea without a cover so they cook more slowly and get a better flavor.

CHICKEN SOUP

The caring that goes into making chicken soup seems to bring the sick back around, but out here it's also good because in winter, it gets so dang-blasted cold. We get long, raw stretches of subzero weather, down to −40° F (actual) and −120° F (wind chill). It's such a bitter, biting cold that icicles form on your face in seconds, and day after day the radio even warns us not to go out, but on the farm we have to. Those nasty days, you can imagine, this soup feels like heaven going down.

MAKES 12 TO 16 SERVINGS

1 fresh chicken, cleaned and cut up
1 teaspoon salt
6 carrots, peeled and cut fine
3/4 bunch celery, cut fine
1 small onion
6 potatoes, cubed
Salt and pepper to taste

1. Put the chicken into a kettle with 1 teaspoon salt and enough water to almost cover, and cook about 1 hour, until tender (see Note).

2. Remove the chicken from the broth (add water if the broth is too thick and rich). Add the vegetables to the broth, season to taste, and cook until they are done.

3. Add as much of the cooked chicken as you'd like; you can save some to cream for another meal.

NOTE: I like to use a 4-quart pressure cooker. If you do, use only about 1 quart of water for cooking the chicken, and cook until tender (about 20 minutes after the pressure regulator starts to jiggle). Remove the chicken from the bones and put the meat and rich broth into a regular kettle; add the vegetables and at least 1 more quart of water and cook all together until vegetables are tender.

CHICKEN DUMPLING SOUP: Follow the recipe for Chicken Soup, and add dumplings (page 24) before adding the cooked chicken.

CHICKEN NOODLE SOUP: Follow the recipe for Chicken Soup, and add noodles (page 24) before adding the cooked chicken.

COUNTRY DUMPLINGS

MAKES ABOUT 24 DEPENDING ON HOW LARGE YOU FORM THEM

1 egg
Pinch of salt
1 cup milk
1/4 teaspoon baking powder
2 cups flour

1. In a medium bowl, beat the egg, salt, and milk together slightly.

2. Add the baking powder and flour, and stir together until well mixed.

3. Drop by teaspoonfuls into the soup (see Note), and cook until done. (To test for doneness, remove a dumpling from the soup, cut in half, and taste. If it tastes gummy, it's not done.)

NOTE: When adding the dumplings, dip the spoon in the hot broth for a little bit, then spoon into the dumpling mixture. That way, the dumpling will fall off the spoon easily.

FARM NOODLES

These are very good added to vegetable-beef or chicken soup.

MAKES A LARGE BATCH

1/2 cup flour
2 egg yolks
1/2 teaspoon salt

1. Mix all the ingredients together in a small bowl, using a wooden spoon.

2. Using a rolling pin, roll the dough out very thin onto a floured board or table.

3. Cut the dough into narrow strips, and let dry a while. (Toss a little to dry them.)

4. Cook in boiling salted water until tender.

HOMEMADE CROUTONS

MAKES A LARGE BATCH

1 loaf day-old bread
Butter, to taste
Garlic (optional; see Note)

1. Preheat the oven to 350° F. Spread the day-old bread with butter. If you like garlic, mince it and add to the butter before spreading.

2. Remove the crusts, and cut into 1/3-inch cubes.

3. Bake once or twice to brown evenly. Bake until nice and brown and dry.

4. Use immediately in a soup or on a salad or store in a tightly sealed plastic bag.

NOTE: If you're in a hurry, garlic powder can be substituted for minced garlic.

There's not much shrinkage on this. You'll get in croutons what you've used in bread.

CHUNKY CREAM OF POTATO SOUP

SERVES 24

16 to 24 peeled potatoes
4 stalks celery
1 small onion
4 carrots (see Note)
1 teaspoon salt
9 pints half-and-half
Salt to taste
Dash of pepper
1 cup (2 sticks) butter

1. Cut or cube the potatoes into a large kettle. Cut the celery into small pieces, and do the same with the onion, and add to the kettle.

2. Peel the carrots, and grate on the coarse side of your grater. Put them in the kettle.

3. Sprinkle 1 teaspoon salt in and add enough water to cover the vegetables. Cook over medium heat until the potatoes are soft and a fork goes through easily (30 to 45 minutes).

4. Drain off the water, and add the half-and-half, salt and pepper to taste, and the butter. Set the kettle back on the stove over low heat, and simmer (do not boil or the milk will curdle) for a couple of hours, until the flavors are well blended. Stir occasionally.

NOTE: The carrots are for color and a little sweetness. For an extragood taste, crumble in a little bacon (fried crisp).

This is a good keeper; it can be kept in a glass container in the refrigerator for up to 1 week.

GARDEN-FRESH TOMATO SOUP

With all our milk out here, we wouldn't think to make tomato soup without it. But don't forget the baking soda or it'll curdle and be a mess. Made right, this is a beautiful soup to look at as well as to taste.

MAKES 4 SERVINGS

1 cup fresh chopped tomatoes
1 stalk celery, chopped
1 tablespoon chopped onion
1/8 teaspoon baking soda
2 cups rich milk or half-and-half
Salt and pepper to taste
1 tablespoon butter

1. Cook the tomatoes fresh from the garden in a medium kettle with the celery and onion over medium heat until the celery is clear in color and the tomatoes have gone to pieces. Stir off and on using a wooden spoon.

2. Stir in the baking soda. (It will turn a little foamy but the foam will disappear.)

3. Gradually add the milk or half-and-half. Heat, but do not boil, and stir occasionally or it will scorch.

4. Season to taste, and stir in the butter. (Butter makes it better.)

FRESH ASPARAGUS SOUP

SERVES 4 TO 6

1 cup water

1 1/2 cups fresh cut-up asparagus

1/2 cup flour

4 cups milk

2 tablespoons butter

1 teaspoon salt

Dash of pepper

4 to 6 slices of American cheese (if desired)

1. In a large kettle, bring the water to a boil, and add the asparagus. Cook about 10 minutes, then drain.

2. Mix flour, milk, butter, and salt and pepper in a large bowl; add this to the asparagus. Let the mixture come to a boil, and serve.

3. If desired, add 1 slice of American cheese to each bowl before serving.

HOT BUTTERED ZUCCHINI SOUP

SERVES 4

1 small onion, minced

3 tablespoons butter

3 tablespoons flour

3 cups milk

1 cup beef broth

3 cups leftover cooked zucchini

Salt and pepper to taste

1. Sauté the onion in the butter in a medium kettle until the onion is clear (about 5 minutes).

2. Add the flour, and stir together. Lower the heat and gradually add the milk, stirring constantly until thick and bubbly (about 1 or 2 minutes).

3. Add the broth and the zucchini, heat thoroughly, and season to taste.

THICK·AND·CREAMY BROCCOLI·CHEESE SOUP

MAKES 6 TO 8 SERVINGS

1 bunch of broccoli

Salt

1 cup (2 sticks) butter

1 cup flour

2 quarts milk

1/2 pound fresh grated American cheese (see Note)

1. Cut up the broccoli and cook in water with a little salt until tender. Drain.

2. Melt the butter in a heavy 4-quart saucepan, add the flour, and stir using a wooden spoon until well mixed. Then gradually add the milk, stirring as it cooks over medium heat.

3. Add the cheese and the cooked broccoli to the milk mixture, and heat together. If the soup gets too thick, thin with more milk.

NOTE: The cheese helps to thicken the soup.

CREAMY CORN SOUP

In place of crackers, buttered popcorn is excellent served with corn soup.

SERVES 8

5 cups home canned or fresh corn
5 cups milk
2 tablespoons flour
2 tablespoons butter
1 teaspoon salt
   Dash of pepper
2 egg yolks

1. In a double boiler, cook the corn with 4 cups of the milk for 20 minutes.

2. Blend together ½ cup of the warm milk, the flour, butter, and salt and pepper to make a white sauce. Add the white sauce to the corn and cook for 5 minutes. Pour the soup through a strainer.

3. Beat the egg yolks and add them to the remaining cup of cold milk.

4. Stir the egg and milk mixture into the soup, and return to heat for about 2 minutes, stirring constantly.

5. Remove from heat, beat real good with a wooden spoon, and serve at once.

CREAM OF CELERY SOUP

SERVES 6 TO 8

1 bunch celery
   Sprinkle of salt
1 tablespoon butter
1 teaspoon chopped onion
1 tablespoon flour
1 quart milk
1 teaspoon salt
   Dash of pepper

1. Wash and slice the celery, and put it in a small saucepan with enough water to cover. Toss in a sprinkle of salt. Cook over medium heat until tender; drain and set aside.

2. Put the butter, onion, and flour in a heavy kettle, and cook, stirring over low heat, until heated well (don't let it burn).

3. Add the milk slowly, then 1 teaspoon salt and the pepper. Cook until nice and creamy, then add the cooked celery, and heat through.

4. Serve piping hot in bowls or use in casseroles.

WISCONSIN CHEESE SOUP

MAKES 4 TO 6 SERVINGS

2 tablespoons butter

1 tablespoon flour

1 tablespoon chopped onion

1 quart milk

1/2 teaspoon salt

1/4 teaspoon pepper

2 slices bacon, fried crisp and crumbled

1 teaspoon chopped pimiento

1/4 pound Wisconsin American cheese, cut up

1. Melt the butter in a medium kettle. Add the flour and onion, and sauté over medium heat until the onions begin to get soft; do not brown.

2. Gradually add the milk, then the salt and pepper. Heat thoroughly over medium heat stirring constantly (don't let the milk curdle), until slightly thickened.

3. Add the bacon, pimiento, and cheese; stir until the cheese melts. Do not boil; heat slowly. Pour into bowls, and serve.

HOME-GROWN VEGETABLE-BEEF SOUP

This is an old-fashioned soup that's been cooking in this area in one form or another since the first year the settlers brought in a crop. In the really hard times of the 1930s, and even in these more recent tough years of the depressed farm economy, some folks have so little meat the women make this soup from a base of a few tablespoons of lard dissolved in seasoned water, and they use water instead of milk for their dumplings.

MAKES 8 SERVINGS

2 beef shanks

2 teaspoons salt

Pepper to taste

1 small onion, chopped fine

8 large carrots, cut small

1/2 bunch celery, cut small

1 small head of cabbage, chopped small

1/2 rutabaga (or not)

6 potatoes, cubed

1. Place the beef shanks in a kettle, and pour in water until the meat is covered (see Note). Add the salt and pepper. Put in the small onion, and cook slowly for 2 hours.

2. Take the soup meat out of the broth, and add water to the broth if it's not enough. Add the carrots, celery, cabbage, and rutabaga to the broth, and cook until the carrots start coming to the top. Then add the potatoes. Cook until tender.

3. Cut the meat off the bone, and add to the soup (see Note). Serve piping hot.

NOTE: I like to use a small pressure cooker for this, and let the meat cook 2 hours.

This soup is also good with Country Dumplings (page 24) added.

A LARGE BATCH OF VEGETABLE-BEEF SOUP: Put 9 beef shanks in a huge kettle, and fill three-quarters full with water. Add 2 medium onions, chopped, and salt and pepper to taste. Cook 2 hours. In a separate kettle cook the vegetables following the recipe for Home-Grown Vegetable-Beef Soup, using 12 pounds of carrots, 3 bunches of celery, 2 heads of cabbage, 1 rutabaga, and 5 pounds of potatoes. (Be sure to add the potatoes last, when the carrots come to the top, or the potatoes will get mushy.) This makes 5 gallons. When serving the soup, take 1 gallon of the meat and broth and mix with 1 gallon of vegetables. Heat together until hot, and season to taste. (I like to use a large pressure cooker for this. I cook the meat for the broth 1 hour, with 10 pounds of pressure.)

HEARTY BEEF STEW SOUP

This is good served with Fair's Choice Baking Powder Biscuits (page 15). It's one of Friday's noon specials at the restaurant.

SERVES 10 TO 12

3 pounds of tenderloin or sirloin tips cut into 2-inch cubes

2 tablespoons Butter Flavor Crisco

1 tablespoon Meat Seasoning (page 41)

2 teaspoons salt

Pepper to taste

6 medium carrots, cut into 1-inch pieces

3 stalks celery, cut into 2-inch slices

1 medium onion, chopped

10 little fresh potatoes

4 tablespoons flour

3/4 cup water

1 cup fresh garden peas

1. Brown the meat and the shortening in a heavy cast-iron skillet. Add the Meat Seasoning, 1 teaspoon of the salt, and the pepper, and stir once in a while. When the meat is well browned, add enough water to cover, lower the heat, and simmer until tender (about 1 1/2 hours) until a fork goes into the meat easily. The slower you simmer, the better.

2. Boil the carrots, celery, onions, and potatoes in a medium kettle over medium heat with enough water to cover and 1 teaspoon of salt. Cook until almost done. Drain, but save the liquid.

3. Remove the meat from the skillet, and add it to the vegetables; leave the juice from the meat in the skillet.

4. Preheat the oven to 350° F. Pour the liquid that you drained from the vegetables into the skillet with the meat juice. Make a paste with the flour and water, and add it to the warm juice. Cook over medium heat, stirring briskly with a wire whisk until it forms a gravy that is thick and smooth.

5. Pour this over the vegetables, add the peas, and place in a small roaster or a large casserole. Bake for 30 to 45 minutes, until bubbling.

FARMERS' CENTRAL SPLIT PEA SOUP

In an old clapboard building next to Ovid Berg's Farm Implement, we had what was called Farmers' Central. The telephone operator lived there, and so there was never any need for a local newspaper. Five or six neighbors shared a telephone line, we all had our own rings (like one long and two short), but it seemed almost everyone listened in on each other if they had a spare minute. And if there was something you didn't hear just right, you could ring in and ask the operator, because most often she was listening, too. Sometimes women would forget themselves and join in on the conversation; that happened quite often. We took it for granted; there was nothing dishonorable or vicious about it. Sometimes when you called someone, the operator wouldn't even put the ring through; she'd just say, "Oh, Cora isn't home today, she's gone to Ladies' Aid." We knew who was down with the flu, what old Doc Leasum or Knutson said about someone's bad heart or a gallbladder operation. We knew so and so ran with whatsamawho's wife or husband, who was pregnant, how much Lars Gunem paid for a new spreader when his wife wanted a wringer washer, and who got drunk and ran over Warren Van Tassel's heifer. But it wasn't all gossip. If the phone rang four or five times in succession, it was a public alert. Everyone would take down their receivers and listen to the operator. Sometimes it was a fire, an accident where blood was needed, a blizzard, tornado, or unannounced church meeting. Anyway, it was all friendly and lent a sense of belonging and community. Sometimes the operator would say,

"Wait a minute, I'm ironing a shirt and have to finish the collar," or "Hold on a sec, I have to add the peas to the soup." In those days, few recipes or even what you were having for supper were secret.

MAKES 12 TO 16 SERVINGS

1 smoked ham hock

3 quarts juice from cooked hock

3 cups green split peas

1 small carrot, coarsely grated

1/2 small onion, finely chopped

1. Put the ham hock in a large kettle, almost cover with water, put a lid on, and cook on medium for 3 hours (but don't let it get as high as a rolling boil).

2. Take the ham hock out of the juice, and take the ham off the bone.

3. Add the split peas, carrots, and onion to the juice.

4. Cut the meat you have taken from the bone into chunks, and add it to the juice. If the juice is too salty or strongly smoked in flavor, add more water now. (You should have 3 quarts of juice.) Add another cup of water.

5. Cook over medium heat for 1 1/2 hours, until nice and thick.

PRIZED CREAMY BEAN SOUP

It may seem surprising to you, but all year long, this is a favorite at the restaurant. I don't know if it's our fat cows or what, but with the half-and-half, this soup tastes almost as though we'd put cheese in it. The waitresses are always saying they get big compliments on the creamy flavor, and people always ask them what kind of cheese is in it. I guess you could make it with cheese, but I just use Trempealeau County half-and-half.

SERVES 6 TO 8

2 cups dried navy beans

6 cups water

1 teaspoon salt

Dash of pepper

2 pints half-and-half

2 slices bacon, fried crisp and crumbled

1. In a large kettle, soak the beans overnight in the water. The next morning, drain the beans, and add enough fresh water to cover.

2. Add the salt and pepper, cover, and cook over medium heat until the beans are tender (20 to 30 minutes). Drain and mash the beans (enough so none is whole).

3. Heat the half-and-half, and add the mashed beans, and the bacon. If too thick, add more half-and-half.

4. Serve hot in bowls with Homemade Croutons (page 24).

NAVY BEAN AND HAM SOUP

SERVES 8 TO 10

2 cups navy beans

6 cups water

1 smoked ham bone with a little meat on it

2 quarts water

Salt and pepper to taste

1. In a large kettle, soak the beans overnight in the water. In the morning, drain the beans, and add enough fresh water to cover. Cover the kettle with a lid and cook over medium heat until tender (20 to 30 minutes). Drain, and mash the beans (enough so that none is whole). Set aside.

2. Cook the ham bone in 2 quarts of water in a large kettle for about 2 hours. Remove the bone from the juice and pick the meat from the bone.

3. Add the beans and the meat to the juice, add salt and pepper to taste, and heat 15 to 20 minutes.

4. Serve in bowls with crackers.

MOCK CHILI

I know this doesn't come close to real chili. A lot of us folks around here would probably either keel over or cry buckets if we ever bit into a real chili or fresh jalapeño pepper. This is the soup we in these parts call chili, and mock as it is, so many travelers ask for it at the restaurant I thought I'd include the recipe.

SERVES ABOUT 4 OR MORE

1 ½ pounds ground beef

½ cup chopped onion

1 teaspoon salt

¼ teaspoon pepper

1 pint homemade tomato soup or 1 (10³/₄-ounce) can store-bought tomato soup

1 (12-ounce) can red kidney beans

1 quart home-canned tomatoes or 1 (12- to 15-ounce) can stewed tomatoes

1 teaspoon celery salt

½ teaspoon chili powder

1. Place the ground beef, onion, salt, and pepper in a heavy cast-iron skillet, and brown the meat.

2. Drain the meat, and pour into a large kettle. Add the tomato soup, kidney beans, and tomatoes, and stir. Add the celery salt and chili powder, and bring to a boil. Let simmer ½ hour on low heat to blend the flavors. Taste, and season as desired.

MILK DUMPLING SOUP

When we were kids and had no potatoes, we always had the chickens and the cows, so we had this soup. I still like it today. It's a good soup for kids and convalescents or for a light meal for the rest of us.

6 SERVINGS

1 egg

Pinch of salt

1 cup milk

2 cups flour

½ teaspoon baking powder

2 quarts milk

1. In a medium bowl, beat the egg, add the salt and 1 cup milk, and mix. Add the flour and the baking powder, and stir until smooth. Set aside.

2. Heat 2 quarts of milk in a large kettle (careful not to scorch); when this is hot, put the dumplings in by teaspoonfuls until all the dough is used. Cook over medium heat until the dumplings are done. They will raise and sort of come to the top when cooked through. (Test by taking one out, cutting it in half, and tasting it. If it's not doughy, it's done and ready to eat.)

YOUNGSTERS' FAVORITE RICE SOUP

When the kids were little, and I was lost for something to make for supper, I made this, and was I ever loved. My family gobbled it down by the bowls full. It filled them up, and they asked for nothing else. Sometimes I put homemade bread and butter and jelly on the table with it, but the kids were so crazy for the soup, they never noticed. I suppose today's mothers wouldn't think it was much of a meal, but we'd had our greens and fruits and meat at our noon dinner, so I never felt I was short-changing them. My grandchildren, even these days, beg for it. (It's also soothing if someone's down in the dumps or under the weather.)

MAKES ABOUT 12 BOWLS

1 cup old-time rice (not instant)

3 cups water

1/2 teaspoon salt

1 quart rich whole milk

Ground nutmeg and cinnamon, and sugar on the table for serving (if desired)

1. In a large kettle, cook the rice in the water and salt until it swells and becomes fluffy and tender and the water is absorbed. (This should yield about 3 cups of rice.)

2. Pour the milk over the rice and place over medium heat until the milk is very warm, but do not let it boil. (If the soup gets too thick, add a little more milk.)

3. Serve in soup bowls while hot (best with nutmeg, cinnamon, and sugar sprinkled on top).

OYSTER STEW

Even though we have no sea or ocean, this is a popular soup in these parts. We get our oysters raw, over the counter at a meat market we trust. Many folks have this as a special treat for Christmas Eve supper. We even have it at church suppers.

SERVES 6 TO 8

1 quart fresh oysters

2 tablespoons butter

2 tablespoons flour

1 teaspoon salt

Dash of pepper

1 quart milk

Oyster crackers (or not)

1. Cook the oysters over medium heat in the liquid they came in until they curl around the edges.

2. Place the butter, flour, salt, and pepper in a 2-quart saucepan, and cook on low heat until creamy. (Be careful not to burn it.) Add the milk gradually, and heat through, but be sure not to boil.

3. Add the oysters and liquid to the milk mixture, stir slightly, and heat through.

4. Serve in bowls, and top with oyster crackers, if you like.

CORN CHOWDER

SERVES 8

1 quart diced potatoes

1 pint boiling water

4 tablespoons diced salt pork (see Note)

1 small onion, chopped

2 cups home-canned corn or fresh corn

1 pint milk

1/2 teaspoon salt

Dash of pepper

2 tablespoons chopped parsley or celery leaves

1. In a large kettle, boil the potatoes in the water for about 10 minutes.

2. Fry the salt pork and onion for about 5 minutes in a small skillet over medium heat. Add this and the corn to the potatoes, and cook over medium heat until the vegetables are tender.

3. Add the milk, salt, and pepper, bring to a boil, then add the parsley or celery leaves.

NOTE: We always had salt pork on hand, but you can substitute some ham (cubed) or crisply fried bacon (crumbled) instead.

FISH OR LUTEFISK CHOWDER

If you tend to go overboard when you cook your family fish, this is a good way to use up the leftovers. It even works for *lutefisk* if you have a lot left over. And if you're thinking what I know you might be, the answer is heck, no. It doesn't taste fishy at all.

SERVES 8 TO 10

1 1/2 pounds cooked fish fillets or lutefisk, cut in bite-size pieces

1/2 cup chopped green onions or yellow onion

3 or 4 potatoes, peeled and cubed

2 carrots, peeled and coarsely shredded

2 stalks celery, cut up small

4 cups water

1 1/2 teaspoons salt

Dash of pepper

4 cups rich whole milk

1 cup whole kernel corn, cooked, or 1 jar of Canned Corn (page 91)

5 slices bacon, fried crisp and crumbled

1. Put the fish, onions, potatoes, carrots, celery, water, salt, and pepper in a large kettle. Cook slowly until the potatoes and carrots are tender.

2. Add the milk and the corn, and heat through, being careful not to let it scorch.

3. Serve with the bacon sprinkled on top.

OUR NEW ENGLAND CLAM CHOWDER

❈

We have land and sky here as far as the eye can see; you couldn't ask for more green in summer or white in winter—and there're no big, tall buildings to block our view. But many of us folks go for years, a lot of us even croak, without ever seeing the ocean. I'm told that all that raging water—the waves and birds and sky—is beautiful and that in some New England towns, fishermen give away lobster the way we do zucchini.

Years ago, Lorraine's relatives were here from the Coast and we liked the chowder they made so much that they were good enough to give us the recipe, and it's kind of funny, even people from Maine who come into the restaurant ask me for it.

Eau Claire, a town about twenty miles north of here, has fresh (as fresh as a trip on the airplane will allow) clams, and that's what we use. It'd be easier to buy a can at the grocery, but it wouldn't have the same flavor.

SERVES ABOUT 8

6 large clams (save liquid; see Note)

1/2 cup minced celery

1/4 cup minced onion

1 quart water

1 cup diced potatoes

8 tablespoons flour

1/2 cup (1 stick) butter

Salt and pepper to taste

1 cup evaporated milk

1. Wash the clams and steam them in a large kettle until they open. Remove the meat from the shell, and chop fine.

2. In a large kettle, cook the celery and the onion in the water until the celery is a little tender. When nearly done, add the potatoes, and cook until done.

3. Add the chopped clams and the clam broth.

4. In a small skillet, blend the flour and the butter over low heat; add it to the soup to thicken. Add the salt and pepper to taste.

5. Pour in the evaporated milk just before serving. If too thick, add more milk. (Be sure not to boil after adding the milk.)

NOTE: Always be careful when buying clams. Look at them closely, making sure they're tight shut and mostly blackish. Once the shells are bleached white, they are aged. Watch out.

ASSORTED MEATS
and
GRAVIES

In the old days, driving from farm to farm on a cold fall day, it wasn't unusual to see fifteen or sixteen chickens hanging from the clothesline, or a cow or pig strung up in a tree. It was often hard for us farm wives to have a Martha or Myrtle or Sy or Gus end up in our kettles, but no matter how attached we got to the animals, butchering was part of farm life. If we wanted something good to eat, we couldn't dwell on it, we took the knife and butchered.

The men folk most often slaughtered the cows and pigs, but chickens, that was women's work, and oh, was that tasty meat. Unlike today's factory chickens that are penned up, force fed, and killed at seven weeks, ours ran free. They clucked around and ate bugs and grass, and scratched at the barnyard and straw stacks for oats and corn until they grew big and round. Their meat was firm and solid, not slimy.

Hard as it was, we chopped their heads off with one sweep, tied a cord or twine around their feet and hung 'em upside down on the clothesline to bleed out so their bones would be white. We scalded their plump, rich yellow bodies in wash tubs, plucked their feathers, and set fire to a newspaper to singe the hair off. Then we cleaned and dressed 'em.

Away from the farm, when you're reaching for a chicken or ham or turkey, or any cut of meat, you may not always remember that the kind of life that animal lived and how it died is all-important to the way it will taste. If you're not raising and butchering your own meat, or you don't have an arrangement with the farmer up the road—if you're city folk, you're at the mercy of your butcher, and you have to find one you can trust.

In this area, there are still a few locker plants and a good number of small meat markets with fresh butchered meats. Just a few miles from here we have Howard Olson's Falls Meat Service (page 262), which is dandy, and about 30 miles down the way (both south from the restaurant), there's another old-time meat heaven, Pat's Country Meat Market (page 262). Pat's been in business twenty-eight years and in that time has won eighty-five national awards and many grand champions. Just as in the old days, twice a week, beef cattle and pigs arrive live at the back door, hauled in from just over the hill where they're raised by a few local, specialized farmers to ensure consistency of feed and life-style. The animals are butchered right there on the kill floor, dressed out, and displayed in a gleaming showcase.

Both Pat and Howard know meat, much the way I know pies, but if you don't have a Pat or Howard and supermarket meat is all you have available, you're on your own with your eyes and good sense. I've jotted down a few hints that might be helpful. As for my recipes, I hope you'll enjoy them and maybe even take time for the bolognas.

You won't find much veal or lamb in this section because it isn't eaten much in these parts, and I believe that has more to do with tradition than price.

Hints

• If you pay practically nothing for something, that's what you're getting, nothing.

• Know the grade of meat you're buying. Go for choice. Pay attention to the dots of fat, that is, the marbling in beef.

> *Utility:* You won't find any.
> *Standard:* You might find a few.
> *Good:* You'll start to get some marbling.
> *Low Choice:* There's marbling.
> *High Choice:* There's quite a bit of marbling.
> *Prime:* It's fat.

• For a good rib eye, you want a lot of marbling. Fat may or may not be good for you, but it's what makes the meat tender and taste good. There are some who don't eat meat much at all but when they do, they have the sense to go for good, fat-marbled meat; otherwise, why bother.

• New York strip and a T-bone are the same piece of meat. On a T-bone, there's a New York strip on one side and a tenderloin on the other. If you take them out separately and you fry them in a pan, they taste different, but if you fry them with the bone in 'em, they taste a little bit better. But everybody's kind of gone to boneless now because you don't have as much shipping cost. But the old-fashioned bone—a lot of the old-time butchers swear there's nothing like that bone to add flavor.

• Ideally, you want a little age on beef so it tenderizes. But unless you know your butcher, in buying beef, especially in a supermarket, look for nice red meat. If it's a little faded, it's getting old. If it's real dark, it's old meat. If I see a showcase where they have all dark meat, I don't buy meat there. It tells me they don't sell much, so their meat isn't much good. However, age in meat, if it's not too old, can add tenderness and flavor. But like I said, you should know the butcher to buy such meat. As long as it's in a clean, cool showcase and you're confident in the market, you might want to choose a steak that's purple over a real bright red one. Some farmers take their beef to the locker to hang for a couple weeks to get that age on it. On the outside, they might have to shave some off, but inside, oh, is it tender. But as a general rule, I look for nice red beef.

• If you have a nice piece of beef and want it to be especially tender, hang it in a cool, dry place for a couple of days until it ages. Air tenderizes the meat. But for gosh sakes, don't let it set or hang there too long or you'll have to do as the old-timers did, either shave the sides off or wipe it with a vinegar-soaked rag.

• Beef cattle ranged one summer, then fed in the feed lot since four months old on corn and no hay, have a good flavor. If they've lived in loose confinement, running around only in the feed lot, and they sleep on good, clean bedding without the fighting or stress of the range, their muscles aren't tightening or developing, so they're tender. Fat, not muscle, makes for flavor and a tender meat. (But cattle these days are slaughtered sooner so age isn't in the meat. While it's tender, it has a little less flavor, so you have to learn to season.)

• Any excitement from heat or rut or from fighting on the range, or stress before slaughter, can cause blood spots. Corpuscles break and leach out into the meat and you'll see red spots, but there's nothing wrong with the meat. (Animals killed by shock rather than bolt action will more often have less blood spots.)

• If hamburger doesn't taste good, it may be either from a silage-fed cow, or a cow with a tipped stomach. A lot of cull cows (cows farmers want to get rid of) are sold at auctions and they might have a tipped stomach (cows have four stomachs), and sometimes gas leaks out into the meat. Inspectors will approve the meat because there's nothing wrong with it, but it will have an off-taste. Rely on a butcher who either gets his livestock all from one farmer or one group, or who knows his cows and steer and has a good eye at the livestock market and auction barn.

• For hamburger, usually I like a higher grade than "ground beef." Ground chuck has a little less fat in it, it's redder, it doesn't have all that white suet in it that ground beef does, and it won't fry away. However, with ground round, an even higher grade (and the most expensive), you don't have enough fat, so it has a tendency to get hard and dry; it's not tender meat and can get to be like flavored sawdust.

• For pork, look for a slightly pinkish, lighter color. Such meat is most often from a younger animal and will be more tender. Generally, an older pig will have more color, although stress before slaughter or prolonged stress can darken the meat of a younger animal.

• Unlike beef, you don't want age in pork. Unless smoked, pork starts to turn bad the day it's butchered.

• You can pick up a sow in heat or a stag in rut by the taste of the meat. If you've noticed a strange odor while frying or baking pork, it could be a boar pig. PHEW! The wrong meat! Get the little feeder pig. Be sure that it's a girl pig, not a boy, unless it is an It. Heat and rut are often responsible for causing an otherwise unexplainable off-taste.

• In the country, ham is a very precious piece of meat. A bone-in ham will have a different flavor from the boneless or semiboneless ham. Get to know the difference and stay with what you like.

• If you're not going to butcher right out back, look for chickens and turkeys that have a certain amount of fat on 'em. At least here in the Midwest, the yellower the chicken, the tenderer it will be. (A chicken fed on cracked corn will be nice and plump and yellow.) A scrawny chicken isn't going to be good. A lot of fryers nowadays don't have yellow skin because they've been pushed (killed at five and a half to seven weeks), and they tend to be white or even gray looking. (Also, if a chicken has been force fed and butchered and bled in a hurry, you can get a lot of red around the bones even after proper cooking. It isn't going to hurt you; it just looks terrible.)

• Taste your meat as it cooks so you know how to season it, and watch out for the number one mistake: overcooking.

Beef and Pork Dishes

and Their Gravies

MEAT SEASONING

**MAKES ENOUGH FOR
ABOUT 4 ROASTS**

1 teaspoon garlic powder

1 teaspoon sugar

1 1/2 teaspoons salt

1 teaspoon turmeric

1 1/2 teaspoons paprika

4 teaspoons onion salt

1 teaspoon pepper

Mix all ingredients together and store in a tightly covered glass container. You don't want to make and store this in real large amounts because it loses its potency.

MEAT LOAF

**MAKES TWO 1½-POUND LOAVES
(ABOUT 16 SERVINGS)**

3 pounds hamburger or ground chuck

3 eggs

1 1/2 cups milk

3 cups soda cracker crumbs

1/2 cup crouton crumbs

1/2 teaspoon salt

1/4 teaspoon pepper

Pinch of dried sage

1 teaspoon mustard

2 teaspoons catsup

1/2 teaspoon Meat Seasoning (at left)

1/4 cup Barbecue Sauce (page 49)

1. Preheat the oven to 375° F. Put the hamburger into a large bowl. Put the eggs in a smaller bowl, and beat them with a wire whisk. Add the milk to the eggs, and mix well. Add the cracker and crouton crumbs to the egg mixture, and stir until well blended.

2. Put the salt, pepper, sage, mustard, catsup, Meat Seasoning, and Barbecue Sauce into the bowl with the meat. Pour the egg mixture over all, and knead until well mixed.

3. Divide in half, and place in two loaf pans. Bake for 1 hour, until meat shrinks away from the sides of the pan and is a nice brown on top.

MEATBALLS

MAKES 30 GOOD-SIZE MEATBALLS

6 pounds hamburger (see Note)

6 eggs (to hold meat together)

2 1/2 cups milk

1 1/2 cups ground soda crackers

1/2 cup ground Homemade Croutons (page 24)

1 teaspoon salt

1/2 teaspoon pepper

1/4 teaspoon dry mustard

1/4 teaspoon ground ginger

1/4 teaspoon dried sage

1 teaspoon Meat Seasoning (page 41)

1 small onion, grated or ground

1 teaspoon celery flakes

4 tablespoons flour

1 cup water

1. Preheat the oven to 375° F. Put the hamburger in a large bowl. In another bowl, put in the eggs, and beat them with a wire whisk.

2. Add the milk to the eggs, and stir until mixed. Add the cracker and crouton crumbs to the eggs, and stir.

3. Put in the salt, pepper, dry mustard, ginger, sage, meat seasoning, onion, and celery flakes in the hamburger, pour the egg mixture on top, and knead using your hands until all the meat is well mixed (dip your fingers in hot water, then the meat won't stick to them).

4. Knead and roll into meat balls.

5. Put the balls in a heavy cake pan (or 2), and bake for 1 hour, until done (see Note). (Sometimes I turn them after 30 minutes, and sometimes I don't.)

6. Remove the balls from the pans, rinse the pans with water, and put the juice into a small kettle. Make a paste with the flour and 1 cup water, and stir into the juices as for Hen House Gravy (page 51). (If you don't have enough drippings, you'll have to add beef broth or potato water.)

NOTE: You can use pork sausage by cutting the hamburger down to 5 pounds and adding 1 pound of pork sausage, but I use only hamburger for these at the Nook.

You can put these on cookie sheets with 1-inch lips instead of cake pans if you wish.

BEEF TIPS

SERVES 10 TO 12

5 pounds tenderloin tips, cut into 2-inch cubes

½ teaspoon salt

Dash of pepper

½ teaspoon Meat Seasoning (page 41)

2 tablespoons Butter Flavor Crisco

Enough potato water or plain water to almost cover meat

4 tablespoons flour

1 cup water

1. Season the tips with salt, pepper, and Meat Seasoning, and brown them in a heavy skillet in the Crisco over medium heat. Stir to brown evenly.

2. Pour water over the meat after browning, enough so it's about ½ inch from the top of the meat. Let it simmer on low heat for about 1 hour.

3. Remove the meat from the juice, and pour either potato water or plain water into the juice to make enough gravy to cover the meat.

4. Thicken the juice with a paste made from the flour and 1 cup water, and cook until smooth. Add the meat, and serve over Mashed Potatoes (page 74), Farm Noodles (page 24), or rice.

SWISS STEAK

SERVES 6 TO 8

½ cup flour

1 teaspoon salt

¼ teaspoon pepper

2 pounds round steak

2 tablespoons Butter Flavor Crisco

1 medium onion, sliced

½ cup water

1. Preheat the oven to 350° F. Mix the flour, salt, and pepper together, and sprinkle on top of the steak.

2. Lay the steak on a breadboard and pound it with a tenderizing mallet. Turn the steak over, and do the same.

3. Cut the steak into 6 or 7 pieces, brown the pieces in a heavy skillet in the Crisco over medium heat, and sprinkle the onions on top. Turn and brown the other side. (The onions will brown in the Crisco with the meat for added flavor.)

4. When brown, put the meat pieces and the onions in a small baking dish. Pour the water into the skillet to rinse out the pan, and pour this good-flavored juice over the meat and onions.

5. Bake for 30 minutes, until tender (a fork goes through easily).

6. Remove the meat from the juice and use the juice to make a tasty gravy.

SUNDAY ROAST AND GRAVY

Sunday was truly a day of rest on the farm. Unless we were racing the weather during planting or harvest, the day was set aside for church and visiting. Women got up early and put dinner in the oven, usually a beef or pork roast. It would cook while they were in church, then they could come home and quickly make the trimmings. To please our families and the men on the farm crew, us ladies were always trying to make better-tasting gravies. One of the secrets my grandmother found was to cook a beef chuck roast (chuck is the best small roast) and a pork roast together. This gives an extraordinary flavor.

At the restaurant, before I close up at night, I put on three twenty-two-pound beef roasts and six twelve-pound pork roasts to cook through until morning. Though simple, hot beef and pork and mashed potatoes and gravy is one of our better sellers. I think you'll like it. Serve with a fresh green salad and a bowl of Cherry or Rhubarb Sauce (pages 82 and 83).

SERVES 8 TO 10

ROAST

2 pounds beef chuck roast

2 pounds pork roast

2 teaspoons salt or enough in hand to taste

2 teaspoons pepper

2 large slices yellow onion

2 or 3 bay leaves

Enough water to cover

SUNDAY GRAVY

1/2 cup flour

A little cold water

Salt to taste

1 tablespoon Meat Seasoning (page 41)

1. *To prepare the roasts:* Preheat the oven to 250° F. Wash the meats and place them together in a roaster. Turn the lean sides down, the fat sides up to keep the meat moist.

2. Sprinkle with the salt and pepper and place a slice of thick, raw onion on each. Add 2 or 3 bay leaves to the top of the pork.

3. Fill the roaster with water to almost cover the meat. Cook slowly for 2½ to 3 hours, until you can poke a fork in easily. (You can either cover this or not, or cover and remove the cover when almost done. It cooks faster when it's covered, and it browns better.)

4. *To make Sunday Gravy:* Remove the roasts from the juice and make a thickening with the flour and a little cold water. (Make sure there's at least a quart of juice left in the pan when you remove the roast. If not, add some water.) Whip this until smooth. Slowly add the thickening to the juice, and whip until thick. Cook on top of the stove over medium heat for 5 minutes, until it comes to a full boil, stirring constantly. Season to taste with salt and meat seasoning. (If the gravy should happen to get too thick, add a little water, but be sure to boil real good to get rid of the flour taste.)

PORK ROAST: Use a 4-pound shoulder or loin roast, and season as for the Sunday Roast. Put in a roaster, add enough water to almost cover, and bake at least 2 hours at 325° F, until the meat comes away from the bone.

SIDE PORK AND MILK GRAVY

If you didn't grow up in the Midwest, some of you might wonder what side pork is. Well, it's sow belly, the exact same cut as bacon, but it's not cured, it's just fresh off the hog. If you like bacon and haven't tried side pork, you must—there's nothing like it. We serve it in the restaurant with whole potatoes and this gravy every January on Hard Times Day, and oh, do people love it.

SERVES 3 OR 4

1 pound fresh side pork (see Note)
2 tablespoons side pork drippings
2 tablespoons flour
1/2 teaspoon salt
Dash of pepper
1 3/4 cups milk

1. Cut the side pork into 8 slices. Place the pieces in a hot, heavy skillet.

2. Brown on both sides, frying until crisp. Place the pieces on a paper towel to drain off the fat. Save 2 tablespoons of the drippings for gravy in the skillet. (It may spatter when it gets too hot, so watch it.)

3. For milk gravy, put the skillet with the drippings back on low heat, and add the flour, salt, and pepper.

4. Add the milk gradually, stirring with a wire whisk until it gets smooth. Taste to see if more salt and pepper are needed. (This gravy is a must with side pork over mashed or whole fresh garden potatoes.)

N O T E : Salt pork is side pork that's been salted but not smoked. It has a whole other flavor, somewhere between side pork and bacon, and is usually fried up in a pan for breakfast. It's also great to use in Firehouse Baked Beans (page 72).

PORK CHOPS AND GRAVY

Years ago it seems people ate more pork than they do now. You kept the cows and fed them well for their milk, but the hogs, we slop-fed them almost anything—warm potato peelings, garden scraps, overripe corn, chicken fat, sour milk—they were our garbage disposal. When they got fat, we butchered.

1 pork chop per person (unless farm appetites)
Salt and pepper to taste
1 tablespoon flour
1/2 cup milk

1. Preheat the oven to 300° F. Sprinkle the chops with salt and pepper. Place in a baking pan, and bake uncovered for about 1 hour.

2. Remove the chops from the pan. If you want a cream gravy, place the baking pan (with the drippings) on a burner over low heat. Sprinkle the flour into the drippings.

3. Using a wire whisk, stir until there are no lumps, and then add the milk slowly to the flour mix. Cook until it gets to be smooth and creamy (about 5 minutes).

STUFFED
PORK CHOPS

1 pocket chop, 1½ inches thick, per person (see Note)

Seventh Heaven Stuffing (page 51)

Salt and pepper to taste

1. Preheat the oven to 350° F. Fill the pocket of each chop with Seventh Heaven Stuffing.

2. Sprinkle on the salt and pepper, place in a baking pan, and bake 1½ hours, until brown and tender.

NOTE: A pocket chop is a thick, fat pork chop with a slit down the fat side nearly to the bone. You can make them yourself (but be sure to cut the holes deep enough) or just ask your butcher for pocket chops.

PORK CHOPS AND
SAUERKRAUT

SERVES 6 TO 8

1 quart Homemade Sauerkraut (page 93), or store-bought, if you must

½ cup brown sugar

2 dashes of ginger

2 dashes of garlic powder

Dash of salt

2 dashes of rosemary

2 or 3 apples, peeled, cored, and diced

6 to 8 pork chops

1. Preheat the oven to 350°F. Sprinkle the kraut into a 9 × 13-inch pan and then sprinkle on the brown sugar, ginger, garlic powder, salt, rosemary, and apples on this. (Do not mix.)

2. Put the chops on top and bake for 1½ hours, or until chops are well done.

BREADED
PORK CHOPS

1 fresh pork chop per person

Salt and pepper to taste

Enough flour to dip chops in

3 eggs, beaten

Enough dry bread crumbs for rolling chops in

Tiny pinch of dried sage

1 teaspoon minced onion

1. Preheat the oven to 325° F. Sprinkle each chop with salt and pepper.

2. Dip each side in flour.

3. Dip each chop into the eggs, then roll in dry bread crumbs. Season again with a little salt and pepper and then the sage and minced onion.

4. Bake in a baking pan for about 1 hour, until tender.

CHERISHED OLD-TIME BAKED HAM

After we butchered, we'd stick willow sticks into the ham to make holes so salt brine could sink into them. We'd put them in the brine, in big crock jars in the basement, then after about three weeks, we'd hang the hams up in the smokehouse, and fire up. If it was winter, the hams could hang there until we ate 'em, but if it was early fall or spring, we'd bury them in the oats in the granary, and three months later, take one out to have for Sunday dinner. Hams were very precious, because it took so much of the pig to get just one, that's why we rarely had ham for breakfast. It was special, something only for Sunday or a holiday occasion.

SERVES 25 TO 30

1 (18-pound) smoked ham (see Note)
Enough whole cloves to stick in diamond shapes
Brown sugar for sprinkling over
Peach Pickle (page 88) or sweet pickle juice for pouring over

1. Preheat the oven to 275° F. Wash the ham well, place in a stainless steel kettle, and almost cover with cold water. Cook slowly (this is important) for about 4 hours. Skim off the broth that forms and leave the ham in the juice in the roaster overnight.

2. The next morning, cut off the outside skin, and place the ham back in the roaster.

3. Preheat the oven to 350° F. Make a few slits through the fat crosswise, making diamond shapes. Stick a clove in the center of each diamond.

4. Sprinkle brown sugar generously over the ham. Moisten with leftover pickle juice from peach or sweet pickles.

5. Bake for 1 hour, then lower the oven to 325° F. Baste the ham often with the drippings from the juice while you continue to bake for about 1 hour.

6. The last 15 minutes, cover with a little more brown sugar, but do not baste. Basting now will form a glaze.

NOTE: For today's ready-to-eat hams, place the ham in a roaster and follow the recipe from step 3 on.

HAM BALLS WITH SWEET-AND-SOUR SAUCE

MAKES 12 TO 16 BALLS, DEPENDING ON THE SIZE YOU ROLL THEM

1 1/2 pounds ground ham

1 1/2 pounds ground pork (see Note)

1 teaspoon salt and pepper

2 eggs

1 cup cracker crumbs

1 cup milk

SWEET-AND-SOUR SAUCE

3/4 cup vinegar

1 cup brown sugar

1/2 cup water

1 teaspoon dry mustard

2 tablespoons flour

1. *To make Ham Balls:* Preheat the oven to 325° F. Mix the ham, pork, salt, and pepper together in a large bowl.

2. Beat the eggs, and add them to the meat.

3. Soak the cracker crumbs in the milk, then add them to the meat and mix well.

4. Form into balls (about the size of a golf ball), and bake in a cake pan or on a rimmed cookie sheet for 2 hours. Turn after 1/2 hour. Cut one in half to see if they're done.

5. *To prepare Sweet-and-Sour Sauce:* Mix all the ingredients together in a medium saucepan, and cook over medium heat until a little thick. Serve with Ham Balls (at left).

NOTE: This is best if you grind the pork from the leftovers of a pork roast and the ham from a leftover ham butt. Grind the meat using the medium blade of the meat grinder (or food chopper).

HAM LOAF

MAKES 1 LOAF

1 1/2 pounds ground ham

3/4 pound fresh ground pork

2 eggs, beaten

1 1/2 cups bread crumbs

1 cup milk

Salt and pepper to taste

3/4 cup packed brown sugar

2 tablespoons flour

1 tablespoon dry mustard

1 tablespoon vinegar

1. Preheat the oven to 325° F. In a large bowl, put the ham and pork. In a smaller bowl, put the eggs. Add the bread crumbs to the eggs, and allow them to soak.

2. Dump the milk and the crumbs into the meat bowl, add the salt and pepper, and mix well. Place in a buttered bread pan.

3. Mix the brown sugar, flour, dry mustard, and vinegar together in a small bowl, and spread on top of the loaf. Bake for 1 1/2 hours, until the meat shrinks away from the edge of the pan.

BARBECUE COUNTRY-STYLE RIBS

SERVES 8 TO 10

1 teaspoon salt

½ teaspoon pepper

½ teaspoon Meat Seasoning (page 41)

8 to 10 country-style ribs (see Note)

BARBECUE SAUCE

1 cup catsup

6 tablespoons vinegar

½ teaspoon smoked salt

2 tablespoons water

4 teaspoons Worcestershire sauce

2 teaspoons prepared mustard

¼ cup brown sugar

¾ cup tomato juice

1. *To prepare the ribs:* Preheat the oven to 350° F. Sprinkle the salt, the pepper, and the Meat Seasoning over the ribs, and bake 1 hour, until a fork goes in easily. Remove the ribs from the oven and turn the heat down to 325° F.

2. *To make Barbecue Sauce:* Mix all the sauce ingredients together in a stainless steel kettle, and heat until it comes to a boil.

3. Put the ribs in a small roaster. Pour the sauce over, and return it to the oven for 1 hour to get the good barbecue flavor into the meat (see Note).

NOTE: Country-style ribs are thicker and have much more meat on them than spareribs.

This sauce may also be used for plain pork chops or spareribs prepared the same way as these country-style ribs.

RIBS AND KRAUT

SERVES 8 TO 10

6 pounds spareribs

Salt and pepper to taste

1 quart Homemade Sauerkraut (page 93)

1. Preheat the oven to 350° F. Cut up the ribs, allowing 2 bones per cut.

2. Put them in a roaster, and sprinkle with the salt and pepper. Place the cover on the roasting pan, and bake 1 hour.

3. Remove the roaster from the oven, pour the sauerkraut over the ribs, and bake 30 minutes longer.

*Turkey,
Chicken,*

*and Their Gravies
and Stuffings*

ROAST TURKEY
OR CHICKEN

✳

In the old days, especially, you really got to know your chickens. You raised Leghorns for eggs, and White Rocks or Rhode Island Reds for meat. Leghorns laid white eggs, Reds and Rocks laid brown ones. The white eggs were a better seller, but I liked the brown ones for the flavor and harder shell. Anyway, the Reds and Rocks were larger-bodied birds, just perfect for roasting, stuffing, and canning. There was meat on those bones, and when stuffed and roasted, they looked like little turkeys.

Reds and Rocks were easygoing, not flighty like Leghorns. If a stranger walked into the coop, Leghorns would fly around and put up an awful fuss. They had a temper, too. When you reached under them in the nest to pick the eggs, they would squawk and peck at you with their sharp beaks. But Reds and Rocks were nice. They'd talk to you in chicken language and they loved to be petted. It was hard to see them go into the kettle.

*1 turkey or large chicken (a White Rock if you
can get it; see Note)*

Seventh Heaven Stuffing (page 51)

Enough soft butter to grease bird

Salt and pepper to taste

1. Preheat the oven to 350° F. Wash the bird thoroughly inside and out, remove the giblets, and save. To drain, set it on its bare bottom. Stuff the bird with Seventh Heaven Stuffing.

2. When done stuffing, plug the opening with the gizzard so the dressing doesn't fall out. Lay the bird on its back in the roaster. (If you don't want its legs to stick up in the air, tie its legs down to the body with some cord, but I never did.)

3. Grease the breast and the legs with butter, sprinkle a little salt and pepper over, and bake in a large roaster for 5 or 6 hours for an 18- to 20-pound turkey; 2 hours for an 8-pound capon or large hen; 1 hour for a 4- to 5-pound chicken.

NOTE: Be sure to remove the giblets. I roast 6 turkeys at a time for the Nook. We have a good laugh removing the necks from the cavity of the turkeys when they're still partially frozen. One of us will hold the turkey while another pulls at the neck. We pull and pull; we start to think they're two feet long by the time we get them out. We call it a necking party. Much bracing is needed.

SEVENTH HEAVEN STUFFING

**ENOUGH STUFFING FOR
AN 18-POUND TURKEY OR
A DOZEN CHOPS
(BUT FOR CHOPS, SEE NOTE)**

1 dry loaf of homemade bread

1/2 pound (2 sticks) butter

1 cup chopped celery

1 small onion, chopped

The heart and liver of a chicken or turkey, chopped

1 quart water

1 teaspoon salt

1/4 teaspoon pepper

2 teaspoons dried sage

1. Break the dry bread into pieces.

2. Brown the butter, celery, onion, heart, and liver in a heavy skillet over medium heat until the celery is clear.

3. Pour the water over this, and let it come to a boil.

4. Place the bread crumbs in a large mixing bowl, and add the salt, pepper, and sage.

5. Pour the boiled mixture over the pieces, and mix until all the bread is wet. Stuff your bird or chops.

NOTE: If you wish to make stuffed pork chops, use this recipe but omit the heart and liver.

HEN HOUSE GRAVY

One thing I notice when making gravy with thickening: Put enough water in the flour right away or it will get lumpy. Start beating, and beat until it gets nice and smooth. It's better to make it a little on the thin side and make it a little smoother; you can always add more thickening.

3 CUPS OF GRAVY

1 pint chicken or turkey broth

1/2 cup flour

1 cup cold water

Seasonings to taste

1. Bring the broth to a boil in a heavy skillet.

2. Put the flour in a small bowl and add the cold water to make the thickening. Then add this to the broth, stirring all the time while adding.

3. Let it come to a rolling boil, reduce the heat, then let it boil for several minutes. If the gravy gets too thick, add more water. Season to your taste.

FRIED CHICKEN

When I was a girl, there were no real fancy proms or outings, but twice a year in the evening and one Sunday afternoon each summer, the community club or church would hold a basket social. The older folks would bring potluck for themselves, and all us young girls would fuss with food for a basket we packed and tied up with fancy ribbon. We'd make sandwiches (or in summer, fried chicken), baked beans, fresh cinnamon buns, cake, or pie, depending on how taken we were with the boys who'd be bidding on our baskets. Our names were hidden amid the food, but if you were especially sweet on someone, you told him what ribbon to look for and hoped he had enough money and liked you enough to outbid the guy who turned your stomach.

This fried chicken was a special treat in those days, and it's a good traveler.

SERVES 4 TO 6

1 chicken

2 cups flour

1 teaspoon salt

Dash of pepper

1/2 teaspoon Meat Seasoning (page 41)

Enough butter or Butter Flavor Crisco to brown chicken

1. Preheat the oven to 350° F. Wash and cut up the chicken, and let the pieces dry on paper toweling.

2. Mix the flour, salt, pepper, and Meat Seasoning together on a plate, and roll each piece of chicken in the flour mixture.

3. Brown the coated chicken over medium heat in a heavy skillet, in the butter or Crisco. (Turn it so it browns evenly.)

4. Place the chicken pieces in a baking pan, and bake for 1 hour, until tender.

CREAMED CHICKEN

This chicken dish is to be served over buttered Company Bread (page 4), Fair's Choice Baking Powder Biscuits (page 15), or Mashed Potatoes (page 74).

MAKES 12 SERVINGS

1 whole chicken

2 stalks celery

1/2 onion

1 teaspoon salt

Dash of pepper

4 tablespoons flour

1 cup water

1. Wash and cut up the chicken. Place it in a large stainless steel kettle, and cover with water. Throw in a couple of stalks of celery (it's not necessary to cut it up). Add the onion, salt, and pepper; cover and cook over medium heat about 1 hour, until tender.

2. Remove the kettle from the stove; remove the chicken from the broth. Pick the meat from the bone, and cut it into small pieces.

3. Strain the broth. Make a paste with the flour and 1 cup water; add this to the broth and cook until smooth. Add the chicken, heat all together on low, and serve.

MOCK CHICKEN LEGS

I'm told that during the Depression, in union towns, this was called "city chicken." Out here in the country we never called it that, but it was always something special.

MAKES 8 TO 12 (6-INCH) SKEWERS

1 pound round steak

1 pound pork steak

Salt and pepper to taste

Enough flour for dusting

2 eggs, beaten

2 cups crushed soda crackers

1/4 cup shortening

Onion (or not)

1 1/2 cups water

1. Preheat the oven to 325° F. Cut the round and pork steak into 2-inch pieces. Arrange the meat alternately, the beef and pork on skewers (see Note), putting large pieces on one end, and small on the other to look like chicken legs. Salt and pepper each leg.

2. Roll each leg in flour, and dip them in the eggs. Then roll them in the cracker crumbs. Brown the legs in a heavy skillet in the shortening over medium heat. Add the onion now, if using, and turn meat to brown all sides.

3. Place in a small roaster and add water. Bake 1 hour, until tender.

NOTE: I use wooden skewers I get at Falls Meat Service (page 262). Wetting them with water before use prevents possible scorching.

BEER BATTER

When using my recipe for beer batter for chicken or fish, allow one can of beer for the batter and one for yourself. If making many batches, you probably won't know what you're doing, but you must be frying lots of chicken or fish. I use this batter for the Friday Night Fish Fry at the Nook.

ENOUGH FOR 1 CUT-UP CHICKEN OR 6 POUNDS FRESH FISH

4 eggs, beaten

1 teaspoon salt

2 cups flour

2 cups beer (to begin with)

Enough Crisco oil to fill deep fryer to one-half full

1. Mix the eggs, salt, flour, and beer together in a flat bowl.

2. Put the oil into a deep fryer and heat. (When a 2-inch cube of bread dropped into the oil browns in 3 minutes, the oil is ready.)

3. Wipe the chicken (or fish) pieces dry, and dip them, one by one into the batter. Place the piece in the fryer. (Chicken will take about 30 minutes, but check because you don't want it pink; fish takes only a few minutes.) Turn over to make sure they are brown on both sides, and well done.

4. When removing the meat from the fat, place it on a paper towel to remove any excess oil. (If the batter gets too thick, add a little more beer. So don't sip too much of it or you'll run short!)

Bolognas, Sausage, Liver,

and Tongue

HOME-GROUND BOLOGNA

There's nothing like the thick scent of hickory as it billows from the smokehouse and hangs in the crisp winter air. Though few and far between now, the old smokehouse out back was a prized place on almost every farm. It was always small and looked like an outhouse. Some were wood, others were concrete block, but there was always a hole in the roof that was covered with a piece of webbed tin or wire so birds and rodents couldn't crawl in. Stones were arranged in the middle of the smokehouse on the ground to form an open fire pit, where the hickory fire was lit and fed every couple hours.

The little puffing shack, if full, could make even the poorest farmer feel like a millionaire.

Inside, sides of bacon, dried beef, bologna rings, and whole hams hung from high iron hooks and caught the smoke on its way up. The secret to good smoking was that top venting so that the opening could be adjusted according to how much smoke flavor a family wanted. It took anywhere from a couple of days to a week before the hickory fire was allowed to die, and if it was late fall or winter, the meat hung there until it was eaten.

Almost every farm has a story about the time the smokehouse caught fire. Even the concrete structures had wooden doors, and as the grease dripped down into the open fire, it didn't take much to ignite the whole shebang. But for every real fire, there was probably at least one false alarm. Many a time townsfolk drove by and ran breathless to the farmhouse door, knocking and calling out, "Your outhouse is afire! Your outhouse is on fire!"

MAKES ABOUT 6 OR 7 RINGS

10 pounds beef (chuck roast is good for this)

3 pounds pork sausage

1 large onion

3 tablespoons salt

1 teaspoon pepper

1 teaspoon ground ginger

Enough natural casings (see Note)

1. Get a partner (someone to turn the grinder handle while you cut up the meat, feed it into the opening, poke it through, and mash it down with a wooden masher).

2. Make sure the knives are sharp on the grinder. Clean the casings (see Note) or buy them at a locker plant or a good meat market.

3. Grind the beef and the sausage twice: first a coarse grind, then a finer one. Let the meat fall into a clean dishpan.

4. Grind the onion into a separate bowl, mix in the salt, pepper, and ginger, and add to the meat in the dishpan. Mix thoroughly using your hands. Squish and mash until completely combined.

5. Remove the knives from the grinder and attach the spout. Slip the casings onto the spout, hold the casings to the spout with one hand, and turn the crank with the other as your partner pokes the meat mixture back through. Allow the meat to flow into the casing until you get enough for a ring of bologna, then give it a twist, and tie with a heavy cord (see Note).

6. Cut off the casing, form into a ring, tie the ends together, and repeat. (If a bubble appears in the ring, prick it with a darning needle.)

7. Hang the rings in the smokehouse (or not), or use a Hasty-Bake charcoal oven and smoke to your taste (see Note).

NOTE: These days you can buy natural casings in a good locker plant or meat market, but in my day, we made our own from the animals we butchered. We took a little knife and scraped the fat off the intestines, but boy, did you have to be careful not to puncture 'em or the meat would squish out. After we'd scraped 'em, we kept on and on, washing and washing those intestines until they were just as snow white as those you buy today. (If buying casings, however, be sure you get the natural casings [most often sheep intestines].)

You must have a sausage stuffer, a simple attachment for your meat grinder or food chopper (page 261), to do this.

If you don't have a smokehouse, don't be discouraged; small modern-day smokers are available. In fact, Hasty-Bake (page 262) is a wonderful small company that makes such high-performing, convenient charcoal ovens —a smoker, grill, and barbecuer all in one— people bequeath them in their wills to their dearest of loved ones. However, if you don't want to do your own smoking but still like to make your own bolognas, ask at your local meat market if they'll do the smoking for you.

This bologna doesn't have to be smoked; it can just be slowly cooked (about 1 hour, until a fork goes through easily) in a large kettle of water (later you can slice and fry it if you like). If you're not smoking or cooking it right away, though, it must be frozen.

PORK SAUSAGE LINKS

MAKES 30 TO 40 LINKS

10 pounds side pork

1/4 cup salt

1 tablespoon pepper

1 tablespoon dried sage

1 teaspoon allspice

1 teaspoon ground ginger

Enough natural casings (see Note, page 55)

1. Grind the pork as for Home-Ground Bologna (page 54) through step 3, then mix all the ingredients (except casings) together thoroughly (see Note).

2. Place the casings on the meat stuffer, and fill. (Care must be taken not to fill too full but rather to pinch, twist, and tie to make link size.)

3. Fry immediately, or refrigerate and fry as needed.

NOTE: Sample this before stuffing the casings by making a little patty and frying it. Add more seasoning if your taste says so.

LIVER BOLOGNA

MAKES ABOUT 2 SMALL RINGS

2 pounds ground liver

1/2 pound ground pork

1/2 pound ground beef

4 teaspoons salt

2 teaspoons sugar

1 teaspoon pepper

8 tablespoons grated onion

1/2 teaspoon allspice

Enough natural casings (see Note, page 55)

1. Grind the liver, pork, and beef together as for the Home-Ground Bologna (page 54) through step 3.

2. Add the salt, sugar, pepper, onion, and allspice to the meat, and mix thoroughly.

3. Stuff into casings as for the Home-Ground Bologna and form into rings.

4. Put the ring into a large kettle with enough water to cover, and cook slowly over medium heat for about 1 hour.

5. Refrigerate, and eat as you like.

ARNOLD'S VENISON BOLOGNA

Every November, about two weeks before Thanksgiving, Wisconsin's woods fill with deer hunters. Even small country markets process more than fifty tons each of venison a year. For many, deer hunting is a sport and a well-earned vacation, but for more and more struggling farm families, that meat makes a big difference in their freezer.

I'm not a hunter; Lorraine is, and she has many stories. One year she was feeding the chickens before she headed to the woods and a rooster flew at her and hit a nerve in her ankle. As bad as it hurt, she was determined to get to the woods, so she dragged out some old crutches, and off she went. She managed to get to her stand while her husband, Arnie, took off across the field on foot to scout. She didn't wait long before a buck came and she shot it, but there was still not a hide-nor-hair sign of her husband. Somehow she struggled and got the deer dressed, but as hard as she tried, with her foot throbbing, she couldn't get the deer strung all the way up in the tree. She'd hoist it up a ways, then it'd drop down; up a ways, and back down. Finally the pain got too much and she sat down by the tree and cried. But before too many tears, here come her husband with a whole group of orange-clad men laughing and laughing. The deer's hinder was touching the ground, and from a distance it looked as if the two of them were just sitting by the tree conversing.

MAKES ABOUT 10 RINGS

15 pounds venison trimmings

5 pounds pork

³/4 pound salt

2 ounces pepper

1 teaspoon garlic powder

¹/4 teaspoon saltpeter

1 teaspoon ground ginger

1 cup grated onion

Enough natural casings (see Note, page 55)

1. Grind the venison and pork together as for Home-Ground Bologna (page 54) through step 3.

2. Mix the salt, pepper, garlic powder, saltpeter, ginger, and onion, and add to the meat mixture. Mix thoroughly.

3. Place casings on the meat stuffer and stuff the casings 18 to 20 inches long; twist and tie both ends. Tie together to make a ring. Smoke (or not) to your taste (see Note).

NOTE: This bologna doesn't have to be smoked; it can just be slowly cooked in a big kettle of water, then later you can slice it and fry it if you like. If not smoking or cooking it right away, though, it must be frozen.

LIVER AND ONIONS

SERVES 6 TO 8

1 cup flour

1/2 teaspoon salt

Dash of pepper

1 pound pork liver, sliced thick

3 tablespoons Butter Flavor Crisco

1 medium onion, sliced

1. Put the flour, salt, and pepper in a flat-bottomed bowl.

2. Lay the pieces of liver, one at a time, in the flour mixture, and dust thoroughly.

3. Place in a heated heavy skillet with the Crisco and fry over medium heat. Put the sliced onion on top of the liver.

4. Fry 8 minutes on each side. (Do not overfry or you can use it for shoe soles.)

VARIATION: I also like this baked with bacon. I usually brown the liver a little bit, put it in a roaster, lay strips of bacon on top (raw), cover it, and bake it in a 325° F oven. But remember, you don't want your liver slices too thin if you're going to stick it in the oven.

BEEF OR PORK TONGUE

MAKES ABOUT 24 SLICES, DEPENDING ON THE SIZE OF THE TONGUE

1 fresh pig or cow tongue

1 teaspoon salt

1/4 teaspoon pepper

1/2 onion, sliced

1. Put the tongue in a large kettle with enough water to cover. Add the salt, pepper, and onion.

2. Cover, and boil over medium heat until tender enough you can stick in a fork easily (about 1 hour because tongue is tough).

3. Remove from broth, and cool. Peel off the skin, and slice the tongue to the thickness you want for sandwiches. (Discard the skin and broth, or feed it to the pigs.)

LIVER POTATO CAKE

This is a simple but good way to use up liver. Any liver will do, but I prefer hog liver because it's not as strong as other livers.

FOR A 9 × 13-INCH CAKE PAN

½ hog liver

1 onion, chopped

1 pound pork

Salt and pepper to taste

6 potatoes

Enough flour to make a biscuit dough consistency

1. Preheat the oven to 325° F. Grind the liver, onion, and pork. Add the salt and pepper, mix, and fry in a heavy skillet until it doesn't have the blood color.

2. Grind or grate the potatoes. (Nowadays I use a blender or food processor for this.) Add them to the skillet, and stir in with the liver.

3. Add the flour until the mixture in the skillet is doughy (like biscuit dough).

4. Remove from heat, put this batter in a 9 × 13-inch cake pan, and bake 1 hour (depending on how thick it is). It is done when it shrinks from the sides of the pan and is nicely browned on top.

LIVER SAUSAGE AND GRAVY DISH

SERVES 4 TO 8

1 pound pork sausage

1 small onion, chopped

1 pound liver

Enough flour for rolling plus 2 tablespoons flour

1 cup water

1 teaspoon salt

⅛ teaspoon pepper

1. Preheat the oven to 350°F.

2. In a skillet brown the sausage, then place in a 2-quart casserole (leave grease in skillet).

3. Brown the onion in the skillet with the sausage drippings over medium heat, then dump it into the casserole (leave drippings in skillet).

4. Cut the liver into strips, roll in flour, and fry in the skillet with the drippings over medium heat until brown, then add the liver to the casserole. (Leave 2 tablespoons of drippings in the skillet. Pour off and save or discard the rest.)

5. Blend the 2 tablespoons of flour and the water together in a cup. Gradually pour this into the skillet (where you left the 2 tablespoons of drippings) and stir with a whisk over medium heat until thick enough for a gravy. Add the salt and pepper and pour over the meat. Bake for 30 minutes, or until well done.

FRESH *and* CANNED
TREASURES
from the
GARDEN
and
WILD PATCHES

Spring to fall on the farm, the garden is a world. Even in winter when it lies frozen and barren under the deep, white drifts, it stands as a promise of better days to come. That plowed square or rectangle, however stubbled, is as real as a child, needing long hours of care, but in return, to farm folks, it can mean the difference between just barely getting along and having a little extra.

Back in the Depression, when an unmailed letter would wait for months on the table for a two-cent stamp, a garden, a few chickens, and a couple of cows got many people through. That's something farm people don't forget. Wild berry patches, the chicken house, the pastures, and the garden remain a precious and main source of food. In our lives, milk comes from a cow, not a carton; potatoes and corn from the ground, not a bag; our meat we get from a fat beef or pig or yesterday's clucking chicken, not from a box or cellophane package.

Even with all of today's modern conveniences, there are still very few things that give me as good a feeling as carrying an apron full of fresh beans in from the garden or going down to the cellar in winter and seeing the shelves full of canning's bright colors—the silvery white of pear sauce; the deep reds of strawberry preserves; the blues, oranges, yellows, and greens of assorted vegetables, berries, and pickles in their shining glass jars.

Some things are just too good to let slip into a past era; that's how I feel about farm freshness and canning. This section is filled with the methods of pickling, cooking, and preserving I learned from my grandmother, who in turn learned from hers. Just remember, for canning, pick a cool morning—and on a subzero day in December, you'll have your reward.

Salads and Dressings

LEAF LETTUCE SALAD

This was a favorite years ago because leaf lettuce was easy to grow. Head lettuce was such a bother to get to grow right, most of us said to heck with it, but we waited and waited for the first fresh, bright leaves of our leaf lettuce. It was a real treat if the rabbits didn't get it first.

SERVES 4 TO 6

1 bunch leaf lettuce
1/4 cup vinegar
1/2 cup sugar
1/2 teaspoon salt

1. Wash and drain the lettuce leaves well.

2. Mix the vinegar, the sugar, and the salt together, and taste to see if you want more sugar.

3. In a bowl, layer the lettuce, pouring a little of the vinegar mixture over each layer. Continue until all the lettuce is used.

4. Refrigerate, and toss before serving.

COLESLAW

SERVES 10 TO 12

1 head fresh cabbage

2 carrots

1 cup sugar

4 eggs

1/2 cup vinegar

1/2 teaspoon salt (to taste)

2 teaspoons celery seed

1 teaspoon mustard if you like it with a kick (or not)

1. Shred the cabbage and the carrots into a big crock or bowl.

2. In a medium saucepan, mix the sugar and the eggs thoroughly, then add the vinegar, salt, celery seed, and mustard (if using). Cook on low heat until thick, stirring constantly.

3. Remove from heat, and cool (see Note). Pour over the carrots and cabbage.

NOTE: This coleslaw dressing may be stored in the refrigerator for quite a while, but not more than a month.

NORSKE NOOK COLESLAW: Shred a large head of cabbage and a big carrot into a large bowl. If you had a rural midwestern childhood, add 2 cups of Miracle Whip and 1/2 cup of sugar, and mix well using a wooden spoon. I mix hard and long enough to almost beat it, so it gets creamy.

BEAN SALAD

SERVES 10 TO 12

2 cups cooked and cooled yellow wax beans

2 cups cooked and cooled green beans

1 (16-ounce) can kidney beans

1/2 cup chopped green pepper

1 cup chopped celery

1/2 cup onion, minced

3/4 cup sugar

1/2 cup vegetable oil

1/2 cup vinegar

1 teaspoon salt

1/2 teaspoon pepper

1. Put the beans, green pepper, celery, and onion into a large bowl.

2. In a separate bowl, mix the sugar, oil, vinegar, salt, and pepper, and pour it over the beans.

3. For a better flavor, store it a day in the refrigerator before serving. (So long as this is refrigerated, it's a good keeper.)

FRENCH DRESSING

❋

MAKES 1 QUART

1 cup catsup

1 cup salad oil

1/3 cup vinegar

3 onions, grated

3 cloves garlic, crushed

3 tablespoons sugar

3 teaspoons paprika

3 teaspoons salt

1 teaspoon celery seed

Pinch of dry mustard

1. Place all the ingredients in a quart jar, or a container with a tight lid, and shake well.

2. Refrigerate.

ROQUEFORT DRESSING

❋

MAKES 3½ CUPS

4 ounces Roquefort cheese

2 tablespoons lemon juice

2 cups Homemade Mayonnaise (at right)

1 cup sour cream

1 clove garlic, minced

1. Break up the cheese in a medium bowl, add the lemon juice, and mix together.

2. Blend in the mayonnaise, sour cream, and garlic. Taste. (You may want to sprinkle in a little salt.)

3. Serve, and store the rest in the refrigerator in a glass jar or any tightly closed container.

HOMEMADE MAYONNAISE

❋

MAKES ½ PINT

1 tablespoon butter

2 tablespoons flour

1/2 cup water

1 egg yolk, well beaten

1/2 teaspoon dry mustard

1/2 teaspoon salt

Dash of paprika

1 tablespoon vinegar

1/2 cup salad oil

1. In a heavy skillet over low heat, melt the butter and stir in the flour, using a wooden spoon to make a white sauce. Add the water, and cook until thick and white.

2. Add the egg yolk, mustard, salt, and paprika, and cook until smooth.

3. Put the vinegar in a medium mixing bowl, add the cooked ingredients, and beat with a mixer on medium speed (see Note). Add the oil slowly until all is mixed.

4. Put into a glass jar or any container with a tight cover, and refrigerate.

NOTE: If you want this more like Miracle Whip, add 1 teaspoon of sugar.

FRESH CREAMED CUCUMBERS

✳

MAKES 1 MEDIUM BOWL

3 (10- to 12-inch) cucumbers, peeled and sliced ⅛ inch thick

1 onion the size of an egg, sliced ⅛ inch thick

1 tablespoon salt to sprinkle on for soaking

½ cup Homemade Mayonnaise (page 64)

Dash of pepper

1. Put the cucumbers and onion slices into a medium bowl, sprinkle with salt, and let them set for several hours. (This will form a juice.)

2. Drain, and add the mayonnaise and pepper. Place in the refrigerator for a couple of hours to marinate.

OLD-TIME CUKES: Prepare the cucumbers as above in step 1, but do not add the mayonnaise. Use ½ cup sweet cream, 1 teaspoon sugar, and 1 tablespoon cider vinegar instead. Add the pepper, and store as in step 2.

POTATO SALAD

✳

MAKES 1 LARGE BOWL

5 pounds potatoes, boiled, cooled, and peeled (see Note)

8 hard-boiled eggs, quartered

1 batch Potato Salad Dressing (at right)

Salt and pepper to taste

2 tablespoons minced fresh onion

1 tablespoon prepared mustard

1. Cut the potatoes into a large bowl. (Cut into large chunks or they'll tend to mush up when you pour the dressing on.) Add the eggs.

2. In a separate medium bowl, combine the dressing, salt, pepper, onion, and mustard together. Taste, and doctor to your liking.

3. Pour the dressing over the potatoes, and gently mix together.

NOTE: It's better to have the potatoes on the firm side. Don't overcook, or they'll get mushy.

POTATO SALAD DRESSING

✳

ENOUGH FOR 1 BIG BOWL OF POTATO SALAD

2 eggs, beaten

1 teaspoon flour

½ cup sugar

½ cup vinegar

½ teaspoon salt

Dash of pepper

3 tablespoons butter

Enough cream to get the consistency you like

1. Combine the eggs, flour, sugar, vinegar, salt, and pepper in a medium saucepan. Boil until thick, stirring as need be. Remove from heat, and add the butter.

2. This will be quite thick, so add cream to it until it gets to be the consistency you like.

3. Add to the salad as directed. (If you are using this on its own, this also keeps very well in the refrigerator.)

RASPBERRY PRETZEL SALAD

Oh, is this ever good!

SERVES 15

2 (3-ounce) packages raspberry gelatin

2 cups boiling water

2½ cups fresh raspberries (or fresh frozen)

½ cup crushed pretzels

¾ cup butter

2 tablespoons sugar

8 ounces cream cheese

1 cup sugar

1 cup freshly whipped cream

1. Put the gelatin in the boiling water in a small bowl, and stir until all the gelatin is dissolved. Place in the refrigerator, and cool until it begins to gel.

2. Add the berries, pour into a serving bowl, and place in the refrigerator to set.

3. Preheat the oven to 350° F. In a separate bowl, mix the pretzels with the melted butter and 2 tablespoons of sugar, and spread into a 9 × 13-inch cake pan. Bake 10 minutes, then remove, stir, and cool (see Note).

4. After the gelatin has set, beat the cream cheese, 1 cup of sugar, and the freshly whipped cream together until it's well blended. Spread over the gelatin, and top with the pretzel mix. Pat down a little on top of the pretzels.

5. Let set in the refrigerator until ready to serve.

NOTE: If you have any crushed pretzel mixture left over, it's delicious over homemade ice cream (pages 218 to 222).

SHOESTRING POTATO SALAD

This is great for a cold lunch or snack.

SERVES 12

1 cup chopped celery

1 cup shredded carrots

1 tablespoon grated onion

2 cups chicken, cut into chunks

1 pint sour cream

1 cup Miracle Whip (see Note)

1 (7-ounce) can shoestring potatoes

1. Mix all the ingredients together. Don't be afraid to use your hands to mix. They do a better job than a spoon.

2. Refrigerate.

NOTE: If you didn't grow up in the Midwest, you might want to use Homemade Mayonnaise (page 64) or store-bought mayonnaise in place of the Miracle Whip.

GLADYS'S COTTAGE CHEESE SALAD

MAKES A LARGE BOWL

1 (9-ounce) can crushed pineapple and its juice

Enough hot water so when added to pineapple juice it will make 1 cup

1 package lime gelatin

2 cups miniature marshmallows

Dash of salt

1 cup small-curd cottage cheese

1 cup freshly whipped cream

1/2 cup chopped walnuts

1. Drain the pineapple juice from the can into a 1-cup measure. Add enough hot water to make 1 cup. Use this to dissolve the lime gelatin in a large bowl.

2. Add the marshmallows and salt, and stir until the marshmallows are dissolved.

3. Place in the refrigerator, and let this start to set. When it begins to gel, add the cottage cheese, cream, and walnuts. Let it set for several hours in the refrigerator before serving.

Vegetables

FRESH GARDEN PEAS

As many fresh, plump garden peas as you want to serve (remember it takes a lot of pods to amount to anything once they're shucked; see Note)

Enough butter to flavor (and/or half-and-half or cream)

Salt and pepper to taste

1. When the peas in the garden are plump (but not too plump, or they'll be tasteless), pick and shuck them, and place them in a heavy kettle with enough salted water to cover.

2. Cook over medium heat about 10 minutes, then drain, and add butter (and/or warmed half-and-half or cream). Season with salt and pepper to taste, and serve in individual dishes.

NOTE: If you don't have a lot of peas once they're shelled, to stretch them, you can put them in a cream sauce made by melting 2 tablespoons of butter in a skillet over medium heat. Stir in 1 tablespoon of flour, and 1 cup of milk to thicken. Shake in salt and pepper to taste. (You can double this for a large batch.)

Another way to stretch the little gems is to steam them with fresh baby carrots.

CORN ON THE COB

There's nothing like corn on the cob when it's picked fresh from the stalk and cooked. But timing is everything. It's time to check for ripeness when its white hair starts to show brown. Carefully pull apart a little of the husk near the tip and gently poke your fingernail into a kernel. If the kernel is a light gold color and milk spurts out, it's ready. It's too ripe if the milk doesn't want to squirt. Then it's only good for canning relish if mixed with less-ripened cobs.

> 2 or 3 ears of corn for each person you're serving
>
> Large kettle of salted or unsalted water (see Note)
>
> Salt and pepper to taste
>
> Lots of butter

1. Remove husks and hair and drop the clean cobs into a large kettle of boiling salted water. Boil until the milk in the kernel does not squirt out (if it does, you'll get a belly ache; see Note).

2. Drain, and pile onto a platter. Sprinkle with salt and pepper to taste.

3. Place the platter on the table near a large dish of butter, so you can be generous with the spreading. (You can also butter bread and rub it over the cobs.)

NOTE: Some folks I know like to cook this in plain water. But out here on the farm, we like it cooked in salted water and topped with so much butter it runs down your arms.

Golden Bantam is the most common type of sweet corn here. We cook it 15 to 20 minutes because we cook 12 to 15 ears at a time. If you're cooking only a few ears or are using a smaller kernel corn, it'll take a lot less time.

FIDDLER'S ESCALLOPED CORN

MAKES A 2-QUART BAKING DISH

> 3 cups home-canned sweet corn (see Note)
>
> 4 egg yolks
>
> 1 teaspoon salt
>
> 1/4 teaspoon pepper
>
> 1/4 pound soda crackers, crushed
>
> 1/2 cup milk
>
> 4 egg whites, beaten

1. Preheat the oven to 375° F. In a large bowl, mix the corn, egg yolks, salt, pepper, and crushed crackers.

2. Add the milk and mix together well using a wooden spoon.

3. Fold in the beaten egg whites.

4. Butter a 2-quart baking dish, and pour in the mixture. Bake about 1 hour, until the center is firm and the top is lightly browned.

NOTE: Be sure your corn was canned when still young enough to be milky, not too yellow and firm, or it won't be right for this recipe. You can use corn fresh off the cob, but you need to boil it first, as for Corn on the Cob (at left), then scrape the cobs as for Canned Corn (page 91) to get all the creamy goodness.

GLAZED BABY BEETS

Beets are usually one of the last vegetables picked, and if they're the size of a golf ball or even smaller, they're delicious this way. Use the larger ones for slicing or for pickles.

SERVES 4 OR 5

16 small beets

1/2 cup sugar

1/2 cup vinegar

1/2 teaspoon salt

2 tablespoons cornstarch

1 cup beet juice, saved from cooking

3 tablespoons butter

1. Scrub the little beets, put them into a medium kettle with enough water to cover, and boil until tender. (Do not remove the greens or cut off the tips, or the beets will bleed.)

2. Drain, and save 1 cup of the juice.

3. Slip the skins off the beets, and now cut off the tops and roots, and discard. Leave the baby beets whole if they're smaller than a golf ball; if not, cut into 1/4-inch slices.

4. Cook the sugar, vinegar, salt, cornstarch, beet juice, and butter in a medium saucepan over medium heat until smooth, and pour this glaze over the beets. Heat through over low heat, and serve.

FOR BUTTERED BEETS: Cook the beets as directed above in steps 1, 2, and 3. Add butter and salt and pepper, and serve.

GLAZED BABY CARROTS

You can never go by the height of the green tops to judge the size of carrots. You have to pull them out of the ground to find out how big or small. If they are real small, wait a little longer. They're best about the size of your ring finger, although the little babies are good too. It's unnecessary to peel them, just scrub them with a stiff vegetable brush like the kind the Fuller Brush man would give away.

SERVES 6

24 or so fresh baby garden carrots (see Note)

1/2 cup (1 stick) butter

1 cup packed brown sugar

1. When the carrots are the right size, dig them up. Remove the tops and the roots, and cook the carrots in a medium saucepan until tender, in enough boiling salted water to cover. Then drain.

2. In a separate small kettle, melt the butter. Add the brown sugar, and cook over low heat until smooth. Pour over the drained carrots, and serve.

NOTE: If you want to get away from refrigerated carrots, you can do as we did and store your fresh-picked carrots in a metal container, in sand in the cellar or anywhere it's cool.

RUTABAGAS

To get good rutabagas, they should be grown in newly broken ground (ground that's never been worked), and they should be dug up after the first frost. If you've never seen one, rutabagas are a large, round, turniplike, bulbous, edible root. They're shades of purple and yellow on the outside, but a beautiful deep orange when peeled and cooked. Rutabagas are a must with *lutefisk* and *lefse*.

SERVES ABOUT 8 (MASHED) OR 14 (SLICED)

4 or 5 good-size 'bagas
 Enough salted water to cover
 Enough butter to cover
 Salt and pepper to taste
 A little sugar (if mashing, which is what I always do)

1. Peel the 'bagas (we call them "beggies"), slice into a large kettle, and cook them in a small amount of salted water over medium heat for 1 hour, until you can easily stick a fork in (cook ½ hour or so if not mashing; see Note).

2. Drain, and serve sliced with a little butter and salt and pepper, or mash them with lots of butter and salt and pepper, and a little sugar.

NOTE: For most vegetables I don't like to use a pressure cooker because I think it zaps the flavor out of 'em. But for rutabagas, a pressure cooker is ideal. Follow the manufacturer's instructions. I've found that for our large cooker, when filled with 'bagas and 2 cups of water, it takes 15 minutes at 10 pounds of pressure.

BUTTERNUT SQUASH

SERVES 8 TO 10

1 large squash
2 tablespoons butter (or more if you like)
 Salt and pepper to taste

1. Preheat the oven to 375° F. Place 1 whole squash in a shallow baking dish and bake for 1 hour or more, until a fork poked into the neck goes in and comes out easily.

2. Remove from the oven, cut in half just above its stomach, peel off the skin, and remove the seeds from its stomach.

3. Add the butter, salt, and pepper, and mash.

VARIATION: Mashed squash can be put in a baking dish and topped with brown sugar and then returned to the oven for 10 minutes.

CREAMED CABBAGE

SERVES 8

1 solid head of cabbage
 Enough cream or half-and-half to cover
1 teaspoon salt
 Dash of pepper
3 tablespoons butter

1. Remove the tough outer leaves of the cabbage. Cut the cabbage in half, then in quarters. Remove the hard center core, and feed it to the pigs or discard.

2. Chop the cabbage into 1-inch pieces.

3. Put the pieces into a large kettle with enough water to cover, and cook until tender (about 20 to 30 minutes, depending on the cabbage); do not overcook. Drain.

4. Add the cream, then the salt, pepper, and butter. Heat, but do not boil. Serve hot in individual sauce dishes.

STEAMED ASPARAGUS

12 STALKS SERVE 3

Before all the herbicides, when I was a kid, not so long after the snow melted and the sleepy sun found its strength in the spring, we'd walk down the road and all along we'd find patches of asparagus popping their little heads out of the ground. We waited for them to grow 6 to 8 inches before we broke them off and ran with them to the house. If you're lucky enough to find a patch today, break them off, rinse them, and cut them up or leave them whole. Put them in a kettle or steamer with a small amount of salted water, cook about 5 to 10 minutes, and serve them either with butter or a cream sauce (page 73).

GREEN BEANS

Green beans and yellow wax beans never seem to stop producing. You can think the season's over when you've picked and cooked and canned until you're tired of them, then lo and behold, come a good rain, they'll start all over again. (If you're picking your own, pick them when the sun is hot and the dew is off, or they'll get rusty.)

2 DOZEN BEANS SERVE 8

As many fresh-picked green beans as you wish to serve

Enough butter or cream to cover

Enough hard, crumbled bacon to cover

1. Pick the beans before they get too fat, or they'll get hard and tough. Remove the stems and either cut the beans up or leave them whole.

2. Place them in a medium kettle with enough boiling salted water to cover, and cook until tender (about 12 to 15 minutes). Take one out of the water and bite it to see if it's done. Drain.

3. Cover the beans with either butter or cream while they're still hot. Sprinkle crumbled bacon on top, and put into individual dishes.

YELLOW WAXED BEANS: Prepare as above, but for these, you can substitute a cream sauce (page 73) for the butter or cream if you like.

FIREHOUSE BAKED BEANS

In small towns and rural areas our fire and rescue people are all volunteer, and years ago especially, a fire was a main event. If farm folks happened to be in town, we even got in on it. The whistle would blow from the city hall, people would roll out of their houses, and the town would be aflurry. The men dropped what they were doing, jumped in their cars, and raced to grab hold of the fire truck as it pulled out of the station. Women shut off their stoves or vacuum cleaners, yelled for the kids, picked up a Grandma Sena or an Aunt Brenda who was waiting on the front porch, and away the town went, neighbor after neighbor, car after car down Highway 10, across town, or on out into the country, chasing after the flashing, blaring truck to see about the fire.

Besides being a popular dish at home, these beans were as common as fresh baked bread at firehouse benefits and summer picnics.

MAKES A FULL 3-QUART OR SCANT 4-QUART BAKING DISH

2 pounds navy beans
1/2 teaspoon baking soda
1/2 pound side pork, cut into 1-inch pieces
1/2 cup molasses
1 teaspoon salt
Dash of pepper
1/2 cup packed brown sugar
1/2 teaspoon dry mustard
1 teaspoon grated onion

1. Soak the beans overnight in a large bowl. Cover with water to at least 3 inches above the beans.

2. The next morning, drain off the water.

3. Preheat the oven to 325° F. Pour the beans into a large kettle, add enough fresh water to cover, add the baking soda, and cook about 1/2 hour, until the beans start to show signs of cracking. (The color of the juice will look sort of greenish.) Drain completely, and pour into a 3- or 4-quart baking dish.

4. Add the side pork, molasses, salt, pepper, brown sugar, mustard, onions, and enough water to cover.

5. Bake slowly for about 3 hours. Check often to be sure they are not getting too dry. If so, add water.

FRIED ZUCCHINI

SERVES 6

1 long (12- to 14-inch) zucchini
1 cup flour for dipping (approximately)
1/2 teaspoon salt
2 eggs, beaten
1/4 cup butter

1. Wash and dry the zucchini (do not peel). Cut into 1/4-inch slices. Mix the flour and salt together in a medium bowl.

2. Dip the zucchini slices in the flour and salt mixture, then into the eggs, then back into the flour again.

3. Put the butter into a heated, heavy cast-iron skillet. Add the zucchini and fry over medium heat. (Be careful so it doesn't get too hot, or the butter will burn.) When browned on the bottom, turn the slices over and brown again. Serve hot.

FRIED GREEN TOMATOES: Do the same.

STEWED TOMATOES

SERVES 6 TO 8

6 to 8 tomatoes

3 tablespoons butter

1 teaspoon salt

Dash of pepper

6 to 8 soda crackers, broken (see Note)

1. Dip the tomatoes in boiling water until the skins crack. Remove from the boiling water, dip into cold water, and slip the skins off.

2. Quarter the tomatoes as you put them into a stainless steel medium kettle, and cook over medium heat about 5 minutes, until tender, so they form their own juice.

3. Add the butter, salt, and pepper and then just before serving, add the broken crackers. Serve in individual dishes.

NOTE: You can use leftover cubed toast or croutons instead of crackers if you'd like. That's good, too.

ESCALLOPED POTATOES

MAKES A 2-QUART CASSEROLE

1/4 cup butter plus butter for dotting

1/4 cup flour

1 teaspoon salt

Dash of pepper

1 teaspoon minced onion

1/4 cup finely chopped celery

1 pint milk and 1 pint cream mixed together

6 to 8 potatoes, peeled and sliced thin

Grated cheese (or not)

Diced or chunked ham (or not)

1. Preheat the oven to 350° F. Place the butter and the flour in a heavy saucepan, and stir together using a wire whisk, until creamy. Add the salt, pepper, onion, celery, milk, and cream, and cook over medium heat until smooth, stirring constantly (see Note).

2. Slice the potatoes thin into a 2-quart buttered casserole.

3. Pour the cream sauce over, dot with butter, and bake 30 to 45 minutes, until a fork goes in easily. (If using cheese or ham, add it to the cream sauce before pouring it over the potatoes.)

NOTE: If you prepare the cream sauce first, as I do here, the potatoes won't get dark while waiting for the sauce.

MASHED POTATOES

In a farm town, if a restaurant doesn't have good homemade mashed potatoes (mashed just right), it might as well close its doors. Out here, it's potatoes for dinner, supper, and sometimes even breakfast. And why not? It's one of nature's wonders how one or two eyes turned under the soil can produce all those potatoes. But like everything else, there's no magic without work. The little characters have to be sectioned, dug down, hoed, hilled, and guarded from sunburn. And of course there're always potato bugs ready for mischief. They can get so bad that at home us kids would go row by row every day and pick them off, or we'd take ash from the wood stove and dust the leaves, until it rained, then we'd have to go at it all over again. Still we loved the potato rows and waited for the vines to be dry, when Dad could take a big, wide fork, press under the earth, and scatter the treasure on top of the ground for us kids to pick. We'd try to guess how many were under each hill, then rush to gather them up into gunnysacks and haul them to their potato bin in the cellar. When the bin was full, we could rest, we felt safe, ready for winter. Maybe that's why we Midwesterners are so fussy—even goofy—about our potatoes.

SERVES 8

1 *dozen potatoes*
1 *teaspoon salt*
1/2 *cup (1 stick) butter*
1/3 *cup fresh cream*
1/2 *cup milk*

1. Peel the potatoes, put them into a kettle, and cover them with water. Add the salt, and cook over medium heat about 30 minutes, until tender. Drain, saving the potato water for gravy (if desired).

2. Add the butter, cream, and milk (you may need more or less depending on the moisture of the potatoes). Mash, and beat real well with a potato masher. Beat until it sounds like horses galloping, and the potatoes are light and fluffy. Serve hot topped with lots of butter or gravy (see Note).

NOTE: If your timing isn't just right, and you need to keep mashed potatoes warm, place the kettle over another kettle of hot water (as for a double boiler).

It's hard to reheat mashed potatoes and have them be good. The best thing I've found to do with them is to put them into a heavy cast-iron skillet, add a little cream and a little American or Cheddar cheese, and heat. Then they'll be something like twice-baked potatoes, quite good.

RAW FRIES

I made this when the kids were little; it's the closest they got to French fries because I couldn't afford much shortening for deep-frying. Instead, I fried them in this small amount of grease so there wasn't much to drain or waste. I turned them often to get them brown and slightly crisp.

SERVES 10

8 *Russet potatoes*
 Enough vegetable oil or lard to measure 1/2 *inch in bottom of large cast-iron skillet*
 Salt to taste

1. Wash the potatoes and peel, if desired. Heat oil or lard in a skillet.

2. Slice the potatoes lengthwise (as thick as you want your fries to be), and wrap them in a clean dish towel to drain off the moisture.

3. Drop them into the heated oil, and turn them to get them brown and a little crisp. (They will take longer to cook than frozen fries.) When they are golden brown, they are ready.

4. Remove them from the skillet and lay them on a brown paper bag to absorb the oil. Salt before serving.

DOUBLE-BAKED POTATOES

SERVES 8

4 *Russet potatoes*
 1/2 *cup cream or half-and-half*
 Salt and pepper to taste
 2 *tablespoons butter*
 Dash of paprika for each
 Grated cheese (or not)

1. Preheat the oven to 350° F. Scrub the potatoes, and wipe them dry.

2. Bake 30 to 45 minutes, until a fork goes into the potatoes easily. Remove them from the oven, and slice in half lengthwise.

3. Carefully remove the pulp and put it into a mixing bowl. Save the shells.

4. Mash the pulp with a potato masher, add the cream, salt, and pepper as you mash, until the pulp is fluffy.

5. Fill the potato shells with the mashed potatoes, and dot with a little butter. Sprinkle a dash of paprika on each.

6. Return them to the oven, and heat through until a light golden color on top. Serve. (If you want cheese, sprinkle it on the top just before putting them back into the oven. Heat until bubbly.)

Hints for Home Canning

• If you've never canned before, consult with the United States Department of Agriculture in Washington, D.C., or your local Extension agent, before tackling such a project. While these recipes are old, and tried and true, this section is by no means a complete instruction guide. While we weren't lucky enough to have them around in the old days, today the USDA should be considered the best source of information.

• Use heavy stainless steel kettles if possible. Never cook vinegar in a cheap aluminum kettle; the kettle turns dark and the vinegar takes on a taste. Also, be sure the kettles you use are large enough for the juices to boil without boiling over, or you'll have a mess.

• Syrups for jams and jellies have a tendency to rise to the top quicker than you can shake a stick, so watch carefully.

• Be sure the tops of the jars are free from any spills that occur when filling them. If you spill, wipe the lip off with either a paper towel or a clean cloth.

• To seal means to screw the covers on firmly according to the manufacturer's instructions.

• When the ingredients are cool, you will hear popping sounds if you're using the two-piece lids. That means the cover has sealed. Press your finger on top, and if the cover is flat, it's okay. If a jar has not sealed, use the contents right away; do not store.

• When I say *jars,* unless I say otherwise, I mean fruit jars, either quarts or pints, whichever suits your family's needs. However, quart jars are a must for large cucumber pickles.

• The number of jars you will get out of a recipe will vary because of the difference in the size and the moisture in the fruits and vegetables.

• Use long-handled wooden spoons for stirring the ingredients.

• Headspace is the unfilled space in the jar above the food and below the lid. I've indicated how much headspace should be left in each recipe. Don't scrimp on this.

• Like most farm women in this area, I've been canning for years the way my mother and grandmothers did, and this never used to include the processing in the boiling-water canner that the USDA recommends today. But we old-timers thought we knew exactly what we were doing with those old methods, and whether by hook or by crook, luckily no one died on us due to botulism. Here however, in this book, I've updated the old recipes and you will notice most often that includes processing in a boiling-water canner or in a pressure canner. This is to make sure of safety, and today *it is a must.* I don't recommend any of our old-time methods anymore. While what's here might take a little extra effort, the finished product will be just as good.

• Using the boiling-water canner method means putting a very large canner on the stove and placing the wire rack in the bottom (I use slats or a rag instead, for more room) so the filled fruit jars will not touch the bottom and crack. The canner should be deep enough so that briskly boiling water will roll up at least one inch above the tops of the jars during processing. If you have an electric stove like I do, a flat-bottom canner must be used, and for proper processing it shouldn't be any more than four inches wider in diameter than the burner.

• To *process in a boiling-water canner* means you should fill the canner halfway up with water, put in the rack (or slats or rag), and preheat the water pretty good (the USDA says 140° F for raw and packed foods and 180° F for hot-packed foods, but not everyone stands and knows the temperature, so let's say "very hot"). Lower the filled jars that you've sealed with rings and lids onto the rack (or on the slats or rag) with a jar lifter, or whatever way you can without burning your hands. Add more boiling water if you need to so the level is at least one inch above the tops of the jars. Boil vigorously, then cover with the canner lid, and lower the heat to keep a gentle boil going for as long as the recipe says to process. Check once in a while so the water doesn't boil away. If there is not enough, add more, but make sure it's boiling, so the heating process doesn't slow down. When the jars have boiled the right amount of time, turn the heat off and remove the canner's cover. Take the jars out with a lifter, or whatever you use so you don't burn your hands, and place the jars on a towel, making sure you leave at least one inch of space between the jars while they cool.

• For pressure canning, always use the pressure canner according to the manufacturer's instructions, and if in doubt or for more general information, get in touch with the USDA.

• Processing times here are for Wisconsin. If you live at a higher or lower altitude, check with your local county Extension agent. Don't be lazy about this because the correct processing times are very important for safety.

• When I say scalded jars, I mean sterilize your empty jars by placing them in a boiling-water canner right side up on the rack. Fill the canner and the jar with water that's hot, not boiling. Make sure the water is one inch above the tops of the jars, and boil for ten minutes if you're at an altitude like us, less than one thousand feet. If you're up there higher, boil an extra minute for each one thousand feet of elevation. Roll them around, then remove them with a rubber-ended nipper, and let them drain upside down on a rack or a towel until they're dry as a sow's ear.

• For all the canned pickles, relishes, and vegetables, do not use iodized salt, or the ingredients will get mushy.

• If you have a smaller family and like to open fresh pickles, when you can, use pint jars.

• Any sweet pickle or relish can be eaten right away, though they have much better flavor the longer they stand. Dill pickles, however, must stand at least two weeks to be good.

Jams
and
Jellies

QUICK RASPBERRY JAM

At home we had a raspberry patch beside the chicken coop, and of all the berries, raspberries were a favorite. But they weren't very plentiful, so a fresh, quick jam that we could eat immediately was a real summer treat. It's great on warm buns or biscuits or on a bowl of ice cream in the evening. Or you might do a farm favorite—spread it on top of a thick slice of Fresh Cream and Bread (page 99) for a cool, old-country breakfast.

1 BATCH MAKES 2 PINT JARS OR A COUPLE ODDS AND ENDS JARS

> *2 cups sugar*
> *1/2 cup water*
> *1 quart raspberries (see Note)*

1. In a saucepan, dump the sugar into the water, stir, and cook over medium heat until it boils and spins a thread.

2. Add the berries, and stir using a wooden spoon. Boil 7 minutes (this is tricky, so watch the clock).

3. Pour into clean, scalded jars. Use the jam immediately, or keep what's left in the refrigerator and use it as long as it lasts. (It goes fast, so don't bother freezing.)

NOTE: If you'd like to have this jam when the snow flies, freeze the berries dry and right off the bush. Of any berry, raspberries freeze the nicest; they don't get wet and mushy. Loosely pack them dry in jars or place them individually on a cookie sheet. After they freeze, put them into an airtight freezer container (a bag or glass jar), and set them back in the freezer. When you're ready to make this jam, take them out. Raspberries out of the freezer taste just like a fresh berry.

FOR BLACKBERRY JAM: Mash 1 quart of berries, and follow the above recipe.

CURRANT JELLY

MAKES ABOUT 6 JELLY GLASSES

> *2 cups water*
> *3 1/2 quarts currants*
> *7 cups juice*
> *1 1/2 ounces Sure-Jell*
> *7 cups sugar*

1. Put the water into a large kettle. Crush the berries, add them to the water, and cook over medium heat for 10 minutes.

2. Strain the juice through a white dish towel. Mix the Sure-Jell with the juice, and bring to a boil. Add the sugar all at once, and boil hard for about 30 seconds, stirring all the while.

3. Remove from heat, and take off the foam. Pour the jelly right away into clean, scalded jelly glasses, leaving 1/4-inch headspace. Seal with 2-piece rings and lids, and process 5 minutes in a boiling-water canner.

APPLE JELLY

If you're buying your apples instead of picking them yourself and you get them in a plastic bag and don't want them to ripen further, remove them from the plastic. When they stand, apples release a gas, and if the plastic is closed, those gases make the apples much more prone to ripening and spoilage.

MAKES 3½ PINTS

5 pounds tart red apples or 5 pounds of peelings from apples

5 cups water

1½ ounces Sure-Jell

7 cups sugar

1. Slice and core the apples. Put the apples and a few peelings (or the peelings only) into a stainless steel kettle, add the water, and simmer about 10 minutes. Then crush with a potato masher, and simmer 5 minutes more.

2. Place the contents into cheesecloth bags or a clean white cloth, and squeeze out the juice. (You should have 7 cups of juice when it all is strained out.)

3. Pour the juice into a large kettle, and add the Sure-Jell. Bring to a hard boil, stirring off and on.

4. Pour the sugar in all at once. Bring to a full, rocking boil (a boil that will not stop boiling when stirred), and boil 1 minute, stirring constantly.

5. Remove from heat, and skim off the foam with a metal spoon.

6. Pour at once into clean, scalded jelly glasses, leaving ¼-inch headspace. Seal with 2-piece covers, and process 5 minutes in a boiling-water canner.

FOR CRABAPPLE JELLY: Quarter the apples (you can leave in the core) and follow the above recipe.

FOR GOOSEBERRY JELLY: Follow the above recipe using enough quarts of berries to make about 5 pounds; use half of the water called for.

APPLE BUTTER

MAKES ABOUT 3 PINTS

4 quarts sweet apple cider

2½ quarts quartered, tart apples

2 cups sugar

1 teaspoon ground cinnamon

½ teaspoon ground cloves

1. Boil down the cider until it is reduced to 2 quarts.

2. Add the apples, and cook until very tender, then rub them through a sieve or mash them.

3. Add the sugar, cinnamon, and cloves, and cook until thick. (Stir it, don't let it scorch.)

4. Pour it into clean, scalded jars, leaving ½-inch headspace, and seal.

5. Process for 10 minutes in a boiling-water canner.

EVIE'S PERFECT PLUM BUTTER

✵

During the Depression, when the ground was so parched and dry and the crops were lost even before the blooming season, food was so precious women would boil apple or plum blossoms and serve them as a meal. To make something extraspecial, they'd dip them in egg batter and fry them.

MAKES ABOUT 3 PINTS

4 pounds plump red plums
One-half as much sugar as you get pulp after cooking plums

1. Wash the plums, put them into a stainless steel kettle, and place it over medium heat. (Crush a few plums to produce a little juice to prevent burning.)

2. Cover, and cook until tender.

3. Rub through a sieve. Remove the skin and pits from the sieve, and discard. Save and measure the pulp.

4. Add one-half the amount of sugar as you have pulp.

5. Return to the kettle, and cook until thick, stirring constantly.

6. Pour into clean, scalded jars, leaving ½-inch headspace, and seal with rings and lids.

7. Process for 5 minutes in a boiling-water canner.

ORANGE MARMALADE

✵

MAKES 3½ PINTS

8 oranges
2 lemons
3 times as much water as cooked pulp and peelings
7 cups sugar (approximately)

1. Wash and dry the fruit, peel, and set aside the fruit.

2. Slice the orange peels very thin into a heavy medium saucepan. Cover them with water, cook 10 minutes, then drain, and set aside.

3. Take the pulp of the fruit (discard the lemon peels or throw them into lemonade), remove the seeds, and slice the fruit very thin. Add the drained orange peel.

4. Measure the pulp and the peelings, and add 3 times as much water, and let stand overnight.

5. The next morning, cook over medium heat for 40 minutes in a large saucepan. Measure the amount of pulp and peelings (in cups), and add the same amount of sugar as pulp (about 7 cups).

6. Cook rapidly (7 to 10 minutes) until it thickens (when a little set aside in a sauce dish is the consistency you like).

7. Pour into clean, scalded jars or glasses, leaving ¼-inch headspace. Seal with lids and rings. Process 5 minutes in a boiling-water canner.

RHUBARB JAM

MAKES 4 OR 5 JELLY GLASSES

1 heaping quart (4 heaping cups) rhubarb

3 cups sugar

1 (3-ounce) package strawberry gelatin

1. In a large kettle, cook ingredients until dissolved (3 minutes at a rolling boil).

2. Scrape off the foam, and pour the jam into clean, scalded jars, leaving ¼-inch headspace. Seal with rings and lids, and when the jars are cool, put them into the freezer.

PEAR JAM

MAKES ABOUT NINE ¾ PINTS

6 pears, peeled, cored, and cubed

6 apples, peeled, cored, and cubed

½ cup water

1 teaspoon butter

1 cinnamon stick

1 box Sure-Jell

3½ cups sugar

1. In a large kettle cook over medium heat the pears, apples, water, butter, and cinnamon stick until fruit is soft.

2. Remove the cinnamon stick. Add the Sure-Jell and cook for about 1 minute, then add the sugar all at once and cook for 3 minutes. Pour immediately into clean, scalded jelly jars, leaving ¼-inch headspace, and seal with rings and lids. Process in a boiling-water canner for 5 minutes.

Fruit Sauces

Fruit sauce is nothing fancy, but out here it's so common, many old-timers wouldn't think of having a midday or evening meal without it. It's served in a small bowl alongside the main plate—just any summer fruit canned in a syrup of sugar and water—another humble pleasure.

PEACH SAUCE

During canning season peaches would come in on the train. They'd stand in wooden crates in the aisles of the grocery store. It was an excuse for women to get together, to break up the isolation of the farm. Even after we were married, my sister and I got together to help each other peel because I never believed in canning water. (It was usually August and so hot in the kitchens with those big, 18-quart copper canners boiling that some ladies would get tired of peeling and they'd skimp on the peaches, and the jars would be more syrup than fruit.) My sister and I would peel and peel until late at night. The different batches would boil in the canner for half an hour all through the day, then we'd take 'em out, and set 'em aside. Sometimes it'd be close to midnight; my sister would go home and I'd go to bed and pretty soon I'd hear "Pop! Pop!" The lids were sealing; they'd snap as they cooled. That was canning season: sweltering heat and "pop, pop" from the kitchen all through the night. →

FOR 12 PINT JARS OR 7 QUARTS

BOILING-WATER CANNER METHOD

1 lug fresh peaches (see Note)
6 cups sugar
12 cups water

1. Peel the peaches. (Blanch by dipping them in hot water and then in cold, so they peel better.) Cut into halves or quarters and put into clean, scalded glass quart or pint jars.

2. Make a sugar syrup to put over the peaches: Mix the sugar and the water, and bring to a good boil. Pour this over the fruit in the jars, leaving ½-inch headspace, and seal with lids and rings (see Note).

3. Place the jars in a large canner. Fill it with enough warm water so the level of the water is at least 1 inch above the tops of the jars, and cook for 30 minutes, counting the time after the water boils around the jars.

4. Remove the jars. Listen for the lids to pop. Store. (The rings will be loose, and you can reuse them.) The USDA recommends removing the rings after the jars have cooled 12 to 24 hours.

NOTE: For peaches, the larger the grade number, the fewer there are in a lug. #70s are considered small, #40s are large. A lug is usually 17 pounds.

If you don't have enough syrup to fill the jars, cook a mixture of 1 part sugar to 2 parts water.

PEACH SYRUP: To use on pancakes or waffles or ice cream, take 1 pound of peach peelings and pits (or whole peaches and the pit) or, if you don't have enough peelings at first, store what you have in a tight container in the refrigerator until you have 1 pound. Add enough water to cover the peelings and the pits in a large kettle, bring to a boil, and simmer 30 minutes or longer. Strain through a cloth as for jelly, squeezing out the juice. Measure 2 cups of juice, add 2 cups of sugar, and bring to a rolling boil for 10 to 15 minutes. Be sure to watch so it doesn't boil over. Stir often. (Do not boil too long, or it'll turn to jelly.) Pour into clean, scalded jars or bottles, leaving ¼-inch headspace, and cap. Process 5 minutes in a boiling-water canner.

PEAR SAUCE: Use the same recipe as for Peach Sauce. Makes about 7 quarts.

APRICOT SAUCE: Use the same recipe as for Peach Sauce, but cut the apricots in half (don't peel). Makes about 5 quarts.

BLUE PLUM SAUCE: Use the same recipe as for Peach Sauce, but prick the plum skins here and there to prevent bursting. Makes about 5 quarts.

CHERRY SAUCE: Use the same recipe as for Peach Sauce, but pit the cherries and increase the sugar to 1 cup of sugar to 1 cup of water. Makes about 5 quarts.

STRAWBERRY SAUCE

It's easy to forget about life's scheme of things, but every so often we're reminded by the state of strawberries. If it's a rainy, rainy spring, the bees stay home in their hives more than is good for the berries, and there's not enough pollination. The berries get green and nubby on the ends, and don't have a good season. So whenever you see a luscious, plump, red berry, don't forget about the bees that aided in their growing.

BOILING-WATER CANNER METHOD

As many strawberries as you want to can (1 quart berries makes 1 quart sauce)

2 cups sugar per quart jar (see Note)

1 quart water for each quart berries

1. Pick over the berries, and wash. Allow 1 quart of berries per quart jar. Set aside.

2. In a kettle, add 2 cups of sugar per jar and 1 quart of water for each quart of berries.

3. Boil the sugar and the water together until it comes to a full boil. Drop the berries in, and cook about 5 minutes. Pour at once into clean, hot jars, leaving ½-inch headspace, and seal with rings and lids.

4. Process in a boiling-water canner for 20 minutes.

NOTE: Use less sugar if you want it less sweet.

RASPBERRY SAUCE: Follow the same recipe as above using raspberries instead of strawberries.

BLACKBERRY SAUCE: Follow the same recipe as above using blackberries.

RHUBARB SAUCE: Follow the same recipe above, only cut the rhubarb into 1-inch pieces. Add a small can of crushed pineapple, if you like. (**NOTE:** In the old days women used a lot of cheap aluminum kettles bought from peddlers, and this sauce, when it cooked, would clean those kettles; it took out all the stains because of its reaction with the aluminum. I don't recommend either a cheap aluminum kettle or cleaning it this way these days.)

BLUEBERRY SAUCE: Follow the above recipe, using ¾ cup water and 1 cup of sugar to a quart of berries. (You can thin it with water when serving if you think it's too rich.) This is very good for settling an upset stomach.

APPLESAUCE

The type of apple you use is all-important to the taste and texture. Years ago, Duchess and Greening Whitneys were popular for sauce and pies. The skins were used for making jelly. It wasn't easy as a kid waiting for them to ripen; we even ate them green and often paid dearly with a stomachache. But in the fall when they were ripe and the cool nights set the juice, the adults would come out and pick them very carefully so as not to bruise them. We'd wrap them individually in a page from the Sears Roebuck catalog and store them in a big box or barrel in the cellar or an unheated room upstairs. →

BOILING-WATER CANNER METHOD

1 peck Duchess or Harvest apples
Sugar to taste (see Note)

1. Peel and core the apples, saving the peelings for jelly. Slice according to how smooth or lumpy you like your sauce, and place in a heavy 10-quart kettle.

2. Pour just enough water in to cover the apples, and cook on medium heat until the apples turn mushy when they are stirred with a wooden spoon. If it becomes too thick, add a little water.

3. Turn down the heat, add sugar to your taste (or none if you prefer), and continue stirring until smooth.

4. Pour directly into clean, hot jars, leaving 1/2-inch headspace, and seal at once with rings and lids. (If you have a little left over, serve it for supper along with your pork roast.)

5. Process in a boiling-water canner for 30 minutes for quarts and 25 minutes for pints.

NOTE: I use about 1/2 cup sugar to each quart (Ernie has a sweet tooth). If your apples are sweet enough, this needs no sugar at all if you'd rather.

SWEET TOMATO SAUCE

This is good both with supper on blustery, cold nights in December or with dinner in a blistering July. But it's especially good with egg salad sandwiches.

BOILING-WATER CANNER METHOD

1 peck fresh tomatoes
1/2 cup sugar per quart of cooked tomatoes
2 tablespoons bottled lemon juice per jar (see Note)

1. Prepare the tomatoes as for Stewed Tomatoes (page 73) except cut into pieces. Place in a large kettle, and bring to a boil (see Note).

2. When it starts to boil, add the sugar and the lemon, and cook real well.

3. Pour the bottled lemon juice into each clean, hot jar; pour in the tomato mixture, leaving 1/2-inch headspace. Seal with rings and lids.

4. Process in a boiling-water canner for 50 minutes.

NOTE: We used to use lemon slices for this in the old days, but now for safety's sake the USDA recommends the bottled lemon juice for a more consistent acid level. So this is by all means what you should use these days.

Get to know your kettle so you know how much you have when the fruit has cooked down.

Pickles, Relishes,

Canned Vegetables, and Mincemeat

ETHELYN'S DILL PICKLES

✸

Dill was a must. Sometimes we planted the seed for it, but if some were left in the garden they would seed themselves and you would have dill here and there all over the garden next year. You usually had to plant the seed about the same time as the cucumber seeds—a little later than the other things in the garden—or it would be overripe by pickling time. Anyway, dill had a pest, a large green worm with one long antenna like a horn on top of its head. We had to keep them picked off or they would strip the plants and all you'd have left were the stems. To get rid of them we walked along the dill row until we saw some black, hard little uneven things on the ground around the plant. We'd pick up the bug, gingerly grasp its antenna in our fingers, and pull it off (it hung on for dear life). Then we'd drop the little culprits into a coffee can we carried along with kerosene in the bottom, and that took care of them. We didn't use pesticides in those days. We were the exterminators.

MAKES ABOUT 6 QUARTS

BOILING·WATER CANNER METHOD

1 peck cucumbers (#2 size or the way you like 'em; see Note)

1 fresh dill plant per quart jar (¹/₂ plant per pint)

1 quart vinegar

2 quarts water

1 cup coarse salt (do not use iodized)

1. Wash the cucumbers. Pack them into clean, scalded glass jars, either quarts or pints (see Note). Put the dill into the jars as you pack the cucumbers.

2. In a saucepan, bring the vinegar, water, and salt to a boil. Boil rapidly, and pour at once over the cukes in the jars; seal by closing jars with rings and lids immediately.

3. Process in a boiling-water canner for 10 minutes, but start counting as soon as you get the jars into the canner.

NOTE: If purchasing cukes, buy a bushel by the straight run, meaning all sizes. Grade the cukes by yourself according to their size. Large, for dill or hamburger dills; medium, for chunk, turmeric, and baby dills; small, for sweet pickles.

#4s are large, #3s are medium, #2s are small, and #1s are tiny.

SWEET CHUNK PICKLES

✳

MAKES ABOUT 8 PINTS

BOILING·WATER CANNER METHOD

20 cucumbers

  Boiling water to pour over cucumbers four times

8 cups sugar

4 cups vinegar

5 teaspoons coarse salt (not iodized)

4 teaspoons pickling spice

1. Wash the cucumbers, and remove the stems and spines. Pour boiling water over the cukes morning and evening for 2 days (four times), draining and adding fresh water each time.

2. Cut the cucumbers into chunks into a large stainless steel or granite kettle.

3. Mix the sugar, vinegar, salt, and pickling spice together in a bowl, then pour it over the cukes, and let them stand for 3 days. (Do not drain.)

4. Put the kettle on the stove over medium heat and bring to a boil.

5. Put the cucumbers into clean, hot jars, pour the juice over to cover the cukes, leaving ½-inch headspace, and seal at once with rings and lids.

6. Process 10 minutes in a boiling-water canner, but start counting as soon as you get the jars into the canner.

BREAD AND BUTTER PICKLES

✳

MAKES ABOUT 12 PINTS

BOILING·WATER CANNER METHOD

1 gallon cucumbers

½ cup coarse salt

8 small onions, sliced

3 sweet green peppers, sliced

3 sweet red peppers, sliced

2 to 3 trays ice cubes

SYRUP

5 cups sugar

1 teaspoon turmeric

2 tablespoons mustard seed

1 teaspoon celery seed

5 cups white vinegar

1. Do not peel the cucumbers. Slice very thin (almost to transparent), and put into a big earthenware bowl with the salt, onions, and green and red peppers.

2. Bury the ice cubes in the mixture, and let it all stand for 3 hours, then drain, and make the syrup.

3. *To make the syrup:* In a large kettle, mix the sugar and turmeric; add the mustard seed, celery seed, and vinegar. Drop the pickle mixture in, and heat to scalding, but do not boil.

4. Put into clean, hot pint jars, leaving ½-inch headspace, and seal. (Pint jars are best for this because the pickles are sliced so thin, a pint goes a long way.)

5. Process 10 minutes in a boiling-water canner, but start counting as soon as you get the jars into the canner.

BEET PICKLES

MAKES 6 TO 8 QUARTS OF SMALL
BEETS (ADJUST FOR
THE AMOUNT YOU HAVE)

BOILING-WATER CANNER METHOD

Enough small beets to pack

6 to 8 quarts (about 32; see Note)

1 teaspoon whole cloves

1 cinnamon stick

1 teaspoon allspice

2 cups sugar

2 cups cider vinegar

2 cups beet juice saved from cooking

1. Wash the beets real good, but do not peel.

2. Put them into a kettle with enough water to cover, and cook 30 to 40 minutes, until tender. Remove the beets from the juice, and slip the skins off. Save the juice.

3. Put the cloves, cinnamon stick, and allspice on a piece of clean, white cloth. Fold the cloth together at the top and tie it with a string to make a bag.

4. Put the spice bag, sugar, vinegar, and beet juice into a kettle, and boil 5 minutes.

5. Add the beets, and simmer for 5 minutes.

6. Remove the spice bag, put the beets and the juice into clean, hot jars, leaving ½-inch headspace, and seal with lids and rings.

7. Process in a boiling-water canner for 35 minutes, but start counting as soon as you get the jars into the canner.

NOTE: If your beets are on the big side, quarter them.

WATERMELON PICKLES

The watermelon patch was usually in a corner of the garden away from the cucumbers, but still once in a while, the pollen from the cucumbers would mix with the melon and the cucumber pollen was stronger than the melons so we'd have beautiful big melons that tasted like cucumbers. You couldn't eat them because the inside never got pink, but they made good watermelon pickles. As a kid, I'd wait and wait for the melons to ripen. I'd go every day to the patch and tap on the wall of the melon with my fingers to hear a hollow sound like an empty room, then it would be ready. If not, it would sound dead. Another way was to cut a little 1-inch square down into the melon and pull out what we called "the plug." If the meat was pink beyond the rind it was ready, if not, you just poked the plug back in and waited for what seemed like forever. When finally they were ripe, we dropped them in the cows' watering tank to cool them. You couldn't beat those melons for relief on an August scorcher.

MAKES ABOUT 7 PINTS →

BOILING·WATER CANNER METHOD

7 pounds watermelon rind

1 stick cinnamon

1 tablespoon whole cloves

7 cups sugar

1 pint water

1 pint vinegar

1. Trim off the dark green skin, and any pink from the rind, and cut into 2-inch squares. Soak overnight in slightly salted water.

2. In the morning, rinse, add fresh water, and parboil until tender. Drain off the water, and set aside.

3. Put the cinnamon and cloves on a small piece of cloth, gather up the sides, and tie together at the top with a string.

4. Put this bag along with the sugar, water, and vinegar into a kettle, and boil for 5 minutes. Add the watermelon rind, and boil 30 minutes, then pour into about 7 clean, hot pint jars, leaving ½-inch headspace, and seal with lids and rings.

5. Process 10 minutes in a boiling-water canner, but start counting as soon as you get the jars into the canner.

PEACH PICKLES

❋

MAKES ABOUT 6 QUART JARS

BOILING·WATER CANNER METHOD

7 cups sugar

1 pint cider vinegar

⅔ lug of #60 peaches (skinned, cut in half, and stone removed; see Note)

1 pint water

18 whole cloves

6 small cinnamon sticks

1. Boil the sugar, vinegar, and water together for 10 minutes in a large kettle.

2. Add the fruit, and boil until tender.

3. To each clean, hot jar, add 3 whole cloves and 1 small cinnamon stick. Put the fruit into the jars, cover the fruit with syrup, leaving ½-inch headspace, and seal with rings and lids (see Note).

4. Process 20 minutes in a boiling-water canner, but start counting as soon as you get the jars into the canner.

NOTE: Save the peelings and the pits and use for Peach Syrup (page 82).

The juice is good for seasoning ham or pork, so save the leftover juice after you've enjoyed the pickles.

GREEN TOMATO RELISH

When frost was predicted, all the tomatoes in the garden were picked. The ripe ones were made into juices or vegetables, the green were used this way. The aroma in the kitchen made your mouth water.

MAKES 6 TO 8 PINTS

BOILING-WATER CANNER METHOD

9 cups coarsely ground green tomatoes

3 apples, ground with tomatoes, unpeeled, but cored

3 cups sugar

1 cup vinegar

2 teaspoons ground cinnamon

1 teaspoon ground cloves

1. Put the ground tomatoes and apples into a heavy stainless steel kettle, and cook with the sugar, vinegar, cinnamon, and cloves until the mixture gets thick and the tomatoes lose their color.

2. Pour into clean, hot pint jars, leaving ½-inch headspace, and seal with rings and lids.

3. Process 10 minutes in a boiling-water canner, but start counting as soon as you get the jars into the canner.

CRANBERRY RELISH

MAKES 1 PINT

2 cups cranberries

1 orange

1½ cups sugar

1. Put the cranberries through the food processor or chopper.

2. Peel the orange and remove the seeds, and put the rind and the orange through the chopper.

3. Mix the cranberries, orange, and sugar all together, cover, and let stand a few hours in the refrigerator before serving.

ZUCCHINI RELISH

✳

MAKES ABOUT 6 PINTS

BOILING·WATER CANNER METHOD

8 cups ground zucchini

6 onions, grated

5 tablespoons coarse salt

4 cups sugar

2¼ cups cider vinegar

1 teaspoon celery seed

1 teaspoon turmeric

1 green pepper, cut up

½ teaspoon nutmeg

1. Let the zucchini, onions, and salt stand overnight in a large earthenware bowl.

2. Drain. Rinse excess salt off the zucchini, and squeeze out the excess water. Set the zucchini aside.

3. Mix the sugar, vinegar, celery seed, turmeric, green pepper, and nutmeg together in a large stainless steel kettle, add the zucchini mix, and simmer for 30 minutes.

4. Pack in clean, hot pint jars, leaving ½-inch headspace, and seal tightly with rings and lids.

5. Process 10 minutes in a boiling-water canner, but start counting as soon as you get the jars into the canner.

CORN RELISH

✳

MAKES ABOUT 5 PINTS

BOILING·WATER CANNER METHOD

18 ears sweet corn

2 large green peppers

2 sweet red peppers

1 small cabbage

4 onions

1 cup chopped celery

1 quart vinegar

2 cups packed brown sugar

2 tablespoons salt

2 tablespoons dry mustard

1. Cut the corn from the cobs. Remove the seeds from the green and red peppers and chop the peppers with the cabbage and the onions. Mix together, and place in a large kettle with the corn.

2. Add the celery, vinegar, brown sugar, salt, and mustard, and stir together.

3. Cook until the corn is tender (20 to 30 minutes), stirring occasionally.

4. Pack into clean, hot jars, leaving ½-inch headspace, and seal with rings and lids.

5. Process 20 minutes in a boiling-water canner, but start counting as soon as you get the jars into the canner.

CANNED CORN

To prepare for canning corn, try to pick a cool day, because it's a long time a-cookin'. First peel off the husks and rub off all the hair using both hands to brush around the cob. Do not wash. It's clean, the husk was its overcoat.

Get a large dishpan and a sharp knife and, holding the stem end in your hand, carefully cut down through to the tip, but be careful not to cut into the cob (you don't want to eat cob). The golden kernels will slide right down into the dish pan. After the kernels are off, carefully scrape the cob with the back of the knife to get all the good creamy goodness that is in the little holes. It's like pulling a tooth; when the tooth is pulled, there's a hole, and these cob holes are full of flavor and an important part of the kernel. When corn is old and dry, the whole kernel will shell out, but fresh, it hasn't let go yet, so don't forget to scrape or you'll be missing something.

PRESSURE CANNER METHOD

Enough fresh corn from the cob to fill as many quart or pint jars as you'd like

1 teaspoon salt per quart jar (¹/₂ teaspoon for pint jars)

1. Cut the corn from the cob, and press into clean, scalded quart or pint jars. Add 1 teaspoon salt per quart (or ¹/₂ teaspoon per pint), then fill the hot jars with boiling water, leaving 1-inch headspace. Seal the jars with rings and lids.

2. Process in a pressure canner at 11 pounds pressure for 55 minutes for pints, or 85 minutes for quarts. Always use the canner according to the manufacturer's instructions.

FROZEN CORN

MAKES 4 PINT-SIZE FREEZER BAGS OR 2 QUART-SIZE FREEZER BAGS

1 cup water

1 teaspoon sugar

1 teaspoon salt

¹/₄ cup (¹/₂ stick) butter

8 cups corn, freshly cut off the cob

1. Heat the water, sugar, salt, and butter together in a kettle over medium heat until boiling.

2. Add the corn and cook 3 minutes. Cool completely and put into freezer bags and freeze.

CANNED TOMATOES

✻

MAKES ABOUT 8 QUARTS

BOILING-WATER CANNER METHOD

1 peck tomatoes
2 tablespoons bottled lemon juice per quart jar

1. Drop a few tomatoes at a time into a kettle of boiling water just long enough for the skin to crack when poked with the tip of a sharp knife.

2. Place the tomatoes in a bowl of cold water (this helps to loosen the skin and makes the tomatoes easier to handle).

3. Remove the skins (they should slide right off if heated enough).

4. Put the lemon juice into clean, hot jars, then add the whole tomatoes (if you want to use them as a vegetable) or slices or chunks (if you want them for soup or hot dishes). Press them down so they form their own juice, and leave ½-inch headspace. Do not add salt. (Add salt when you use them.)

5. Seal with rubber rings and lids, and process in a boiling-water canner for 85 minutes.

CANNED BEETS

✻

PRESSURE CANNER METHOD

As many beets as you want to can

1. Cook the beets in a large kettle with enough water to cover for about 30 minutes, until tender.

2. Peel the beets, and cut them into slices or cubes.

3. Put the beets into clean, hot pint or quart jars, leaving ½-inch headspace. Then pour boiling water into the jars again, leaving ½-inch headspace.

4. Seal the jars with rings and lids.

5. Put into the pressure canner and process 30 minutes for pints, or 35 minutes for quarts, at 11 pounds pressure according to the manufacturer's instructions.

6. Remove from the canner, cool in a draft-free area, and store on the pantry shelf.

MINCEMEAT

MAKES ABOUT 18 PINTS

PRESSURE CANNER METHOD

3 pounds lean beef (see Note)

1/2 pound suet

6 pounds apples, peeled and cored

1/2 cup citron, minced

1 teaspoon ground nutmeg

2 pounds sugar

1 pint Rhubarb Sauce (page 83)

1 pint Strawberry Sauce (page 83)

1 tablespoon ground cloves

1 teaspoon ground cinnamon

1 teaspoon mace

1 tablespoon salt

2 cups meat broth

1. Cut the meat into 2-inch chunks, put in a large kettle, cover with water, and simmer until tender. Cool, and save the juice.

2. Grind the meat, suet, and apples together. Add the citron, nutmeg, sugar, sauces, cloves, cinnamon, mace, salt, and broth, and simmer in a heavy large kettle (not aluminum) for 1 hour, stirring frequently.

3. Stuff into clean, hot pint jars, leaving 1-inch headspace, and seal with rings and lids.

4. Process in a pressure canner for 75 minutes at 11 pounds of pressure according to the manufacturer's instructions.

NOTE: The heart and tongue are good to use in this.

HOMEMADE SAUERKRAUT

When I was a kid, we made sauerkraut in 30-gallon earthenware jugs. We'd take all the cabbage heads out of the garden and go to work on it, shredding it with a big wooden shredder that had three or four knives in it. We'd stuff the cabbage into the jug, cover it with about ¾ cup coarse (not iodized) salt, and stomp it down with a wooden stomper until the juice started coming. Then we'd cover it with a wooden board, and let it stand in the cellar a few days before using it. Today we make it in small batches, in quart jars.

As much cabbage as you have to harvest

1 teaspoon coarse salt (not iodized) per clean, scalded quart jar

1. Clean and shred as much cabbage as you want.

2. As you pack the cabbage into the quart jars, add the salt.

3. Pack the cabbage up to the neck of the jar, pressing down with a wooden spoon as you go. The juice will start to form once the salt is added.

4. When the cabbage is stuffed in up to the neck, cover the jars with rings and lids, and let them stand for a few days (in a cool place) to work.

5. Store on a very cool shelf or refrigerate until ready to use.

FARM MEALS

When we women went out to milk in the morning, our heads were always tied up in a kerchief, our hair was tucked under, and even in summer we maybe had on big, high rubber boots. It was usually five o'clock, with the sun just peeking up over the horizon, the coffeepot on, and the rooster crowing off-key on the fence post. No matter how tired we were or how sore our arms were from carrying the little ones along as we hiked down the cow trail, the air was always fresh and served to wake us. The men would be in the barn laying down feed, and we'd shoo the cows lazily back up from the pasture. It wasn't a hurry-up time. Back then we sat down when we milked; that's why we wore kerchiefs, so we could lean our heads against the cow's bellies and still keep our hair clean. As we squeezed the plump, warm udders, that's when we rested, before our long, full day of work. We'd talk about rain or crops, or who needed a new pair of shoes or patches on their britches, but our minds would inevitably wander to the day's meals. We needed as many calories as possible to get us through the tough physical work of summer and the punishing cold of winter.

On the farm, women still have to plan not for three but for six meals a day. Up at five, we grab coffee or milk and a cookie on the way to the barn; around seven o'clock we're back in for breakfast; nine thirty or ten, there's morning lunch; noon, we have dinner; three o'clock, afternoon lunch; four thirty or five o'clock, grab something to chew on and off to the barn again; seven o'clock (depending on how the cows have milked or if a machine's broken down) we're back in for supper; nine o'clock, we have evening lunch if company is over to visit.

City folks might think it's a holy fright all this food, but it's our way of life—it's both our sustenance, and the center of family and neighborly togetherness.

Country Breakfasts

YEAR-ROUND PANCAKES

In the back kitchen of the restaurant, tacked up above the sink, there's a slopped-up sales slip with my scribbling on it. I copied this recipe out of my head and tacked it there long ago for each cook so both local folks and travelers always get the same cakes they depend on.

**MAKES 25 TO 30
(8-INCH) CAKES**

4 cups white flour

6 tablespoons sugar

3 teaspoons baking powder

2 teaspoons baking soda

6 to 8 egg yolks (depending on how good the hen)

1 teaspoon salt

2 1/2 cups half-and-half

2 1/2 cups buttermilk

2 tablespoons melted butter

1. Combine the flour, sugar, baking powder, baking soda, egg yolks, salt, half-and-half, buttermilk, and butter together in a large bowl, and stir using a wire whisk. When you first stir the batter together, stir up from underneath. If it remains lumpy, don't worry; farm pancakes should have a few air bubbles.

2. Drop by mixing-spoonfuls onto a lightly greased griddle or into a buttered cast-iron skillet, fry on both sides, and serve covered with butter and Homemade Syrup (below) or fresh homemade jams (pages 78 to 81) or white or brown sugar.

BLUEBERRY PANCAKES: Fold about 1 cup of fresh picked blueberries (or frozen if you must) into the batter just before frying.

HOMEMADE SYRUP

Even if we could get to town and afford to buy store-bought Karo syrup, we made this. My mother did, and so did I after I was married. Everybody did. It's truly an old, everyday country favorite (see Note).

MAKES 1½ CUPS SYRUP

1½ cups brown sugar
½ cup water

1. In a small, heavy saucepan, boil the sugar and water together over medium heat.

2. If you like your syrup on the thin side, leave it on just until it boils good. If you want it thick, boil it longer until it starts to spin a thread (see Note).

NOTE: We also sometimes used sorghum as a topping. Sorghum was a crop we used to grow and cut like sugarcane. Then we'd haul the tough stalks in a horse and buggy to the sorghum plant where the juice was crushed out and cooked down to a syrup.

If not feared, a little maple flavoring may be added, if you have it. Stir in 1 teaspoon just before removing from the stove.

MA'S FRY BREAD

Y

If my mother was up and had the bread set before the sun rose, we'd have this after morning chores with breakfast. Otherwise we'd have to wait till midmorning when the bread raised and was ready for the loaf pan. No matter how common, we never failed to nag and beg for it.

A hunk of fresh Company Bread dough
(page 4) the size of a rubber ball (make
sure dough has raised twice)

1. Take the hunk of dough and stretch it out with both hands to oblong or round until about ½ to 1 inch thick—don't be fussy—and fry it on the wood cookstove top or in a lightly buttered cast-iron skillet over medium heat.

2. Fry on both sides until golden brown, then cover it with butter, and eat it when it's still warm. (It's also good with butter and your favorite homemade jam, but try at least one hunk with only butter so you get the true, full flavor.)

FRY TOAST

We had this because we didn't have toasters. But now once someone tries it, they're hooked; they always come back for more.

As many thick slices of Company Bread (page 4) or Dark Bread (page 6) as you want to serve

Butter (see Note)

1. Butter your homemade bread on both sides, and lay the slices in a heavy cast-iron skillet on medium heat until golden brown on both sides.

2. Serve with just butter, butter and homemade jams (pages 78 to 81), or rich, thick peanut butter.

NOTE: It's best to fry this in butter, but make sure it's fresh, not the cold storage stuff; and be careful so the heat isn't so hot that the butter burns.

MY OLD-COUNTRY FRENCH TOAST

MAKES 6 OR MORE SERVINGS

8 egg yolks

1 whole egg

1/2 teaspoon salt

1 teaspoon sugar

2/3 cup whole milk

6 or more thick slices homemade bread

1. Combine the egg yolks, whole egg, salt, sugar, and milk in a flat bowl, and stir together using a wooden spoon.

2. Dip the bread into the batter, cover both sides, and fry in a buttered, heavy cast-iron skillet (be careful because butter will easily burn). Top with fresh butter and Homemade Syrup (page 97).

VARIATION: Many serve this with a little cinnamon in the batter, and then roll it in powdered sugar after the frying. You might like to try that, but be careful if you're using good, farm-fresh ingredients so you don't cover up that simple, pure taste.

OLD-TIME WAFFLES

Even in the toughest times, if you were on the farm, you usually had eggs, flour, and milk. Topped with plump fresh strawberries and thick whipped cream, these waffles could make even the sorest hearts sing. When I put them on the menu at the restaurant, they were a hit right off the bat for both breakfast and supper.

MAKES 10 SMALL OR 6 LARGE WAFFLES

2 cups flour

3 teaspoons baking powder

1 teaspoon salt

2 tablespoons sugar

4 tablespoons melted butter

1 3/4 cups milk

2 egg yolks

2 egg whites

1. Combine the flour, baking powder, salt, sugar, butter, milk, and egg yolks in a medium bowl, and mix all together using a wire whisk.

2. Beat the egg whites separately in a bowl until stiff, then fold them into the batter. Do not overmix. It may be lumpy, and that's okay. Bake by big tablespoonfuls in a big waffle iron, and lesser spoonfuls (according to common sense) for a small iron.

3. Serve with fresh strawberries and whipped cream or with butter and syrup.

FRESH CREAM AND BREAD

✳

This is our old-fashioned fast food. It takes no time to have a plate of rich cream and bread on the table, and it's always delicious. We skim the warm, sweet cream right off the top of the milk can so it's good and thick. But if you're in the city and aren't lucky enough that you can run to the barn, you can substitute whipping cream; that's what I use when we have it at the restaurant.

Waffles, pancakes, french toast, and this cream and bread are also common as suppers on the farm.

> *Day-old homemade bread, cut into thick slices (see Note)*
>
> *Thick cream*
>
> *Homemade jam or white or brown sugar*

1. Put one thick slice of day-old homemade bread on each plate you want to serve.

2. Pour the thick cream over, and top with a little of your favorite homemade jam, or white or brown sugar, and eat to your heart's content.

NOTE: You must have homemade bread for this or you might as well forget it; it won't be right.

Hints for Country Eggs

• For the perfect *fried egg,* put a little butter, bacon grease, or side pork fat into a cast-iron skillet (I like my pan warm, but not hot unless I want a crust around the egg). If you want it sunny-side up, put a cover on and the steam will take care of the egg. If you want it over easy, flip the egg over, and count to five slowly. Leave it longer if you like the yolks hard.

• For *scrambled eggs,* throw 1 or 2 eggs into a bowl for each person you're serving, beat with a wire whisk, add a little milk (¼ cup) and salt and pepper, and fry in bacon or side pork grease over medium heat. Pour the eggs in, and as they start to set, stir until a little dry, or as desired. (Add chopped cheese, bacon, onion, or whatever you like when the eggs are almost ready.)

• For *poached eggs,* put water and a little salt in a saucepan over medium heat (don't have that boiling too hard or they'll boil all to heck). Carefully break the egg into the boiling salted water, cover tightly, and cook as long as or as short as you want the egg hard or soft (about 3 minutes for soft). Using a slotted spoon or turner, lift the egg out of the water, and place it on a slice of homemade fry bread or toast or on pancakes, or eat them alone with bacon or sausage.

There's a lot of discussion on how to keep the whites of poached eggs from going to feather if not using a poacher. You have to have the water boiling just right, not too hard when you drop in the egg, but we never had that trouble in the old days. Some say add a splash of vinegar, but I never do. I believe that feathering has mostly to do with the eggs having been in storage too long. If you do get a certain amount of the stringy stuff, accept that because with today's eggs, unless they're farm fresh, you just want what sticks onto the egg after it's poached anyway.

• For *hard-boiled eggs,* put eggs in a kettle of cold water with 1 teaspoon of salt. Place over medium heat, and let them come to a full boil. Boil for 5 minutes.

• For *soft-boiled eggs,* boil for about 3 minutes and pour the hot water off immediately after you remove them from the heat.

• It's been in the newspapers about salmonella these days, and although the cases still are rare, if you aren't raising your own hens, it's hard to tell from just looking whether your eggs are worth a hoot, so if you like your eggs runny, be very careful about salmonella.

THRESHERS' BREAKFAST

If you're city folks, even if you've never been on a farm, you might get a kick out of making a Saturday or Sunday brunch from this old Threshers' Breakfast. Today we have huge, huge combines that roll through the fields at harvest, but in the old days, the main threshers traveled the countryside in their big caboose and steam engine. They'd roar into the yard, the neighbors would gather, and so would begin the day's reaping. Women would scurry all over the kitchen preparing meals for twenty people. And at night those with the engine slept over, either in the caboose or hay mow— four or five men, and a water boy. The next morning, those traveling men would come in for breakfast, so with your own men you had eight to ten workers to feed before sun up.

• For a true threshers' breakfast, to serve ten, fry 1½ pounds side pork (page 45) in a cast-iron skillet, then a dozen boiled, chopped potatoes in the drippings, and 10 to 20 scrambled eggs (page 99), and put out a bowl of home-made fruit sauce (pages 81 to 84) for each guest.

• To prepare threshers' potatoes, save enough of the side pork drippings (or bacon fat) to have a tasty grease to generously coat the bottom of a cast-iron skillet. Place over medium heat and when the pan is hot, add a dozen boiled potatoes. As they begin to fry, chop them up with a paring knife. When one side is golden brown, flip them over with a pancake turner to keep them from getting mushy. Fry until golden on both sides, then carefully stir, and fry a little longer if you want them crisp.

Remember to allow time to boil the potatoes, if you have none left over from the day before.

We used to chop these boiled potatoes with the sharp edge of a Calumet baking powder can, but you can also slice them if you wish. Slices are pretty, and fry up nice.

If you like a little onion, slice it in while frying.

Farm Lunches

Women have been packing sandwiches with cake and cookies into lunch boxes and old tin syrup pails, stowing them in wicker clothes baskets, and hauling them out to the fields ever since planted seed started growing in this ground. We used to wrap coffee jugs in newspaper to keep them hot, then trudge the few miles on foot, or in horse and wagon, to where the men were working. Now, we have Thermoses and zipper-seal bags, and rumble out with the pickup, but these lunch breaks—whether around the table in winter, or on the steps of a combine at harvest—give everyone energy and a lift in order to keep going.

FARMERS' FAVORITE GROUND RING BOLOGNA SANDWICHES

ENOUGH FOR A DOZEN DOUBLE SANDWICHES, OR 2 DOZEN OPEN-FACED

1 ring Home-Ground Bologna (page 54)

½ cup ground sweet pickles

3 hard-boiled eggs, chopped fine

1 cup Homemade Mayonnaise (page 64; see Note)

Enough fresh butter to spread onto bread as thick as desired

24 thick slices Company Bread (page 4)

1. Grind bologna into a large bowl.

2. Add the pickles, eggs, and mayonnaise, and stir together using a wooden spoon. Mix well.

3. Butter the bread, and spread the mayonnaise mixture on top. If you are making double sandwiches, spread the bologna mixture on very thick, then cover with a top slice of buttered bread. (Open-faced doesn't need to be as thick.)

NOTE: If you like it, you can use Miracle Whip instead of mayonnaise.

If you need to stretch this, add more eggs.

RICH HAKKE KJAT

ENOUGH FOR 12 SLICES OF BREAD OR BUNS

2 cups leftover roast beef, ground (see Note)

2 cups leftover roast pork, ground (see Note)

1 cup meat juice

1 1/2 tablespoons finely chopped onion

1/4 teaspoon pepper

1/2 teaspoon salt

Dash of ground ginger

1. Put the ground meat into a large saucepan over medium heat. Add the juice, onion, pepper, salt, and ginger, and cook on medium heat until the onion is tender.

2. Remove from heat, cool slightly, and spread on buttered bread or buns, or put in an airtight container and let it get cold in the refrigerator.

NOTE: This should be made from leftover roast that's been cooked in larger amounts (page 44) or it won't be as good.

Allowing this dish to be in the refrigerator for a day seems to set the flavor.

DENVER

The U.S. Congressperson from this district is a small-town boy who grew up about 10 miles from the restaurant. When he has visitors in these parts, he brings them in, and he has a Denver because he says he can't get one like it anywhere else. I guess in some places they call this a Western, but that's a little different, because it's made with green pepper.

ENOUGH FOR 1 DENVER

2 eggs

1 1/2 tablespoons diced baked ham

1/2 teaspoon finely chopped onion

Salt and pepper to taste

1 tablespoon butter

2 slices homemade bread (toasted or not)

1. Beat the eggs together in a small dish, add the ham, onion, and seasonings, and mix.

2. Put the butter in a skillet over medium heat, and let it melt. Pour the egg mixture in, and heat until it sets on one side. Flip over with a pancake turner, and fry the other side.

3. Put on buttered bread.

AMERICAN CHEESY BEEF-TOMATO SPREAD

This may not look or sound like anything at all, but taste it.

ENOUGH FOR 12 SANDWICHES

1/4 cup dried beef

1 pound fresh American cheese

1 cup Garden-Fresh Tomato Soup (page 25)

24 thick slices homemade bread

Enough fresh butter to cover bread

1. Grind meat and cheese together, and moisten with as much tomato soup as you desire.

2. Spread 12 slices of bread with a layer of fresh butter, then with a generous layer of this spread. Butter the remaining slices and use as tops to make 12 sandwiches. This spread is a good keeper in the refrigerator.

LADIES' AID SANDWICH SPREAD

ENOUGH FOR 48 OPEN-FACED SANDWICHES

1 cup salad dressing

2 tablespoons sugar

2 tablespoons vinegar

1 teaspoon salt

1 small onion, grated

3 raw carrots, grated

1 cup Spam, ground

1 small green pepper, chopped

6 hard-boiled eggs, mashed

   Thick-sliced homemade bread

   Enough fresh butter to cover

1. Mix all the ingredients except the bread and the butter together in the order given.

2. Place in an airtight container in the refrigerator until chilled.

3. Spread thick-sliced bread with a layer of fresh butter, and cover with the chilled spread.

DREAMS-OF-HOME SALMON SALAD SANDWICHES

Folks from Norway really missed the fresh salmon of the Old Country when they first settled here. Later, when towns sprung up and there was a grocery, to buy a can of salmon was a special treat, and it still is for all of us living by these seas of corn.

MAKES 1 DOZEN OPEN-FACED SANDWICHES

1 (6- to 7-ounce) can salmon (see Note)

2 hard-boiled eggs, chopped fine

1/4 cup celery, chopped fine

1/2 teaspoon finely grated onion

3 tablespoons Homemade Mayonnaise (page 64; see Note)

   Enough fresh butter to cover bread

12 thick slices Company Bread (page 4) or Golden Butter Rolls (page 10)

1. Remove the bones from the salmon; using a fork, mix together with the eggs, celery, onion, and mayonnaise.

2. Spread a layer of fresh butter on the bread, and cover with this spread.

NOTE: This is also good using tuna.

If you had a rural Midwest childhood and have a taste for Miracle Whip, you can use that instead of mayonnaise.

BEEF OR PORK TONGUE SANDWICHES

ENOUGH FOR 18 OPEN-FACED SANDWICHES

1 medium tongue

Enough butter to spread on bread

Company Bread (page 4) or Golden Butter Rolls (page 10)

1. Prepare the tongue (page 58) or go to a good meat market or delicatessen and buy one.

2. Spread butter thick onto homemade bread, and slice the tongue onto it.

3. Season to your own taste.

MILK MAID'S HAM AND RELISH SANDWICH

ENOUGH FOR A DOZEN SANDWICHES

½ pound cream cheese

¾ pound boiled or baked ham

2 large dill pickles or 4 small, sweet pickles

1 small onion

1 pimiento

Fresh, thick whipping cream or homemade mayonnaise

24 thin slices homemade bread

Enough fresh butter to cover

1. Grind together the cream cheese, ham, pickles, onion, and pimiento.

2. Add the cream until spreadable. Stir together using a wooden spoon, and mix well.

3. Cover 12 slices of the bread with a layer of fresh butter, then a generous layer of the ham spread. Top with another slice of buttered bread.

NORSKE NOOK SANDWICH

ENOUGH FOR 1 SANDWICH

1 generous slice American cheese (see Note)

1 slice ham

2 slices bacon, fried the way you like it

2 slices homemade bread with a layer of butter on one side of each

1. Place the cheese, ham, and bacon on the unbuttered side of homemade bread, then place the other slice on top with the buttered side out.

2. Grill on medium heat until golden brown on both sides.

NOTE: You can make this with just cheese, or just ham and cheese, or just cheese and bacon. But the Norske Nook way is a favorite with travelers.

SAVING GRACE SIDE PORK AND SYRUP SANDWICH

In a pinch, if there was nothing else in the pantry to make a good sandwich, farm ladies often tried this. It kind of started out as a last resort, poor-man's kind of thing, but men especially seemed to love it, and it became a country favorite.

1 DOUBLE SANDWICH OR 2 OPEN-FACED

6 to 8 pieces side pork (page 45)

2 thick slices homemade bread spread with butter or home-rendered lard (see Note)

Enough Homemade Syrup (page 97) to cover (as much as you like)

1. Fry the side pork, and place it on two slices of bread spread with butter or home-rendered lard.

2. Cover the side pork with as much syrup as you like, place one slice of bread on top of the other, and cut the sandwich in half or eat open-faced.

NOTE: Many also ate home-rendered lard and syrup sandwiches or butter and syrup sandwiches. Just plain lard sandwiches filled many a lunch bucket, too.

OTHER COW-COUNTRY SANDWICHES

All these sandwiches are made with thick-sliced homemade bread spread with a layer of home-rendered lard or butter.

Thick-sliced Meat Loaf (an old Ladies' Aid treat; page 41)

Firehouse Baked Beans (page 72)

Primost (page 246)

Homeground Bologna (page 54) or sausage, sliced 1/4 inch thick

Dried beef

Fried egg and salad dressing

Plain mustard

Sliced radish

Fresh cucumber and onion

Sliced strawberry

Brown sugar or grilled cheese and brown sugar

Thickly spread butter and homemade jam

Peanut butter and banana

*Everyday
Dinners*

As I've said, our main meal is at noon. Everyday we have a dinner special at the Nook. Most often there are at least two meats to choose from. I put those menus together from what we'd have on the farm, and I've included some of them here. However, please check the yields to make sure they suit your own needs.

MONDAY

Swiss Steak and gravy (page 43)

Mashed Potatoes (page 74)

Green Beans (page 71)

Bread and butter

Gelatin, pudding, or pie

TUESDAY

Meat Loaf (page 41)

Mashed Potatoes (page 74) and butter

Glazed Baby Carrots (page 69)

Bread and butter

Gladys's Cottage Cheese Salad (page 67)

Apple Pie (page 128) or other fruit pie

WEDNESDAY

Meatballs (page 42)

Mashed Potatoes (page 74) and gravy

Fiddler's Escalloped Corn (page 68)

Bread and butter

Leaf Lettuce Salad (page 62)

Cherry Torte (page 142)

THURSDAY

Stuffed Pork Chops (page 46)

Mashed Potatoes (page 74) and gravy

Glazed Baby Carrots (page 69)

Peach or Pear Sauce (pages 81 and 82)

Banana Cream Pie (page 136)

FRIDAY

Beef Tips (page 43) over Farm Noodles (page 24)

Golden Butter Rolls (page 10)

Coleslaw (page 63)

Quick Lemon Pie (page 131)

SATURDAY

Creamed Chicken (page 52) over Fair's Choice Baking Powder Biscuits (page 15)

Fresh Garden Peas (page 67)

Fresh Strawberry Pie (page 124) or Raspberry Torte (page 142)

For Sunday and holiday dinners, see pages 110 to 113.

Farm Suppers

COMMUNITY CLUB CHICKEN HOT DISH

FOR A 9 × 13-INCH CAKE PAN

1 stewing chicken (3 or 4 pounds)
2 teaspoons salt
Dash of pepper
1 onion, chopped
5 eggs, beaten
Salt and pepper to taste
1/2 teaspoon dried sage
1 quart chicken broth
1 loaf bread, torn into pieces
1 cup cracker crumbs

1. Cook the chicken in 2 teaspoons salt, a dash of pepper, and enough water to cover. Cook over medium heat for 1 hour, until tender. Drain, and save the juice.

2. Remove the chicken from the bones when cool, and cut into bite-size pieces.

3. Preheat the oven to 350° F. Mix the onion, eggs, salt, pepper, sage, and chicken broth, and add the bread and chicken.

4. Place in a greased 9 × 13-inch pan, and sprinkle the cracker crumbs on top. Bake 1 hour, until the juice bubbles. If it becomes a little dry, add a little hot water. (This is good with chicken gravy poured over as it's served.)

W aste not, want not" is as sacred as the Bible on the farm, so supper is usually a matter of thrift and imagination because by evening we have leftovers to use up, and we still want to please those coming in hungry from the fields or barn. Hashes, stews, potato pancakes, and soups are common—even pancakes or waffles—usually something warm but simple, because our heavy work for the day is done. Whether we're in from the barn or fields at seven o'clock in the winter, or nine or ten in the summer, supper is our time to wind down. Unless, of course, we're having supper with our neighbors at community club, then a few favorite hot dishes (which I've included here) are put together in the midafternoon, and toted down the road after everyone has hurried in, washed up, and changed clothes from chores.

HOMESTEAD FRIED POTATOES AND RING BOLOGNA

This is served with fresh sliced tomatoes and peach sauce. In the country, at day's end, this is enough for supper.

SERVES 4

4 tablespoons butter and enough to grease another skillet

1 ring Home-Ground Bologna (page 54)

7 or 8 leftover boiled potatoes

Salt and pepper to taste

2 fresh, large tomatoes

4 to 8 thick slices Company Bread (page 4)

4 bowls Peach Sauce (page 81)

1. Melt the butter in a cast-iron skillet over medium heat. (To keep the meat from spattering, sprinkle salt into the skillet before adding the butter.)

2. Grease a separate skillet, cut up the bologna, and fry until brown.

3. Meanwhile, in the skillet with the butter, slice up the leftover boiled potatoes. Slice either thick or thin. (I like mine thick.) Season with salt and pepper, and fry on low heat until golden brown. (Don't stir, or they'll get mushy.) Flip using a pancake turner, and brown all around.

4. Put the potatoes and the bologna together on plates, and slice up fresh tomatoes on the side. Top with a little sugar, or salt and pepper.

5. Put out a plate of Company Bread and 4 saucers of Peach Sauce.

LORRAINE'S STRETCH POTATOES : Melt a little leftover bacon grease in a cast-iron skillet, put in 4 or 5 leftover boiled potatoes (whole, halved, or quartered, whatever makes 4 or 5), chop them with a paring knife or the rim of a Calumet can (as we did), break up a slice or two of Company Bread (page 4), drop it into the pan with the potatoes, and fry all together. Oh, are these good, and they make the potatoes go a little farther.

VARIATION: In the old days, when we cooked cornmeal for breakfast, we let what was left over stand and get cold like pudding. Then for supper, we would slice it and fry it, letting it get brown on both sides in bacon or side pork drippings. We ate it hot, covered with butter and Homemade Syrup (page 97).

QUICK BOLOGNA-AND-PEA SUPPER

1 ring Home-Ground Bologna (page 54)

2 cups fresh peas (or frozen or canned, if you must)

2 cups cream sauce (page 73)

Toast or mashed potatoes

1. Cook the bologna until heated through. Drain it and then cool enough so you can peel off the skin.

2. Cut the bologna into 1-inch pieces.

3. Warm the peas in a little water (or their own juice, if canned) over low heat, then drain off the liquid.

4. Add the peas and bologna chunks to the prepared cream sauce. Heat again and serve over toast or mashed potatoes.

GARDEN-FRESH FARMERS' HOT DISH

ENOUGH FOR A 2-QUART CASSEROLE

2 cups sliced raw potatoes

2 cups sliced raw carrots

1/2 cup sliced onions

1 cup chopped celery

2 cups raw hamburger

2 teaspoons salt

Dash of pepper

1 pint jar tomato soup or 1 can store-bought

1. Preheat the oven to 350° to 375° F. Place all ingredients in a 2-quart casserole in the order given.

2. Bake for 1 hour, until the vegetables are as you like them.

DRIED BEEF CASSEROLE

ENOUGH FOR A 3-QUART CASSEROLE

1/4 pound dried beef

1 cup boiling water

1 cup cubed cheese

1 cup diced celery

1 can cream of mushroom soup

1 cup milk

1 cup water

1 small onion, diced

1 (11-ounce) package noodles, broken (not cooked)

1. Preheat the oven to 325° F. Mix all the ingredients together in a 3-quart buttered casserole.

2. Bake 1 1/2 hours, until it bubbles.

*Sunday
Dinners,*

*Holiday Menus,
and a
Country Picnic*

On the farm, dinner is at noon. And how many farm women sit in the pew at church on Sunday and wonder how it's going back home with the oven? Because we tend to really fuss all day Saturday and early Sunday, by the time we go out the kitchen door to church, Sunday dinner's all set. Either a Sunday Roast (page 44), a nice plump chicken, or a Cherished Old-Time Baked Ham (page 47) is in the oven; the potatoes and vegetables are peeled and soaking in water to be put on to cook when we return; the dessert and the rolls sit out on the counter, ready from the day before. For women, Sunday's songs and sermons are laced with images and second guessings: Did I forget the pepper? For Pete's sake, I must've turned on the oven, didn't I? Was that enough water on the roast so it won't go dry . . .

THANKSGIVING

"Over the river and through the woods, to Grandmother's house we go. The horse knows the way to carry the sleigh, through the white and drifted snow, oh . . ." Every schoolchild hereabouts still learns that song, and it really does have meaning for us. By Thanksgiving the fields that were so green in summer usually lie covered in the thick blanket of white that is so important in nourishing and protecting next year's crop. The plows and balers and combines stand silent in their sheds, the silos and granaries are filled, and our pace has slowed to the rhythms of winter's work. Whether we've had a good harvest or had to battle weather or had poor market prices, for whatever the land gives us each year, we're thankful. It, and Our Maker, are in most farmers' hearts as we sit around the table. And this is how we celebrate. (Please check the yields to make sure they suit your own needs.)

> *A big Roast Turkey (page 50)*
> *Mashed Potatoes (page 74)*
> *Hen House Gravy (page 51)*
> *Rutabagas (page 70)*
> *Cranberry Relish (page 89)*
> *Sweet Chunk Pickles (page 86)*
> *Lefse (page 243)*
> *Golden Butter Rolls (page 10)*
> *Gladys's Cottage Cheese Salad (page 67) or
> any other Midwestern gelatin or sweet salad*
> *Pumpkin Pie (page 131)*

VARIATION: On Sundays we have a scaled-down version of this, with roast chicken instead of turkey, corn instead of rutabagas, usually no relish or *lefse,* and whatever pie's in season.

CHRISTMAS

About all that remains of yesteryear's Christmases is this menu. Back then, Christmas was a feeling in the pit of your stomach; we could get warm and teary eyed over a sleigh ride, "Silent Night," and a scrawny tree coming to life on that special eve. Our gift was a candy cane or carameled apple or, in a good year, a dollar bill, a baby doll shared with two sisters, or a ball made from cord wound around a walnut and hand sewn with leather from an old glove or shoe.

Now the stores light up the last week of October, the music starts, and people are hog wild, running their legs off buying gifts through November and December. You ask kids, "What'd you get for Christmas?" "I don't know—Nintendo, and a TV—that's about it," or "Oh, just a snowmobile, not too much else but clothes." The same wonderful old tunes are sung, and we eat the same food, but everything is rush, rush, toward that bursting cloud of ripped paper. Only in these last years of tougher times, when people just don't have the money to match their fits of generosity and good intentions, have we started to get back to good folks getting together over a good meal and the true meaning of Christmas.

(Please check the yields to make sure they suit your own needs.)

APPETIZER

Egg nog or wine and Christmas baked goods (see Note)

FIRST COURSE

Sødt Suppe (page 249)

MAIN COURSE

Lutefisk (page 242) and Meatballs (page 42)

Mashed Potatoes (page 74)

Gravy (page 42, step 6)

Melted butter for the Lutefisk

Rutabagas (page 70)

Cranberry Relish (page 89)

Sweet Chunk Pickles (page 86)

Raspberry Pretzel Salad (page 66)

Lefse (page 243)

Golden Butter Rolls (page 10)

Steamed Cranberry Pudding (page 148) or Grandma's Risk Risingrøt (page 248) or Rommegrøt (page 247)

DESSERT

Homemade Mincemeat Pie with Hot Rum Sauce (page 132)

Pumpkin Pie (page 131) or Apple Pie (page 128)

NOTE: Some have Oyster Stew (page 33) on Christmas Eve and some form of the preceding menu on Christmas Day. Others, like us, have this menu on Christmas Eve and leftovers Christmas Day.

NEW YEAR'S DAY BUFFET

❋

In the old days, if they had any energy left from the night before, folks used to run through the countryside, from neighbor to neighbor, Christmas Fooling. But nowadays, more and more people seem to just gather with family and friends for a quiet afternoon buffet. We enjoy these hot and cold beverages, finger foods, and desserts. We visit, and maybe watch a little college football. And, of course, we discuss our hopes for our favorite pro team, the Green Bay Packers. It can get to be a merry affair, but is nothing like the old days when we were probably still singing "Auld Lang Sy."

BEVERAGES

Brandy Slush (page 233)

Wine (pages 232 and 233)

Egg nog

Egg Coffee for Ladies' Aid or Company (page 230)

Root Beer in the Fruit Jar (page 227)

FINGER FOOD

LEFSEBUSSE: Lefse (page 243) filled with meatball miniatures (make very tiny meatballs, page 42). For other fillings, we use sliced and fried homemade bologna (page 54), sliced and fried homemade sausage links (page 56), and wieners (cut up small, or mini-wienies) grilled in barbecue sauce (page 49). Roll these fillings in *lefse* to make a good assortment of *lefsebusse*. Here we serve all four types of *lefsebusse* on New Year's.

CHICKEN WINGS: Marinate the wings in Worcestershire or barbecue sauce (page 49) for 1 hour in the refrigerator. Then brown them in shortening in a heavy skillet over medium heat. Bake in a 300° F oven for 1 hour, or until done and tender.

FRESH BACON AND WATER CHESTNUTS: Wrap raw bacon around whole water chestnuts that have been marinated in Worcestershire sauce. Fasten the bacon with toothpicks and broil until the bacon is done.

FRUIT PIZZA: To make this, use ½ recipe of White Sugar Cookies dough (page 199). Press the dough onto a pizza or jelly roll pan until it is about the thickness of a cookie. Bake in a 350° F oven for 10 to 12 minutes, then cool. Mix an 8-ounce package of cream cheese and 1 cup Fresh Whipped Cream (page 192) together and spread the mixture on the crust. Arrange assorted fresh fruit on top. Cook 2 cups of any fruit juice and 2 tablespoons of cornstarch together in a heavy skillet over low heat until smooth. Cool a little, then pour this over the top of the pizza to keep the fruit topping looking fresh and inviting.

DESSERTS

Rosettes (page 253)

Sandbakkels (page 252)

Fattigmand (page 254)

Ernie's Favorite Three-Layer Devil's Food Cake with Date Filling (page 171)

Pumpkin Pie (page 131)

Homemade Mincemeat Pie with Hot Rum Sauce (page 132)

EASTER

In the country, when the farm market was good, Easter was a time the womenfolk, young and old, got new dresses. Mothers would put a little money away each month for fabric, then sit late into the night over their sewing machines. With money we saved from selling hatching eggs, we bought gloves and maybe a pink-and-yellow bonnet. And, somehow, with a few fresh plucked hens we peddled to town-folks, we managed to get bright, shiny shoes, and some years, even patent leather.

We cut up old aprons into strips and strings and set our hair in rag curls or ringlets. Then off we'd go to church, happy not only for our new clothes but that we could sit and appreciate our neighbors'. After services, we tried to remember what Easter was really about when we sat down and said Grace over this dinner.

(Please check the yields to make sure they suit your own needs.)

> *Cherished Old-Time Baked Ham (page 47)*
>
> *Mashed Potatoes (page 74)*
>
> *Gravy from the ham juice (see Note)*
>
> *Fiddler's Escalloped Corn (page 68)*
>
> *Cranberry Relish (page 89)*
>
> *Golden Butter Rolls (page 10)*
>
> *Sweet Chunk Pickles (page 86)*
>
> *Pineapple Torte (page 139)*

NOTE: For this gravy, follow the recipe for Side Pork and Milk Gravy (page 45); just use ham juice in place of side pork drippings, but be sure to brown it real good (you don't want a white gravy with ham).

A COUNTRY PICNIC

There wasn't anything much more special than the picnic we took along to eat on the way to the Fair. On December days, our minds would wander to a blanket spread out under a shade tree, to the butterflies that nipped at our stomachs as we counted the miles to the gates of the steamy fairgrounds with all that bustle, the bright carnival colors, and noise. My girl-friends and I would talk about this fried chicken, the potato salad and just how we'd make it, and we'd argue and wonder who our beaux would be there in that fresh summer air. Virgil McCune? Nels Goodegger? Charley Finn? Would they have enough money for us to go on the rides and in the Fun House, too? Would they want a kiss at the top of the creaking Ferris wheel or would they wait till we were breathless from the day, and they dropped us at our doors?

(Please check the yields to make sure they suit your own needs.)

> *Fried Chicken (brought out in a roaster; page 52)*
>
> *Firehouse Baked Beans (page 72)*
>
> *Potato Salad (page 65) or Escalloped Potatoes (page 73)*
>
> *Mixed fruit salad*
>
> *Coleslaw (page 63)*
>
> *Lorraine's Refrigerator Buns (page 7) topped with Rich Hakke Kjat (page 102) or just buttered*
>
> *Apple Pie (page 128)*
>
> *Lemonade in the Milk Can (page 226)*
>
> *Homemade ice cream (kept frozen in packed ice; pages 218 to 222)*

PIES, TORTES, PAN DESSERTS, and PUDDINGS

It might be true I've made enough pies in my life to be in *The Guinness Book of World Records,* but I certainly didn't start out as "The Natural." When people call me the "Queen of Pies," the "Pie Piper," the "Pie Lady," I have to kind of laugh at Life.

The first time I tried to make a pie I was sixteen and was hired out as a housekeeper for the minister's wife, who was recovering from surgery. When I rolled the dough out, I could tell right away it was really bad. It was tough, just like tire rubber. In those days, it was not only terrible but a sin to waste, so I couldn't just put it in the garbage. I hurried and rolled it back up, wrapped it in newspaper, stuffed it in my suitcase, kept it till the weekend, then took it home with me, and threw it away in secret.

The next time I thought to put pie dough into a suitcase, I had become "A Rare Treasure." It was forty-three years later. I was on my way to the David Letterman show. I figured I could use the dough as a backup in case things got hectic in the studio.

But all the attention, all my fancy new names, what do they mean? When you've made as many pies as I have, you're either bound to be good at it, or you're hopeless. When I first took over the restaurant, I made what the woman before me had always made, four pies a day: one custard, one lemon, one apple, and one banana cream. I gradually got up to seven, and by some twist of fate added Sour Cream Raisin. Like I said, it was that pie that caught Jane and Michael Stern's attention when they happened by in 1976, and it was Sour Cream Raisin that *Esquire* featured two years later. When such a magazine ranks your restaurant as one of the United States's ten best and deems your baking "some of the best pies and cakes in the world," business tends to boom, even in a small cow town like Osseo. I was soon making twenty pies a day, working from sunup on past midnight; that's when I had to bring in Lorraine. By 1983 we were up to seventy-five pies a day; by 1985, one hundred; and by 1988, one hundred and fifty!

Now at the restaurant a typical summer day includes ten lemon, eighteen strawberry, ten raspberry, twenty-two banana cream, five coconut, eighteen sour cream raisin, six pumpkin, twelve apple, twelve rhubarb, ten pecan, six butterscotch, twelve chocolate, twelve blueberry, three custard, and six peach. For me, that's 210 crusts every day from April to December, during the very busy season, plus about half that every day in the off-peak months.

The secret to these "world famous pies" is all in this section, but like most of my life, there's nothing fancy about it. I've improved since that first bad crust in the minister's kitchen, but through the years, if there's a mistake that could have been made, I've probably made it. I've baked pies and used cornstarch instead of flour, baking soda in place of cream of tartar, cinnamon instead of nutmeg; I've dropped pies, forgotten the sugar, and baked in a cold oven. Maybe people are right when they call my pies "nothing less than miracles," but I believe I've learned the best lesson—you gotta relax and laugh at your failures.

I've made the pies in this section so many times, I no longer even measure. I throw in a little bit of this and a little bit of that and think to myself "that looks right." So when following a recipe, do the best you can to be precise, but remember, nothing turns out if you're too fussy.

Hints for Pies

• As I've said, for pies especially, dig in. Use your hands and fingers.

• Taste everything as you go. In fact, I taste it twice to get the true flavor. Your taste buds are on the back of your tongue so to really taste you have to swallow. And use a finger instead of a spoon. Ingredients change flavor when they hit metal or wood.

• Revere Ware makes beautiful stainless steel pie tins, so you can't go wrong on that, but if you're using aluminum, use heavy aluminum, flat-finish pie tins such as those made by Kaiser Bakeware; they're very good. Thin, shiny aluminum that you get at the hardware store will reflect the heat and keep the bottom crust from browning. Glass is no good either. It heats too quickly and is easily broken. (However, if you have only Pyrex, lower your oven by 15° to 25° F. You'll have to experiment.)

• If a recipe calls for milk, by all means use whole milk. As is, store-bought whole milk doesn't have the butterfat we get on the farm, but it'll be fine.

• The sugar is white unless otherwise specified. The flour is all-purpose.

• Be sure your rolling pin is wood and is heavy enough. Some are like toys, they're too light. A medium rolling pin, about five pounds, works fine.

• If a recipe calls for a cup, don't put in a rounded cup. Unless it says "heaping," use a level measure.

• I've always believed in fat pies. Heap the filling into the crust. I've never liked a skinny pie.

• No matter how little salt a recipe calls for, if I list salt, add salt. It's there for a reason.

• If you like your pies not quite as sweet as I do, cut down on the sugar.

• Insert a knife into the slits of a double-crust pie, and it should come out clear. If it is sugary, it needs more baking.

• What I call a "licker" is one of the best tools for pies. It's a rubber spatula and if you're going to make pies, you must have one.

• If you're strapped for time and don't want to make fresh whipped cream or if the pie has to travel or is going to stand a while before it is served—if you're going to substitute—I recommend Cool Whip. It isn't as good as the real thing, but it's the best of store-bought whipped toppings, and it will not separate. Where a recipe calls for two cups freshly whipped cream, use twelve ounces of Cool Whip.

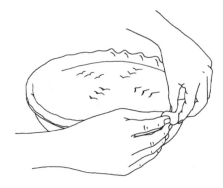

• *Fluting:* Everyone is different; I learned from my mother and this is how I flute: Whether for a single or a double crust, the dough should be one inch larger all around than the tin. If not, trim it with a paring knife. Do not fold under. Pull up what's hanging over, get it even, and press all around on the top of the rim of the pie tin so you get about one-half inch height to flute (see illustration above). Use your two forefingers and thumbs. Take the thumb of your left hand and push the edge out away from you. Your right forefinger will press toward you on the right side of that left thumb while the thumb of the right hand is under your right forefinger pressing against the pan so the dough doesn't slide down. The forefinger of your left hand will hold the dough against the top of the tin while that left thumb is pushing the dough out. Repeat, working around as you go. (I've found this is the best method. Others, such as twisting and scalloping, allow the dough to shrink into the tin more as it bakes, and the fork method is not as pretty and is hard

to dish out of the pan.) If you're just starting, it takes practice, so don't get discouraged.

• When fluting a double-crust pie, remember the thumb of your right hand is down lower on the rim to be sure a ditch forms so the juice from the filling has a place to go and it doesn't run over.

• When measuring shortening for pie crust, wet the cup first, and the shortening will slide right out.

• Always use your fingers to mix pie dough. But keep them loose; don't "squeeze" like you're milking a cow, and don't mix too long or the crust will get tough.

• Use plenty of flour on your hands, on the rolling pin, and on the board or table, so your dough is easy to handle.

• Make your "tennis balls" nice and round so they roll out without getting cracked or scalloped.

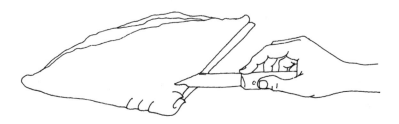

• When rolling out the dough, make sure you roll in every direction or the crust will not be round. You'll get Africa, and it'll be hard to fit into the pan.

• Any dough left over can be rolled out, sprinkled with cinnamon and sugar, and baked for about 10 minutes.

• When rolling crust, I can get five very thin crusts from my Basic Pie Crust recipe (page 120), but if you haven't rolled for as many years as I have, you may get only three or four—just keep rolling and you'll get there.

• Using a fork, poke a lot of holes into the bottom and the sides of a crust that is to be baked without filling, or it will bubble and shrink. If you poke no holes, it'll blow up like a football.

• For better flavor, your crusts should be well browned. This also keeps them from getting mushy when you add the filling.

• *To make the slits for your double crusts:* Fold your rolled-out top crust dough in half, then half again, then half again. Take a paring knife and cut a little slit ¼ inch long on the folds about 1 inch from the center, then ½ inch from that, make another, and ½ inch from that, another (see illustration above). Unfold the slitted crust over the filling, and flute. (The slits keep the pie from bubbling over.)

• If you have baked crusts for future use for a single-crust pie, be sure to cover the crust tightly with plastic wrap so it does not absorb flavors from the air. Also, if saving dough for the following day, wrap it up in plastic and refrigerate until you are ready to use it. But take it out a few minutes before rolling.

Pie Crusts

BASIC PIE CRUST

There are a lot of different recipes in this world for pie crust, some with egg, some with vinegar. I still say it's in the mixing. I just use flour, vegetable shortening, salt, and cold water. For many years, I used lard. You can't beat pie crust that's made with home-rendered lard, but it's almost impossible to get anymore, and store-bought lard is awful. So now, in the restaurant, I use Butter Flavor Crisco. But I find that it's flat, so you have to add salt. Spry is more waxy, so don't use that, it'll go all to pieces when you roll it. (If you're not scared off by cholesterol and would like to recover the taste of what I think makes the best pies, go to a locker plant or a good meat market and try to get home-rendered lard. Or if you know someone who is butchering and you can get a fatted pig skin, try our recipe, page 257.)

**MAKES 4 (10-INCH)
VERY THIN CRUSTS**

2 cups flour

1 cup Butter Flavor Crisco (or 1 scant cup lard)

Enough salt in hand to scatter in

½ cup cold water

1. In a bowl, using your fingers, mix the flour, shortening, and salt together until it gets to be a crumbly mixture. Add the cold water, and mix until smooth. (Don't overmix.)

2. Place the dough on a floured table or board. Cover your hands with flour and knead the dough back and forth a few times like you would bread, then spank it.

3. Divide: Take a ball about the size of a tennis ball, make it nice and round in your hand, set it on the floured board, then flatten it, keeping it round.

4. There's no fancy way to roll a crust, just take a floured, wooden rolling pin and roll in every direction so the crust stays round. Keep rolling until the crust is 1 inch bigger all around than the pie tin.

5. Lay the bottom crust in the pan. If for a baked single crust, take a fork and poke holes all around in the bottom and on the sides. (This will keep it from bulging or bubbling while it bakes.) Now, take your fingers and make a fluted edge around the pie rim. Press your hands around the side of the fluting to get rid of the excess pie crust. Bake at 350° to 375° F for 10 to 15 minutes, depending on your oven. I like mine nicely browned, not white. Let it cool, then put the filling in.

6. If you're making an unbaked single crust, lay the bottom crust in the tin (do not poke holes), flute the top, and add the filling. If you're making a double crust, lay the bottom crust in the tin, add the filling, then roll out the top crust and make slits (page 119). Unfold over the filling, and flute (page 118). Bake according to the recipe.

VARIATION: This is the basic recipe. If you want a crust not quite so tender—a crust that won't break quite so easily—just add a little more flour.

For a quick treat, roll out any excess dough as cookies, no fancy shape; sprinkle with sugar and a little cinnamon, and bake.

GRAHAM CRACKER CRUST

FOR A 10-INCH PIE TIN
(OR A 9 × 13-INCH
TORTE CRUST)

2 cups crushed graham cracker crumbs (see Note)

1/2 cup powdered sugar

1/2 cup (1 stick) soft butter

1. Mix the graham cracker crumbs and the powdered sugar together in a bowl.

2. Add the butter, and mix, using your fingers, until it becomes a crumbly mixture. Don't overmix.

3. Press into the pie tin, covering the sides and the bottom (see Note).

4. For pie, put the crust in the refrigerator to set until it's good and cold. (Be sure it is well set or it'll get mushy when the filling is added.) For a torte, press the crust into the bottom of a 9 × 13-inch cake pan. (Do not press on the sides.)

NOTE: To crush graham crackers, place the crackers on waxed paper or a brown paper sack, and roll with a rolling pin. Roll until they're good and crushed, but don't pulverize. (Aim for finer than gravel and coarser than sand.)

It's easy to make your crust too thick where the sides of the tin curve upward. To avoid this, take two fingers and press them lengthwise against the inside of the rim all the way to bottom, and all the way round. Then press with your fingertips all the way around once again.

CRUSHED OREO COOKIE CRUST

FOR A 10-INCH PIE TIN

2 cups crushed Oreo cookies

1/4 cup (1/2 stick) butter, melted

1. Put the cookies in a plastic bag and crush them with a rolling pin as fine as you can. Put the crushed cookies in a small bowl, and using your hands, mix well with the melted butter.

2. Press into the bottom and the sides of the tin. Put the crust into the refrigerator or the freezer, and allow it to chill and set completely (about 10 minutes in the freezer, at least 30 minutes in the refrigerator).

Hints for Meringues

MERINGUE

FOR A 10-INCH PIE TIN

12 medium egg whites (see Note)

¼ heaping teaspoon cream of tartar

2 cups powdered sugar

• Meringues are the one thing you need to be fussy about.

• When making meringue, be sure the bowls are completely clean, not a speck of grease or soap residue on anything, not on the bowl or the mixer. And be sure no egg yolk drips into the egg white. It won't be worth a darn if you get grease or egg yolk in there.

• If you beat the whites too long before you add the powdered sugar, the meringue won't have a nice firm texture.

• After you've added the powdered sugar, beat it until it's so thick and smooth that when you take a spatula and run it through the meringue, it will part and stay that way, like the Red Sea. (Don't overmix.)

• When putting meringue on the pie, spread it around with a "licker" to get the bubbles out. Don't dump it on all at once; add about ¼ inch at a time.

• Use very thin pot holders when removing a meringued pie from the oven. Thick holders will bunch up and tear the meringue.

1. Preheat the oven to 400° F. Read "Hints for Meringues" (at left). Separate the yolks from the whites, being careful not to drip any yellow in the whites or they won't beat up. Put into a bowl. Add the cream of tartar, and beat until stiff, using an electric mixer on high speed continually.

2. Add the powdered sugar and beat until it forms soft peaks.

3. Using a licker, spread a layer of meringue onto the pie. Make a good seal over the filling. Spread until it meets the edge of the crust to keep the meringue from shrinking as it stands or bakes. Repeat until the meringue is used up, then gently swirl the top to make it pretty. Bake about 15 to 20 minutes, until golden brown.

NOTE: Large eggs make poor meringue. Small eggs do not necessarily have less egg white and are preferable to large if you can't get medium.

Do not double the recipe.

Pies

SOUR CREAM RAISIN PIE

❈

In Wisconsin, our license plates say "America's Dairyland." Some are personalized, "WE-FARM," "MOOOO," or "EAT-CHZ." If you're traveling anywhere Interstate 94 stretches into the countryside, you can see them—big, beautiful milk cows in every direction. They'll be just standin' there, lazily chompin' grass. They're the ones to thank for making this pie, and every other dessert I make, good.

I'm so used to getting these pure milk products from our milkman, I never had to make any adjustment with this recipe until I tried it in New York. In the studio before the David Letterman show, they brought me two different brands of sour cream to use, but both were poor. When I put the flour and sugar and everything in, it was just like the sour cream melted, and when I put it on the stove to cook, it turned brown instead of white. In Wisconsin, our sour cream is real thick and when we stir it in, it stays white. Here at home, I use four teaspoons of flour to thicken the filling; out there I was using tablespoons instead of teaspoons to get the same effect. So depending on the quality of your ingredients, you may have

to experiment and adjust the amount of flour to get it right. If the filling seems runny at first, don't worry, you can mend it; just add a little flour at a time as the filling cooks, and it'll turn out fine.

FOR ONE 10-INCH PIE TIN

2 cups sour cream
4 egg yolks (save whites for meringue)
1³⁄4 cups sugar
4 heaping teaspoons flour
1¹⁄2 cups raisins
1 baked single crust (page 120)
1 recipe Meringue (page 122)

1. Stir the sour cream and the egg yolks together in a heavy medium saucepan.

2. Add the sugar. Dump in the flour, then the raisins, and mix using a wooden spoon.

3. Cook over medium heat until the raisins are plump and the filling is glossy (about 5 minutes after a full boil, or just a little longer, depending on your burner).

4. Cool the filling slightly, then pour it into the cool crust.

5. Preheat the oven to 400° F. Prepare the Meringue and spread it onto the pie.

6. Put the pie in the oven. Watch closely for 15 to 20 minutes, then take it out when the peaks are golden brown. Let it cool. Eat immediately or keep in a cool room. Do not refrigerate unless keeping it overnight.

FRESH STRAWBERRY PIE

✳

It's funny what you think about in a time of crisis. The night of June 13, 1983, just after I'd gotten home from the restaurant and was getting into bed, I got a call that the Nook was on fire. I sped back to town; there were fire trucks and people all over. Lorraine was already there, but there was nothing we could do. We went and sat on the steps of the store across the street just like two orphans. It was the height of the season and we were way underinsured; flames were shooting up, there was water all over, firemen were chopping holes in the roof and busting the windows, but what Lorraine and I talked about were the twelve strawberry pies we'd made that night so we wouldn't have to rush so much the next morning. We kept saying "Now those pies are going to burn up with the new refrigerator." After the place was gutted and rebuilt, and we were back in business, we laughed at ourselves, and still laugh at just how much we thought of our strawberry pies.

FOR ONE 10-INCH PIE

JUICE

1 pint fresh strawberries (see Note)
2 cups water

PIE

2 cups strawberry juice
2 cups sugar
1/3 cup strawberry gelatin

3 heaping tablespoons cornstarch
1 baked 10-inch single crust (page 120)
1 1/2 quarts strawberries (stems removed, washed, and drained; see Note)
2 cups Fresh Whipped Cream (page 192)

1. *To make the juice:* Cook in a stainless steel saucepan over medium heat until the berries are pale (about 5 minutes). Strain and reserve the juice.

2. *To make the pie:* Combine the strawberry juice and the sugar, and boil for a couple of minutes until the sugar is dissolved completely.

3. Add the gelatin, and stir until it boils. Dissolve the cornstarch in a little cold water, add quickly to the above mixture and cook, stirring slowly until a clear bubble forms (about 5 minutes). Cool until it's as thick as molasses.

4. Pour just enough juice into the baked pie crust to cover the bottom.

5. Arrange the berries over the crust. (Cut the large berries in half.) Pour on the remaining juice, making sure to cover the berries completely.

6. Refrigerate and when ready to serve, top with Fresh Whipped Cream.

NOTE: For everything else I recommend home-grown berries, but for this pie I suggest you use firm, store-bought California or Florida berries. The pie will keep much better. (But for shortcake or anything else, home-grown berries taste much better.)

RASPBERRY PIE: Use raspberries instead of strawberries, and follow the above recipe.

RHUBARB PIE

FOR ONE 10-INCH PIE

*4 or 5 cups fresh or frozen rhubarb, cut into
⅔-inch pieces*

2 cups sugar and a little to sprinkle over

⅓ cup flour

Dash of ground nutmeg

3 eggs

1 double crust (page 120)

4 tablespoons butter

1. Preheat the oven to 350° F. Place the rhubarb in a large bowl. Pour the sugar over, add the flour and nutmeg, and mix it together a little on top of the rhubarb.

2. Using your hands, in the center of this mixture, make a well for the eggs. Crack the eggs into the well and beat them with a fork.

3. When the eggs are mixed, gradually blend them into the rhubarb and flour mixture until the rhubarb is partially coated. (Do not overmix.)

4. Using your hands, put the filling into the pie crust and dot with thinly sliced butter. This may seem to be a heaping pie tin, but rhubarb shrinks a lot.

5. Cover with the slitted top crust, and flute (page 118). Sprinkle with a little sugar, and bake 1 hour for fresh rhubarb, 1½ hours for frozen.

RHUBARB CREAM PIE

FOR ONE 10-INCH PIE

½ cup (1 stick) butter

4 cups fresh rhubarb, cut into ¾-inch pieces

2 cups sugar

3 egg yolks (save whites for Meringue)

½ cup flour

½ cup cream

1 baked single crust (page 120)

1 recipe Meringue (page 122)

1. Put the butter in a heavy saucepan and place on the stove on low heat to melt.

2. Add the rhubarb to the butter and cook together over medium heat until the rhubarb is well coated.

3. Add 1½ cups of the sugar, and cook until soft.

4. In a separate bowl, while the rhubarb mixture cooks, combine the egg yolks, ½ cup of the sugar, the flour, and cream, and mix until smooth.

5. Pour this into the hot rhubarb, and cook until thick. Remove from heat, and cool.

6. Preheat the oven to 400° F. Pour into a cooled crust. Make the Meringue and cover the filling. (Be sure the rhubarb is completely cooled.) Bake 15 to 20 minutes, until the Meringue is golden brown.

STRAWBERRY-RHUBARB PIE

❈

FOR ONE 10-INCH PIE

1 double crust (page 120)

3 cups rhubarb, cut into ¾-inch pieces

2 cups strawberries, stemmed and halved

2 cups sugar

⅓ cup flour

Dash of nutmeg

3 eggs

6 tablespoons butter

Sugar, for sprinkling

1. Preheat the oven to 350°F. Press the bottom crust into a pie tin.

2. In a large bowl, combine the rhubarb and strawberries. Onto the top, dump the sugar, flour, and nutmeg. In the center of this mixture, make a well. Break the eggs into the well and mix using a fork. Beat the eggs thoroughly, then gradually work them into the rhubarb and berries. (Do not overmix.)

3. Use your hands to put this mixture into the bottom pie crust. Dot with thinly sliced butter.

4. Cover with the top crust, and slit the crust decoratively. Flute (page 118), then sprinkle with sugar, and bake for 1 hour, or until a knife inserted in a slit comes out clean.

CHERRY PIE

❈

FOR ONE 10-INCH PIE

1 double crust (page 120)

5 heaping cups pitted, sour cherries, fresh or frozen (enough to make a fat pie; see Note)

⅓ cup flour

2 cups sugar and a little to sprinkle over

1 tablespoon cornstarch

1 tablespoon rum (see Note)

4 tablespoons butter

1. Preheat the oven to 350° F. Place the bottom crust in the bottom of the tin, and cover it with the cherries.

2. In a small bowl, mix the flour, sugar, and cornstarch together, using your fingers, and sprinkle this over the top of the cherries.

3. Pour the rum on top of this mixture, and dot with thin slices of butter.

4. Cover with the slitted top crust, and flute (page 118).

5. Sprinkle with sugar, and bake for 1 hour or more, until the juice is clear (see Note).

NOTE: It's a slow job to pit the cherries by hand, but that's how we do it.

Rum sweetens or takes tartness out; do not substitute.

This is juicy, so bake it slowly so the juice doesn't boil out of the crust. Insert a knife in one of the slits; if it comes out sugary, the pie needs to bake longer.

BLUEBERRY PIE

FOR ONE 10-INCH PIE

1 double crust (page 120)

5 heaping cups blueberries, fresh or frozen
(enough to make a heaping pie)

½ cup flour

2 cups sugar and a little to sprinkle over

1 heaping tablespoon cornstarch

4 tablespoons butter

1. Preheat the oven to 350° F. Press the bottom crust into the bottom of the tin, and heap with blueberries.

2. In a small bowl, using your fingers, mix the flour, sugar, and cornstarch together. Sprinkle this over the berries, and dot with thin slices of butter. There's nothing wrong with adding a little brandy, but don't overdo it (a scant capful).

3. Cover with the slitted top crust, and flute, making a deep ditch (page 118).

4. Sprinkle with a little sugar, and bake 1 hour, until a knife stuck into a slit does not come out sugary (see Note).

NOTE: Bake slowly so the juice doesn't boil out of the crust.

OPEN-FACE NORWEGIAN DUTCH APPLE PIE

FOR ONE 10-INCH PIE

1 unbaked pie crust (page 120)

5 heaping cups sliced McIntosh or Cortland
apples (enough for a fat pie)

1½ cups white sugar

1 teaspoon ground cinnamon

1 teaspoon ground nutmeg

½ cup packed brown sugar

¾ cup flour

½ cup (1 stick) butter

1. Preheat the oven to 400° F. Press the crust into the bottom of the tin, and cover with half of the apples.

2. In a small bowl, mix 1 cup of the white sugar with the cinnamon and nutmeg. Sprinkle half of this mixture on the apples, then make another layer of apples, and do the same.

3. In a separate bowl, mix ½ cup of white sugar, the brown sugar, flour, and butter together, and work, using your fingers, until crumbly.

4. Sprinkle this over the apples, and bake for 15 minutes. Then turn down the oven to 350° F, and bake 45 minutes longer, until a knife comes out clear (not sugary). Serve with homemade ice cream (pages 218 to 222) or as is.

APPLE PIE

When the threshing crews would come to help with harvest, oh, that was a big time. The women would cook and bake all day—breakfast, morning lunch, noon dinner, afternoon lunch, and supper—usually about eighteen or twenty men to feed, and there'd always be pie. Ordinary as it was, apple was a favorite with threshers. They liked it served with a slice of Longhorn cheese. If I close my eyes I can still see and hear them there at the table—sunbrowned, hands swollen with work, bits of chaff in their hair, but never too tired to tease: "What is apple pie without a slice of cheese? Like a kiss, my dear, without a little squeeze."

FOR ONE 10-INCH PIE

1 double crust (page 120)

8 or 9 fresh apples, peeled, cored, and sliced (enough to make a fat pie; see Note)

2 cups sugar and a little to sprinkle over

1/4 cup flour

1 teaspoon ground cinnamon

Dash of ground nutmeg

3 tablespoons butter

1. Preheat the oven to 375° F. Press the bottom crust into the pie tin, and fill with sliced apples.

2. In a small bowl, using your fingers, mix the sugar, flour, cinnamon, and nutmeg together.

3. Sprinkle this around and around the apples on top of the pie, and dot with thin slices of butter.

4. Cover with the slitted top crust, and flute (page 118).

5. Sprinkle with a little sugar, and bake 1 hour, until a knife comes out clear.

NOTE: Our McIntosh or Cortland apples are the best for this pie. They cook well, and don't go to mush.

GOVERNOR'S FAVORITE CRAN-APPLE PIE

Like most farm towns across America, for the last decade Osseo has struggled to stay alive. The once bustling three-block main street where the Nook stands used to house a large general store, a farm equipment dealership, a feed mill, three groceries, a bank, two doctor's offices, two hardware stores, a dime store, two barbershops, two shoe stores, a pharmacy, four cafes, four taverns, a dress shop, a locker plant, and a bakery. Of those, the pharmacy, the feed mill, three taverns, the dress shop, the farm equipment dealership, the bank, and a barber shop remain.

By bringing in tourists, the Norske Nook has helped, but with the farm economy as it is, this town, like so many others, has had to scurry to try to attract small industry. To help with that, the governor, a few years ago, flew up and presented Osseo with a grant for an industrial park. It got to be a big deal; the band came out, the men wore suits, there were banners of every color, and almost all of the town's fourteen hundred gathered in the park. I was part of the program, handing the governor the pie his office had called ahead and requested. This is the recipe.

1 double crust (page 120)

3 heaping cups apples, peeled and sliced (see Note)

2 heaping cups cranberries, cut in half (see Note)

2 cups sugar and a little to sprinkle over

¼ cup flour

½ cup nutmeats, coarsely chopped

Dash of ground cinnamon

2 tablespoons butter

1 tablespoon rum

1. Preheat the oven to 350° F. Press the bottom crust into the tin.

2. In a large bowl, mix the apples, cranberries, sugar, flour, nutmeats, and cinnamon together, and pour into the crust.

3. Top with thin slices of butter and the rum.

4. Cover with the slitted top crust, and flute (page 118). Sprinkle with a little sugar, and bake 1 hour, until a knife comes out clear.

NOTE: Our McIntosh or Cortland apples are best for this. The type of apple will affect the sweetness. My mother uses 2 cups of apples and 4 cups of cranberries (all of the other measures are the same).

Cut the cranberries in half by hand. If you put them through a chopper, they get too fine.

GLAZED PEACH PIE

❈

6 or 7 fresh 3½-inch peaches, their skins, and 1 stone

3 cups water

2 cups sugar

1 (3-ounce) package orange gelatin

3 tablespoons cornstarch

1 baked single crust (page 120)

2 cups Fresh Whipped Cream (page 192)

1. Peel the peaches and set aside.

2. Cook the skins and the peach stone in the water in a medium saucepan. Boil for 5 minutes, then strain. (This should make about 2½ cups of juice; if not, add water.)

3. Add the sugar and bring to a boil. Add the orange gelatin, and let it come to a boil again.

4. Dissolve the cornstarch in a little water, and add it to the boiling syrup. Cook until clear, stirring often. Remove from the stove, and cool until the mixture is like half-set gelatin.

5. Slice the peaches, and place two-thirds of them in the bottom of the baked pie shell. Pour one-half of the syrup over the peaches. On top of this, arrange the rest of the peaches in a neat fan design, and pour the remaining syrup over.

6. Refrigerate until set, then take it out and top with Fresh Whipped Cream when ready to serve.

PEACH PIE

FOR ONE 10-INCH PIE

1 double crust (page 120)

*10 or 12 peaches (depends on size), peeled
and sliced*

*1³/₄ cups sugar and a little to sprinkle
over*

¹/₄ cup flour

2¹/₂ tablespoons cornstarch

Dash of ground nutmeg

1¹/₂ tablespoons butter

1. Preheat the oven to 375° F. Press the bottom crust into the tin, and place a heaping pile of sliced peaches over the top.

2. In a small bowl, using your fingers, mix the sugar, flour, cornstarch, and nutmeg together. Sprinkle over the peaches, and dot with thinly sliced butter.

3. Cover with the slitted top crust, and flute (page 118). Sprinkle with a little sugar, and bake 45 minutes, until a knife comes out clear (see Note).

NOTE: Peaches cook quickly.

OPEN PEACH CREAM PIE

This doesn't look real pretty, but oh, is it good.

FOR ONE 10-INCH PIE

1 unbaked single crust (page 120)

1¹/₂ cups sugar

3 tablespoons flour

3 tablespoons cornstarch

Dash of ground nutmeg

Dash of salt

7 or 8 peaches, peeled and sliced

³/₄ cup cream

1. Preheat the oven to 375° F. Press the crust into the bottom of the tin.

2. In a small bowl, using your fingers, mix the sugar, flour, cornstarch, nutmeg, and salt together.

3. Put about three-quarters of this mixture into the crust, pushing some of it up onto the sides. Heap the peach slices over this.

4. Take the remaining flour mixture and sprinkle it on top of the peaches.

5. Pour fresh cream over all, and bake for 45 minutes, until the peaches are tender.

PUMPKIN PIE

As I must have said a million times in my life, tasting is the key to good cooking, and stirring up pumpkin is a perfect example. If you stick your finger in it, and it's bitter, you know you've forgotten the salt. You can stand and add sugar till the cows come home, but if you've forgotten the salt, pumpkin'll still have an edge of bitterness.

Whatever you're making, tasting can prevent a lot of failures; at the restaurant, I've even found lemonade in the gravy. One of the cooks reached for potato water when a same-size jug of lemonade was standing alongside, and in went the lemonade. No one realized it until I stuck my finger in. So even if you're an expert, you gotta taste. And don't underestimate salt when it comes to pumpkin.

FOR ONE 10-INCH PIE

3 cups pumpkin puree

3/4 cup brown sugar

3/4 cup white sugar

1 tablespoon pumpkin pie spice (see Note)

1 teaspoon salt

4 eggs

1 3/4 cups milk

1 unbaked single crust (page 120)

1. Preheat the oven to 350° F. Using a whisk, mix the pumpkin, sugars, spice, salt, and eggs together well in a large bowl until blended. (Don't overmix.)

2. Add the milk, and stir again.

3. Pour into the unbaked pie shell, and bake for 45 minutes, until when you touch a finger to the top, it does not stick. (Top with Boss's Vanilla Ice Cream, page 218, if desired.)

NOTE: If you don't have pumpkin pie spice, use 1 teaspoon ground cinnamon, 1 teaspoon ground nutmeg, a dab of ground cloves, and a dab of allspice.

QUICK LEMON PIE

FOR ONE 10-INCH PIE

1 batch Miss Little's Lemon Pudding (page 152)

1 baked single crust (page 120)

1 recipe Meringue (page 122)

1. Preheat the oven to 400° F. In a heavy saucepan, prepare the pudding as directed and cool.

2. Pour into the baked pie crust, top with Meringue, and bake for 20 minutes, until golden brown.

HOMEMADE MINCEMEAT PIE WITH HOT RUM SAUCE

FOR ONE 10-INCH PIE

1 double crust (page 120)

3 apples, peeled (see Note)

1 pint home-canned Mincemeat (page 93; see Note)

1/2 cup sugar and a little to sprinkle over

1 tablespoon butter

1 tablespoon rum (see Note)

1 tablespoon brandy (see Note)

1. Preheat the oven to 375° F. Press the bottom crust into the tin.

2. Slice the apples into a mixing bowl and chop them into small pieces. Add the Mincemeat and sugar, and mix well.

3. Pour into the bottom crust, and dot with thin slices of butter. Pour the rum and the brandy over all. (Use your fingers to poke the butter into the filling.)

4. Cover with the slitted top crust, and flute (page 118). Sprinkle with a little sugar and bake 45 minutes, until the crust is nice and brown (see Note). Serve with Hot Rum Sauce (following recipe).

NOTE: Use McIntosh or Cortland apples.

Rum and brandy smooths the meat taste.

If you have no home-canned Mincemeat, I recommend Borden's store-bought mincemeat, but of course, it's not as good as what you'd can yourself.

Canned mincemeat cooks quickly.

HOT RUM SAUCE

MAKES ABOUT 1 QUART

2 cups sugar

4 tablespoons cornstarch

3 cups boiling water

3/4 cup (1 1/2 sticks) butter

1 cup brandy (or less to suit taste; see Note)

3/4 scant cup rum (see Note)

1. With a whisk, mix the sugar and cornstarch in a heavy medium saucepan. Add the boiling water and cook on medium heat until clear, stirring occasionally.

2. Add the butter, and cook until it's melted. Remove from heat.

3. Add the brandy and rum and stir. Serve hot over pie or homemade ice cream (pages 218 to 222; see Note).

NOTE: Always use less rum than brandy.

Cool the sauce slightly when using it for ice cream shakes or sundaes.

FRESH GREEN TOMATO MINCEMEAT PIE

This is a mock mincemeat. It's great for vegetarians or people who don't have the time and aren't able to butcher and can the real thing. Try to get home-grown fresh green tomatoes, though. They'll make all the difference. If you're not growing your own, and don't know a farmer up the road, try an open, outdoor market. They should have green tomatoes. If not, ask, and maybe they'll bring you some. There is no substitute.

FOR ONE 10-INCH PIE

1 double crust (page 120)

6 medium (3 1/4-inch) green tomatoes

2 tablespoons water

1/2 lemon, sliced with rind

1 cup sugar

2 tablespoons cornstarch

Pinch of salt

1/4 teaspoon ground cinnamon

2 tablespoons butter

1. Preheat the oven to 375° F. Press the bottom crust into the tin.

2. Wash the tomatoes, remove both ends, cut into thin slices, and cook in a stainless steel saucepan over medium heat with the water and lemon until almost soft. Drain, and save the juice. Set both the tomato/lemon mixture and the juice aside to cool.

3. In a small bowl, mix the sugar, cornstarch, and salt together.

4. In a heavy medium saucepan, combine the juice and the sugar mixture, and cook until thick. Add the tomatoes, cinnamon, and butter, and blend thoroughly. Cool.

5. Pour into the bottom crust. Cover with the slitted top crust, seal, and flute (page 118). Bake 30 minutes, until golden brown.

LIGHT PRUNE PIE

FOR ONE 10-INCH PIE

6 egg whites

2/3 cup sugar

2 cups cooked prunes, pitted and chopped

1/4 teaspoon salt

1 tablespoon lemon juice

Heaping 1/4 cup chopped pecans

1 baked single crust (page 120)

2 cups Fresh Whipped Cream (page 192)

1. With an electric mixer on high speed, beat the egg whites until foamy, gradually adding the sugar. Beat until stiff.

2. On slow speed, add the prunes, salt, lemon juice, and pecans. Then beat on full speed for about 5 minutes.

3. Pour into a cooled baked pie shell, and chill in the refrigerator for 1 hour to be sure it's set.

4. Garnish with Fresh Whipped Cream, and serve. You can also serve this as a pudding without the crust.

CUSTARD PIE

In the old days, almost every farm had chickens. You could write away to the hatchery in Winona, Minnesota, and a few weeks later the mailman would bring an order of baby chicks to the house. Of course, it isn't legal today, but back then, for us country folks, that was quite the thing, getting our chickens by mail. Townspeople would go the post office, and they'd hear "peep, peep, peep," from the back room; one of us farmers was getting a brood.

Chickens helped a lot in hard times—no matter how little you had, at least hens and eggs were plentiful, and no part of an egg went unused. In those days, the shells went back to the chickens or pigs for food, and if a recipe called only for whites, the yolks were used for something else. Sponge cake, or this custard pie, was usually my something else.

FOR ONE 10-INCH PIE

14 egg yolks

1 cup sugar

1 teaspoon salt

1 teaspoon vanilla extract

3 cups milk

1 unbaked single crust (page 120)

Dash of ground nutmeg

1. Preheat the oven to 325° F. Using a whisk, beat the egg yolks, sugar, salt, and vanilla together in a big bowl.

2. Add the milk, and mix well.

3. Pour into an unbaked pie shell. Put a dash of nutmeg on top, and swirl it around with a whisk. Bake about 45 minutes, until set.

CUSTARD PUDDING: Follow the same recipe, only put custard into custard cups on a cake pan with a little water in the bottom, and bake 30 minutes in a 325° F oven until set.

OLD-FASHIONED COCOA PIE

Farm women years ago had miles and miles to go to town and usually couldn't afford to have many fancy things on hand to bake with. We weren't accustomed to having chocolate chips, peppermint sticks, maraschino cherries, or even coconut and nutmeats in our cupboards. Unless it was for something special like Ladies' Aid, a wedding, a barn dance, a funeral, or threshing, we rarely thought to use anything but the basics. Cocoa, however, was an old standby, and this is how we always made our chocolate pie.

FOR ONE 10-INCH PIE

½ cup cocoa

1 cup sugar

½ cup flour

3 cups milk

2 tablespoons butter

1 teaspoon vanilla extract

1 baked single crust (page 120)

2 cups Fresh Whipped Cream (page 192)

Enough chocolate shavings to sprinkle on (see Note)

1. Mix the cocoa, sugar, and flour together in a small bowl.

2. Heat the milk in a heavy medium saucepan.

3. Using a whisk, add the dry ingredients, and mix. Cook over medium heat until thick and smooth, stirring with a licker so it doesn't scorch.

4. Remove from heat, then stir in the butter and vanilla. Cool and put into a cooled pie crust. Top with Fresh Whipped Cream, then sprinkle with chocolate shavings.

NOTE: To make chocolate shavings, rub a chocolate candy bar over a grater or slice the bar with a potato peeler.

CHOCOLATE PIE

FOR ONE 10-INCH PIE

1 baked single crust (page 120)
1 batch Basic Chocolate Pudding (page 150)
2 cups Fresh Whipped Cream (page 192)
    Enough chocolate shavings to sprinkle on (see Note)

1. Prepare a batch of chocolate pudding, cool to lukewarm, and pour into a cooled pie crust.

2. Top with Fresh Whipped Cream. Sprinkle with chocolate shavings.

NOTE: Make chocolate shavings by rubbing a chocolate candy bar over a grater, or slice the bar with a potato peeler.

COUNTRY MUD PIE

I can't make this pie without thinking back to being a little girl and playing in the granary. Boy, did I have a fancy house! I took gunnysacks and pieced 'em together with shingle nails and hung 'em from the ceiling to divide out rooms. I draped grain sacks over hen crates for beds; a chick incubator was my stove. I made cookies, had rocks for potatoes, and ragweed for coffee. I even smoked, using twigs from the big maple. But the best was when I'd find a tiny egg a chicken had laid by mistake. I'd grab it as if it were a dollar bill, mix it with three or four handfuls of fresh mud, and pour in sand from an old rusted spice tin. Then I'd run and try to treat the shiny black crows that strutted along the barnyard. That mud pie maybe wasn't as delicious as this one, but boy, was I proud.

FOR ONE 10-INCH PIE

1/2 gallon homemade Coffee Ice Cream (page 220)
1 Crushed Oreo Cookie Crust (page 121)
3/4 cup hot fudge sauce
2 cups Fresh Whipped Cream (page 192)
1/4 cup toasted slivered almonds

1. Pack the ice cream into a chilled cookie shell, making sure the surface is smooth.

2. Cover with the hot fudge sauce, and freeze until firm.

3. Top with Fresh Whipped Cream, sprinkle with almonds, and serve.

BANANA CREAM PIE

If this pie is to be meringued, put it in a baked pie shell. If it's to be topped with whipped cream, put it into a graham cracker crust.

FOR ONE 10-INCH PIE

1 batch Basic Vanilla Pudding (page 150)

1 baked single crust (page 120) or 1 Graham Cracker Crust (page 121)

3 large (or 4 small) bananas, sliced (see Note)
Meringue (page 122) or Fresh Whipped Cream (page 192)

1. If using the meringue topping, preheat the oven to 400° F. Prepare the vanilla pudding, cool to lukewarm, and spread a layer over the pie crust.

2. Add a layer of sliced bananas, then another layer of the filling, making sure you cover each banana completely, or the bananas will turn dark. (Be sure there's enough filling to completely cover the top.)

3. If this is for a baked single crust, top with Meringue, and place in the oven 15 to 20 minutes, until the peaks are golden brown. If this is for a Graham Cracker Crust, refrigerate before topping with Fresh Whipped Cream.

NOTE: Don't overdo the bananas or they'll fall out and turn dark when the pie's cut.

GRAHAM CRACKER CREAM PIE: Follow the same recipe, using a Graham Cracker Crust, but do not add the bananas in step 2. Top as for the Graham Cracker Crust in step 3.

COCONUT CREAM PIE: Follow the Banana Cream Pie recipe, using a baked single crust, but do not add the bananas in step 2. Instead, while the pudding is still on the stove, after it has thickened, add 1 cup of flaked coconut, and cook for a minute or so (so the oil gets cooked in). Cool slightly, pour into the crust, and top with Meringue. Sprinkle the Meringue with flaked coconut before baking as directed.

GRASSHOPPER PIE

FOR ONE 10-INCH PIE

1 (16-ounce) package of miniature marshmallows

1/3 cup milk

1/4 cup crème de cacao

1/3 cup crème de menthe

2 cups whipped cream

1 Crushed Oreo Cookie Crust (page 121; see Note)

1/4 cup pecan halves

1. Heat the marshmallows and the milk together in a heavy medium saucepan over hot water until the marshmallows are melted.

2. Remove from heat, and add the crème de cacao and crème de menthe to the mixture while hot.

3. Cool completely, and fold in the whipped cream.

4. Put into the crust (see Note), and decorate with pecan halves around the edges.

NOTE: If you want a pie that's less rich, use Graham Cracker Crust (page 121).

PECAN PIE

To me this is the easiest pie to make, but I've tried to teach people, and they've had a heck of a time. It's either too hard or too syrupy on top, or it's boiling over in the oven. I never dreamed anyone could have so much trouble with a pie that's so quick to stir up. But it's as much in the mixing as in the ingredients. Here's a few hints that I hope will enable you to breeze right through: When you're dumping in the syrup, don't absolutely drain the cups, use a scant measure; make sure the melted butter is warm so it beats up (butter is more oily nowadays, that makes a difference); be careful on the beating, don't overbeat (or the pie will run in the oven) or underbeat (or syrup will form on top). Stop when it's just on the verge of turning a light color, when it starts to take on a creamy look. You have to use sound judgment, because if it gets thick like sea foam it's too late, it's ruined, it'll all be in the oven. Beware of these things, have confidence, and it'll turn out.

FOR ONE 10-INCH PIE

5 eggs

1 cup sugar

1 1/2 scant cups dark Karo syrup

3/4 cup warm melted butter

1 unbaked single crust (page 120)

1 1/2 cups pecans, chopped (enough to cover the top completely)

1. Preheat the oven to 325° F. Using an electric mixer on high speed, beat together all the ingredients except the pecans. Beat until thick and the mixture just begins to get a light color.

2. Pour into the unbaked pie shell.

3. Sprinkle the chopped pecans on top, and bake for about 45 minutes, until set and not wiggly.

BUTTERSCOTCH PIE

FOR ONE 10-INCH PIE

2 cups packed brown sugar

3 tablespoons flour

3 tablespoons cornstarch

3 egg yolks

3 cups milk

3/8 cup (3/4 stick) butter

1 capful maple flavoring

1 baked single crust (page 120)

Meringue (page 122) or Fresh Whipped Cream (page 192) for topping (see Note)

1. Using your fingers, mix the sugar, flour, and cornstarch in a heavy saucepan. Work these dry ingredients well together, then add the egg yolks and milk, and mix, using a whisk.

2. Add the butter and cook on medium heat until thick and glossy. (Cook well, stirring all the while with a "licker.")

3. Remove from the stove, add the maple flavoring, and stir.

4. Cool, and pour into a baked pie crust. Top with Meringue (and bake for 15 to 20 minutes, until golden brown) or whipped cream.

NOTE: If you use whipped cream, sprinkle ground nuts around the edge to make it fancy.

Tortes,
Pan
Desserts,

and Puddings

In these parts, *torte* means a rich, four-layered pan dessert. It looks a little fancy and is oh, so good, with its thick bottom crust, two layers of creamy fillings, and a billowy topping of whipped cream.

NUT CRUST FOR
TORTES

FOR A 9 × 13-INCH CAKE PAN

2 cups flour

1/2 cup (1 stick) butter

2 handfuls chopped walnuts

1. Preheat the oven to 375° F. Dump the ingredients into a bowl, and using your fingers, mix until crumbly.

2. Press into the bottom of the cake pan, and bake about 20 minutes, until lightly brown and the crust has little crooked cracks running through like a creek.

CREAM CHEESE
FILLING FOR
NUT CRUST TORTES

FOR A 9 × 13-INCH CAKE PAN

8 ounces cream cheese

1 1/2 cups powdered sugar

2 cups Fresh Whipped Cream (page 192)

1 Baked Nut Crust for Tortes (at left)

1. Combine the ingredients together in a large mixing bowl, and beat on high speed until well blended and smooth.

2. Spread onto the *cold* baked crust.

CHOCOLATE TORTE: Prepare a nut crust (see Note) and the cream cheese filling (above). Spread 1 batch of Basic Chocolate Pudding (page 150) on top of the cream cheese filling, and top with Fresh Whipped Cream (page 192) and a few sprinkles of grated chocolate bar or chocolate chips.

PEANUT BUTTER–CHOCOLATE TORTE: Do the same as for the Chocolate Torte (see Note), but beat 1/2 cup of peanut butter into the cream cheese filling before spreading it onto the nut crust. Add the chocolate pudding and the whipped cream as above, but instead of grated chocolate, sprinkle chopped salted peanuts on top of the whipped cream.

VARIATION: If you try the Peanut Butter–Chocolate Torte a few times and decide you want it even richer, here's a delicious variation; but be warned—it's expensive and quite thick. Follow the recipe to prepare the Peanut Butter–Chocolate Torte (above), but instead of spreading it onto the nut crust, spread it over the Graham Cracker Crust (page 121) that is already prepared with the cream cheese filling (at right). It's more work and money, but it's hard to beat.

COCONUT CREAM TORTE: Prepare a nut crust (see Note) and the cream cheese filling (page 138), and spread with the Coconut Cream Pie filling (page 136). Top with whipped cream, and sprinkle with toasted, flaked coconut. To toast the flakes, put a handful in a pie tin, place it in the oven under the broiler, watch like a chicken hawk for just a couple of minutes, stir, and watch again until light brown; it will take about 5 minutes all together.

LEMON TORTE: Prepare a nut crust (see Note) and the cream cheese filling (page 138), spread a batch of Miss Little's Lemon Pudding (page 152) on top, and top with Fresh Whipped Cream (page 192). This is very refreshing in the summertime.

PINEAPPLE TORTE: Prepare a nut crust (see Note) and the cream cheese filling (page 138). Follow the recipe for Basic Vanilla Pudding (page 150), and as the pudding is cooking, add 1 cup of drained crushed unsweetened pineapple. Heat thoroughly, and cool until cold. Pour onto the cream cheese filling, and top with Fresh Whipped Cream (page 192).

NOTE: All of these tortes go onto the nut crust, not the Graham Cracker Crust, because with the cracker crust, they'd be much too rich.

CREAM CHEESE FILLING FOR GRAHAM CRACKER CRUST TORTE

FOR A 9 × 13-INCH CAKE PAN

8 ounces cream cheese

1 cup sugar

2 eggs

1 teaspoon vanilla extract

1 Graham Cracker Crust (page 121) pressed into a 9 × 13-inch cake pan

1. Preheat the oven to 350° F. Combine all ingredients in a large mixing bowl, and beat on high speed until well blended and smooth.

2. Pour over the Graham Cracker Crust, and bake 25 minutes, until lightly browned.

3. Top with whatever torte filling you desire.

PUMPKIN TORTE

Today most people think of pumpkins as glowing jack-o'-lanterns, but in past days on the farm, they had many uses. We didn't always have the nice pie pumpkins that folks now grow in their gardens; we had field pumpkins. They were planted between the corn rows, and when fall spread a killing white frost and the corn froze, there they would be, round and huge.

They weren't a favorite, though, with women because they were tough; we had to split 'em with an ax. Inside, they were coarse and stringy and not as bright an orange as pie pumpkin, but that's what we had, so that's what we used. We canned, and we baked our breads and pies and tortes, and gave the rinds to the chickens and pigs for food. In winter, there was another use. We'd chop a pumpkin in half and hang it up with twine in the hen house so the chickens could jump and peck to keep warm in the nasty cold.

FOR A 9 × 13-INCH CAKE PAN

> 2 cups pumpkin puree
>
> 1½ cups sugar
>
> 3 eggs, separated
>
> 2 teaspoons ground cinnamon
>
> 1 teaspoon salt
>
> ½ cup cream
>
> 1 package Knox gelatin
>
> ¼ cup cold water
>
> 1 prepared and baked recipe Cream Cheese Filling for Graham Cracker Crust Torte (page 139)
>
> 2 cups Fresh Whipped Cream (page 192)

1. Combine the pumpkin, 1 cup of the sugar, the egg yolks, cinnamon, salt, and cream in a heavy saucepan, and cook on medium heat until thick (about 15 minutes). Remove from heat.

2. Dissolve the gelatin in the cold water, and add to the hot mixture. Mix well, and set aside to cool.

3. Beat the egg whites until stiff, add ½ cup of the sugar, and continue beating. Fold well into the pumpkin mixture, and pour onto the prepared crust and filling.

4. Cool until set, and top with Fresh Whipped Cream.

LEMON TORN ANGEL FOOD

FOR AN ANGEL FOOD TIN OR A 9 × 13-INCH CAKE PAN

> 2 egg yolks
>
> 1 cup water
>
> Juice of 1 lemon
>
> A few drops of yellow food coloring
>
> 2 tablespoons cornstarch
>
> 1 cup sugar
>
> 3 tablespoons flour
>
> 1 lemon rind, grated
>
> 1 baked Bride's White Angel Food Cake (page 169) torn into about 1½-inch pieces
>
> 2 cups Fresh Whipped Cream (page 192) plus whipped cream for garnish

1. In a bowl, beat the egg yolks, water, and lemon juice together. If not feared, add the food coloring, or the cake will be pale looking. Set aside.

2. In a saucepan, using your fingers, mix the cornstarch, sugar, flour, and grated rind.

3. With a whisk, mix in the egg mixture and cook over medium heat until thick and clear, stirring constantly with a licker. Remove from heat and cool to lukewarm.

4. Fold in the whipped cream.

5. Cover the bottom of a cake pan with torn angel food and pour ½ of the filling over the pieces.

6. Add another layer of torn angel food, pour the remaining filling over, and refrigerate.

7. When ready to serve, cut into squares and garnish with a dab of whipped cream.

RING'S BLUEBERRY TORTE

A lot of farmers will tell you farming doesn't allow for getting attached to animals, but ask any country veterinarian. Whenever they drive onto a farm and want to find the people, they look for the dog. The dog I'll never forget when I was growing up was Ring—all black with a white collar. Around milking time, "Ring," we'd say, "go get the cows," and off he'd go. We'd climb the hill and watch down through the valley, and it wasn't long before one lazy cow came walking after another, with Ring behind wagging his tail. It was sad the day he died, because for each of us kids he'd been the loyal baby-sitter. From the day we were born,

wherever she laid us, my mother said—the front-room cot, the kitchen table, a blanket on the blueberry bluff—wherever she put us, there Ring would be standing guard till we could walk. To this day, whenever I have anything with blueberries, I think of my mother's stories of Ring and that bluff.

FOR A 9 × 13-INCH CAKE PAN

> *6 tablespoons cornstarch*
>
> *2 cups sugar*
>
> *4 cups fresh blueberries*
>
> *4 tablespoons (½ stick) butter*
>
> *1 tablespoon rum*
>
> *1 prepared and baked recipe Cream Cheese Filling for Graham Cracker Crust Torte (page 139)*
>
> *2 cups Fresh Whipped Cream (page 192)*
>
> *Chopped nuts for garnish (or not)*

1. In a heavy large saucepan, combine the cornstarch and sugar, and mix using your fingers.

2. Add the blueberries and cook on medium heat until thick. Stir enough so it doesn't scorch.

3. Add the butter and the rum, and stir until the butter melts. Remove from heat, and cool.

4. Pour over the prepared crust, and top with the whipped cream. Garnish with chopped nuts if desired.

CHERRY TORTE

FOR A 9 × 13-INCH CAKE PAN

6 tablespoons cornstarch

2 cups sugar

4 cups pitted cherries

4 tablespoons (1/2 stick) butter

1 tablespoon rum

1 prepared and baked recipe Cream Cheese Filling for Graham Cracker Crust Torte (page 139)

2 cups Fresh Whipped Cream (page 192)

1. In a heavy large saucepan, combine the cornstarch and sugar, and mix using your fingers.

2. Add the cherries and cook on medium-low heat until thick. Stir gently using a licker or a wooden spoon so you don't crush the cherries.

3. Add the butter and rum, and stir until the butter melts. Remove from heat, and cool.

4. Pour over the prepared crust and filling, and top with Fresh Whipped Cream.

NOTE: Don't boil this heavily or the cherries'll go to mush.

RASPBERRY TORTE

FOR A 9 × 13-INCH CAKE PAN

1 (6-ounce) box raspberry gelatin

1 1/4 cups boiling water

1 1/2 quarts fresh raspberries or 1 1/2 pounds frozen berries

1 prepared and baked recipe Cream Cheese Filling for Graham Cracker Crust Torte (page 139)

TOPPING

25 large marshmallows

1/2 cup milk

1/2 pint whipping cream

1. Dissolve the gelatin in the boiling water.

2. Add the berries to the gelatin (thaw the berries slightly if frozen).

3. When halfway set, pour the gelatin on top of the baked cream cheese filling, and spread with the topping.

4. *To prepare the topping:* In a double boiler, melt the marshmallows with the milk. Cool. Beat the whipping cream until stiff and fold into the marshmallow mixture.

5. Refrigerate until ready to serve.

STRAWBERRY TORN ANGEL FOOD

"What life is this? Who stuck me on this farm with no telephone?" There's a farm woman poem that starts off something like that, and maybe the women didn't always say it, but they thought it. Who wouldn't, month after month of cruel weather and the nearest neighbor so far down the road? In those days, what we called Ladies' Aid at the church was something to look forward to. Husbands could refuse to let their wives go to a quilting bee, a baby shower, or even a wedding, but miss Ladies' Aid? No. Women made the most of it, and still do in many farm communities. We put on our best dress, prepare a pretty dish, and off we go. Usually someone reads from the Bible, another sings a solo, and there might be a skit or two, but the important thing to most is being together over a large lunch. This torn angel food was always one of my favorite desserts to tote along.

FOR AN ANGEL FOOD TIN OR A 9 × 13-INCH CAKE PAN

1 (6-ounce) package strawberry gelatin

1 1/2 cups boiling water

1 quart fresh strawberries or 1 pound sliced frozen strawberries (thawed)

1 tablespoon sugar

Pinch of salt

1/2 pint whipping cream

1 baked Bride's White Angel Food Cake (page 169) torn into about 1 1/2-inch pieces (see Note)

1. Dissolve the gelatin in the boiling water, and stir in the strawberries, sugar, and salt. Cool at room temperature until it starts to gel.

2. Beat the whipping cream until stiff, and fold it into the berry mixture.

3. Cover the bottom of the tin with the torn angel food.

4. Pour one-half of the gelatin mixture over the pieces, add another layer of torn angel food pieces, and pour the remaining filling over.

5. Refrigerate, and when ready to serve, remove from the refrigerator, take it from the tin, cut into 12 slices, and garnish each slice with a dab of whipped cream and part of a whole strawberry.

NOTE: Tear the angel food and put it back into the angel food tin or into the cake pan, then follow the recipe.

SCRUMPTIOUS CHOCOLATE NUT DELIGHT

FOR A 9 × 13-INCH CAKE PAN

1 (12-ounce) box vanilla wafers

1 cup powdered sugar

1/2 cup (1 stick) butter

3 eggs, separated

2 squares unsweetened chocolate, melted

1 teaspoon vanilla extract

1/4 cup chopped walnuts and a few more for garnish

1/2 pint whipping cream

1. Crush the vanilla wafers until coarser than sand and finer than gravel, and place in a 9 × 13-inch cake pan.

2. In a bowl, beat the powdered sugar and the butter together until creamy.

3. Separate the eggs. Add the egg yolks one at a time to the sugar mixture, beating after each. Add the melted chocolate and the vanilla, mix, and add the nuts.

4. Beat the egg whites until stiff and fold them into the mixture, being patient because it's hard to do.

5. Carefully spread the mixture over the crushed vanilla wafers. (This takes care because they're not set.)

6. Whip the cream until stiff (don't sweeten) and spread over all. Garnish with chopped nuts or crushed vanilla wafers.

FARM SHORTCAKE DUMPLINGS

At home we had a raspberry patch behind the barn. In the evening, when it was a little cooler, we'd go out and pick, and we'd get big dishpans full of raspberries. There were so many that after we froze 'em or canned 'em, or made sauce, we'd wonder what to do with 'em. I thought they were too seedy for pie, so those hot nights, I'd fuss around on the porch until late, after the house cooled; then I'd fire up the wood stove and experiment with this recipe. It soon became a favorite. They aren't really dumplings, but for some reason that's what we called 'em, so that's what they remain.

FOR A 9 × 13-INCH CAKE PAN

2 1/2 cups flour

2 tablespoons sugar

3 teaspoons baking powder

1 teaspoon salt

1/2 cup (1 stick) butter

1 egg

3/4 cup milk

Your choice of filling (pages 145 and 146)

1. Preheat the oven to 375° F. Using your fingers, mix the flour, sugar, baking powder, salt, and butter together in a large bowl and work as you would a pie crust, until crumbly.

2. Crack the egg into the milk, mix together, and pour into the flour mixture. Stir with a fork until thoroughly moistened.

3. Knead the dough on a floured board or table, and form it into a rectangle.

4. Using a floured rolling pin, roll the dough out on a floured board or table until about ½ inch thick.

5. Prepare your choice of filling.

6. Spoon the filling over the rolled-out dough, saving some to set aside.

7. Roll the dough up like a jelly roll and pinch the ends to seal in the fruit. Cut into 1-inch slices.

8. Pour the remaining fruit filling into the bottom of a cake pan, and take the 1-inch slices and set them in it.

9. Bake about 25 to 30 minutes, until a toothpick comes out dry.

10. With a pancake turner, put the dumplings into dessert dishes and spoon some of the warmed filling from the bottom of the pan over the dumplings. Serve.

BLACKBERRY FILLING

ENOUGH TO FILL 1 BATCH OF FARM DUMPLINGS (10 TO 12 DUMPLINGS)

1 quart fresh blackberries

2 cups sugar

½ cup water

4 tablespoons cornstarch

4 tablespoons butter

1. In a heavy saucepan, boil the berries, sugar, and water together for a few minutes.

2. Dissolve the cornstarch in a little cold water, and add to the boiled berries. Cook until thick (about 3 to 5 minutes).

3. Add the butter and swirl until melted, then set aside to cool.

4. Use for filling the shortcake (page 144).

RASPBERRY FILLING: Use 1 quart of fresh raspberries instead of blackberries.

STRAWBERRY FILLING: Use 1 quart of fresh strawberries instead of blackberries.

APPLE FILLING

**ENOUGH TO FILL 1 BATCH
OF FARM DUMPLINGS
(10 TO 12 DUMPLINGS)**

5 large apples, peeled and sliced (see Note)

1 cup water

1 cup sugar

3 tablespoons cornstarch

2 tablespoons butter

1 teaspoon hot cinnamon candies or 2 teaspoons cinnamon with a couple drops red food coloring (if not feared)

1. In a heavy large saucepan, combine the sliced apples, water, and sugar, and bring to a boil over medium heat.

2. Dissolve the cornstarch in a little cold water, and stir it into the apples using a wire whisk. Boil about 3 to 5 minutes, until thick and clear.

3. Add the butter, and the hot candies or cinnamon, and swirl until the butter melts.

4. Use for filling the shortcake (page 144).

NOTE: Our Cortland or McIntosh apples are best for this, but do not overboil.

STRAWBERRY-RHUBARB FILLING

**ENOUGH TO FILL 1 BATCH
OF FARM DUMPLINGS
(10 TO 12 DUMPLINGS)**

1/2 cup (1 stick) butter

2 cups fresh sliced strawberries

3 cups fresh sliced rhubarb

2 cups sugar

1/2 cup (1 stick) butter

5 tablespoons cornstarch

1. Melt the butter in the bottom of a heavy large saucepan.

2. Add the strawberries, rhubarb, and sugar and cook about 10 minutes over medium heat, until soft.

3. Dissolve the cornstarch in a little cold water, stir it into the fruit, and cook until thickened. Cool.

4. Use for filling the shortcake (page 144).

JOHN LESTER'S BREAD PUDDING

FOR A 2-QUART BAKING DISH

5 cups dry Company Bread (page 4)

1 cup raisins (or not)

5 eggs

3/4 cup sugar

4 cups milk

1 teaspoon vanilla extract

1/2 teaspoon salt

Dash of ground nutmeg

Fresh cream or half-and-half to pour over

1. Preheat the oven to 350° F. Butter a 2-quart baking dish. Break the bread up into pieces (not cubes), and add the raisins if desired; put into the baking dish.

2. In a separate bowl, beat the eggs slightly; stir in the sugar, milk, vanilla, salt, and nutmeg. Mix well, and pour over the bread in the baking dish. (Using a licker, poke down into the bread pieces to make sure they're saturated.)

3. Bake for 45 to 50 minutes, until a knife stuck in comes out clean. Serve warm, covered with fresh cream or half-and-half.

EMMA'S FLOATING CLOUD PUDDING

It's strange the places small kids can find heaven. When I was little, I'd wait for the chance to go visit my godmother, Emma Anderson, and part of the thrill was this simple little dessert she'd fix for dinner.

SERVES 3

2 egg whites

2 tablespoons sugar

1 teaspoon vanilla extract

3/4 cup milk

1. In a small bowl, beat the egg whites until stiff.

2. Add the sugar and continue beating. Slowly add the vanilla while beating.

3. Take 3 custard cups, put 1/4 cup of milk in the bottom of each, and spoon the pudding onto the top. Serve. (Top with fresh fruit, if desired.)

STEAMED CRANBERRY PUDDING

Years ago we got coffee in low, wide, 1-pound cans with metal covers. Mid-December, whenever the wind howled and the blizzard snows blew in with those who'd fought their way back from the barn, I'd take out one of those coffee cans and make this cranberry pudding. I'd set a big kettle of water on the back of the wood stove, close the lid tight on the coffee can, and let the pudding steam there for three hours. It became part of the magic of those snowbound days and such a treat that my son, Dennis, still asks for it when he comes home at Christmas.

SERVES 10 (VERY RICH); FOR A 1-POUND COFFEE CAN (SEE NOTE)

> 2 tablespoons sugar
> 1/2 cup molasses
> 1 teaspoon baking soda in 1/2 cup hot water
> 1/2 teaspoon salt
> 1 cup cranberries, cut in half
> 1 1/2 cups flour
> Warm Butter Sauce (at right)

1. Using a wooden spoon, combine the sugar and molasses in a medium bowl. Mix the soda in hot water, and pour it into the sugar mixture.

2. Add the salt and the cranberries, and stir well. Add the flour, and mix.

3. Butter a 1-pound coffee can. Pour the dough in, and put the cover on. Place in a deep kettle of hot water. Put the lid on the kettle, and steam for 3 hours, keeping the water in the kettle simmering. (Watch so this doesn't simmer dry. Add water to the kettle if necessary, but be careful no water gets into the pudding can.)

4. Top with Warm Butter Sauce.

NOTE: If you can't get a low, 1-pound coffee can, and don't have a tall kettle, use a double boiler instead of the coffee can.

WARM BUTTER SAUCE

MAKES 2 CUPS

> 1/2 cup butter
> 1/2 cup cream
> 1 cup sugar
> 1 teaspoon vanilla extract

1. In a heavy saucepan, combine the butter, cream, and sugar.

2. Boil on medium heat until clear. Stir in the vanilla, and serve hot over hot cranberry pudding.

LARGE PEARL TAPIOCA PUDDING WITH COCONUT MERINGUE

FOR 1 BREAD LOAF PAN

1 cup large pearl tapioca (see Note)

1/2 cup water

2 1/2 cups milk

Dash of salt

3 eggs, separated

1 cup sugar

1 teaspoon vanilla extract

1/2 cup cold milk

3 tablespoons sugar

1 cup coconut

Fresh cream (or not)

1. Soak the tapioca in the water for 1/2 hour (longer—1 to 2 hours—if you don't get sick of waiting for it).

2. In a double boiler, combine 2 1/2 cups milk, the salt, and pearl tapioca, and cook on medium heat about 1/2 hour, until the tapioca is almost clear.

3. In a separate bowl, mix the egg yolks, 1 cup of sugar, and the vanilla together with 1/2 cup of cold milk.

4. When the tapioca is clear, pour the egg mixture into the tapioca and bring to a boil. Cook for 10 minutes, stirring constantly until thick. Remove from heat, and cool.

5. Preheat the oven to 350° F. In another bowl, beat the egg whites until stiff. Add 3 tablespoons sugar, and continue beating until mixed.

6. Take the tapioca mixture and pour it into the loaf pan, spread the beaten egg whites on top, and sprinkle with the coconut.

7. Put into the oven, and bake 20 to 25 minutes, until brown. Dish up, and serve right out of the oven with fresh cream, half-and-half, or milk. Or serve cold. This is a good keeper.

NOTE: Be sure that you are not using minute tapioca.

BASIC VANILLA PUDDING

SERVES 6 TO 8, OR USE FOR A 10-INCH PIE

1½ cups sugar

¼ cup flour

3 tablespoons cornstarch

3 egg yolks

3 cups milk

1 tablespoon butter

1 teaspoon vanilla extract

Fresh cream or whipped cream and nut-meats for garnish (if for pudding)

1. In a heavy saucepan, combine the sugar, flour, and cornstarch, and mix together a little using a whisk.

2. Add the egg yolks, but do not mix yet. Gradually add the milk, and stir all together thoroughly with a whipper.

3. Place over medium heat, and cook until thick and smooth, stirring constantly with a licker.

4. Remove from heat, and add the butter and vanilla. Stir well.

5. Put into bowls. Serve warm with fresh cream, or cool and top with whipped cream and nutmeats. (If for pie, follow the directions in the recipe.)

BASIC CHOCOLATE PUDDING

Unless it's for something special—confirmation or graduation—we don't pay much attention to what dish we use for what on the farm. We usually grab the biggest dish and fill it, because everybody's hungry. So if you're in town and serving these puddings, they'll probably go a lot farther than they do when feeding someone who's spent hours trying to deliver a calf or hustle a bull away from the cows and into the barn.

SERVES 6 TO 8, OR USE FOR A 10-INCH PIE

3 cups milk

2 squares bittersweet chocolate

1 cup sugar

3 tablespoons flour

3 tablespoons cornstarch

Dash of salt

1 teaspoon vanilla extract

Fresh cream or whipped cream and ground nuts or chocolate shavings for garnish (if for pudding)

1. Pour the milk into a heavy large saucepan, add the chocolate, and heat until the chocolate melts.

2. In a small bowl, combine the sugar, flour, cornstarch, and salt, and mix, using your fingers.

3. Gradually add this to the hot milk mixture, and stir constantly using a whisk. Cook on medium heat about 5 minutes, until thick and smooth.

4. Mix in the vanilla, stir, and remove from heat.

5. Put into bowls. Serve warm with fresh cream, or cool and top with whipped cream and nuts or chocolate shavings. (If for pie, follow the directions in the recipe.)

ORANGE CREAM PUDDING

SERVES 6 TO 8

2 cups milk

1¼ cups sugar

¼ cup cornstarch

Pinch of salt

1 egg, slightly beaten

½ teaspoon vanilla

3 or 4 oranges

Fresh cream or whipped cream

1. In a heavy saucepan over medium heat, scald the milk (do not scorch).

2. In a small bowl, combine ¾ cup of the sugar, the cornstarch, and salt with ¼ cup of the milk and the egg. Stir together and add to the remaining scalded milk. Cook until thick, stir in the vanilla, and cool.

3. Peel the oranges and cut in chunks into a nice glass bowl.

4. Sprinkle on the remaining ½ cup sugar and allow to stand.

5. Pour the cooled pudding over the oranges. Serve with fresh cream.

MISS LITTLE'S LEMON PUDDING

✳

My mother's eighty-nine, and she still talks about the hard time she and my dad had trying to get me to start school. As tough as times were, they promised me a new dress, candy, new shoes, and still I wouldn't go. Then one day the superintendent came out. Mom had just made lemon pudding, and we were outside sweeping the porch and here comes Miss Little in her coupe. There was a steep bank along the driveway by the field, and she was driving kind of fast around the corner when—*zoom*—that coupe flew right down the bank, rolled over, and landed right side up in our yard. But that didn't stop Miss Little; she got out, brushed herself off, and walked calmly to the house. "Weren't you scared?" my mom said, even before "hello." "Nah," Miss Little said. "You better try to get Helen to go to school." Good sense told me to run and hide, because I was afraid she'd take me away, but I just stood there and marveled. She didn't stay for coffee or the lemon pudding like any other visitor would have. She just got in her coupe and took off real fast down the road. Two days later, I started school, and ever since that morning, I don't think I've ever made lemon pudding without thinking of Miss Little and her coupe.

SERVES 6 TO 8

2 egg yolks

3 cups water

Juice of 1 lemon (save and grate the rind)

2 tablespoons cornstarch

1 cup sugar

3 tablespoons flour

1. In a medium bowl, beat the egg yolks, water, and lemon juice, and set aside.

2. In a heavy medium saucepan, using your hands, mix the cornstarch, sugar, flour, and grated rind.

3. Using a wire whisk, mix the egg mixture into the pan, and cook about 5 minutes over medium heat, until it is thick and clear (see Note).

4. Cool, and serve in individual dishes.

NOTE: If you don't have a nice yellow color, add a drop or two of yellow food coloring (if not feared). It looks a little sick if you don't.

RHUBARB PUDDING

SERVES 6 TO 8

2 cups rhubarb, cut into ¾-inch pieces
1½ cups sugar
Dash of salt

THICKENING

½ cup sugar
⅓ cup flour
2 eggs
¼ cup cream
Fresh cream to cover when serving (or not)

1. In a heavy saucepan over medium heat, cook the rhubarb, sugar, and salt.

2. *To make the thickening:* In a small bowl, and using your fingers, mix the sugar and flour. Stir in the eggs and cream, using a whisk.

3. When the rhubarb in the saucepan is soft, add the thickening; cook over medium heat, stirring constantly until thick.

4. Pour into dessert dishes or bowls. Cool or serve hot with fresh cream, if desired.

RICE PUDDING

SERVES 6 TO 8

1 cup rice
2 cups water
1 cup raisins (or not)
2 eggs
1 cup sugar
1 teaspoon vanilla
Dash of salt
Fresh cream or half-and-half

1. In a heavy saucepan over medium heat, cook the rice and water until the rice is tender. (If it gets dry and is not done, add a small amount of water and cook longer.) If using raisins, add now.

2. Meanwhile, beat the eggs in a small bowl. Add the sugar, vanilla, and salt, and mix well. Pour this mixture into the rice in the saucepan. Cook, stirring occasionally, until thick and cooked through.

3. Remove from heat and pour into dessert dishes. Top with fresh cream.

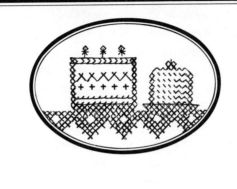

CAKES, BARS,
and
FROSTINGS

Talk about lowly beginnings: The cakes I baked when I was first a hired girl went to the dogs—night after night after night.

It wasn't as bad as that sounds, though. It was all part of the deal when I worked at the minister's. They had purebred Chesapeakes. No dog I knew had ever gotten anything to eat but unstrained milk and table scraps, so you can imagine how dumb I thought it was when every night I had to mix up a mush, put it in a cake pan, bake it, crumble it, cover it with milk, and hike it on out to those dogs. "Everyone starts somewhere," my mother would say, and she was right; eventually I baked for the minister and his guests, but I still had to feed those Chesapeakes.

As it turned out, it was good practice because cakes were all-important in a farm woman's life. They still are, but in those days it was "You are what you bake," and cakes were at the heart of what you served your hired hands and neighbors.

Even though we helped in the fields and had endless chores in the house, there always had to be a cake. Cake for morning coffee, afternoon coffee, evening coffee—everyday cakes and special cakes—cakes for weddings, showers, birthdays, funerals, barn dances, Ladies' Aid, Community Club, basket socials, and school programs. We were so used to stirring up cake that even though we had to stand and beat them by hand, it took less time than opening up a cake mix box today and reading what goes in it.

In summer, we'd sit outside in the evening, and when we'd see a car coming down the road, it was a big thrill—"We're getting company! Hurry up and make a cake!" We'd practically fall over each other trying to get inside to get that cake started. We had no fancy recipes or measuring; we'd throw it all in a bowl and have it almost in the oven before whoever it was got to the door. We made what we called "everyday cake," either yellow, molasses, or cocoa—plain, down-to-earth cake. And most often, in that kind of a hurry, we wouldn't bother with frosting. Instead, one of us would sneak to the barn and skim a couple cups of thick, fresh cream from the raw milk in the milk cans. We'd run with it back to the house, whip it, and top the cake, warm, right out of the oven. Even if we had a cake on hand, we'd do this so there'd be something fresh for the neighbors. It made everyone feel good.

In telling you these things, I hope to encourage you to stay away from cake mix no matter what your hurry. These days you can fool a lot of people with all the well-researched, time-tested imitations, but you'll never really fool anyone who knows cake.

The recipes here, for the most part, are not time-consuming. If you relax, your kitchen will fill with the sweet smell of days gone by, and the making of the cakes will provide you with one of life's simple pleasures. Don't be too fussy, but don't tear through these recipes, either. Remember, the real satisfaction is in the doing; it's private, so don't depend on everyone always to appreciate or compliment your efforts. Through the years, I've gotten more than my share of praise for my cakes—my children have gobbled them up, jokers have proposed, tourists and magazines have asked for recipes, but I've never once seen a gleam as bright as that in the eyes of those dogs, way back when, at the minister's.

Hints for Cakes

and Bars

• Use the highest-quality and freshest ingredients you can get. Cakes rely heavily on eggs and dairy products, so here we have very little trouble with quality or freshness. But if you're in the city, choose your butter, cream, and eggs carefully. Especially watch out for what we call cold-storage eggs. That's eggs that have been in the cooler too long. They become watery, and don't hold their shape in the pan, and of course their flavor is not as fresh.

• Do not substitute with milk when a recipe calls for cream; likewise, don't substitute with 2 percent milk when a recipe calls for whole. As I said in the pie section, store-bought, whole milk already doesn't have the rich butterfat that farm-fresh milk has, so don't tamper further with it—use what the recipe calls for.

• If a recipe calls for cake flour, use cake flour, not all-purpose, presifted flour. Cake flour is a finer ground and a heavier packed flour. Also, there's a difference between commercial and regular flour. Commercial flour is not as heavily bleached, so it's fluffier than what you get in the store. If you're accustomed to commercial flour and want to use it in these recipes, use generous measures.

• Home-rendered lard is what we used to use for shortening, and in a few of these recipes I feel it's still necessary. But for heaven's sakes, don't go to a grocery store and buy lard; it's awful. Get real home-rendered lard at a good meat market if you're not going to make your own (page 257). If there's no way around it, substitute butter using the same measurement.

• If you plan ahead, try to have all your ingredients at room temperature.

• If a recipe calls for sour milk, and you have none on hand, what you can do is put 1 tablespoon of vinegar into 1 cup of milk. It will curdle immediately.

• There's a lot of talk about cakes falling. Some say if you aren't careful with the oven door or if you touch a cake in the middle or even look at it the wrong way, it'll fall. But as far as I'm concerned, there's only two reasons for such a flop. Either you took it out of the oven too early, or you beat it wrong—too much or not enough.

• The feel, consistency, and texture of batters will differ, depending on what cake you're making. But as a rule, your batter should be smooth and creamy like thick, freshly beaten cream. (Recipes that include fruit are of course thicker, brownies are thicker, and upside-down cake is heavier.) If the batter looks sugary, or some shortening shows, or maybe some egg shows, it's not beaten enough, and the cake as it bakes will fall. However, if you overbeat a cake, the ingredients will start to separate again, and the cake'll get coarse, and it also falls as it bakes. (If you're nervous and new at this, err the way of under- rather than overbeating.)

• If you don't have an electric mixer, these recipes can be done by hand, but you have to beat it like a fright (about 350 strokes) for the first beating of the sugar, butter, and egg, then fold in the rest of the ingredients.

• When using an electric mixer, shut it off a time or two while beating and scrape around the bowl a little bit with a licker. It's impossible for the beater to get completely around the edges and the bottom. Get it all beaten in good so the batter is smooth and alive.

• In the old days we used to stand and beat these cakes by hand; now we even have the convenience of the Cadillac of mixers, the KitchenAid. Even though I now most often use a KitchenAid, the speeds in my recipes are for a regular electric mixer. If you're using a KitchenAid (or any of the other top-grade universal mixers such as Bosch), decrease the speed called for.

• If you're short of time and have to hurry things up, as we often have to do in the country, you don't necessarily have to follow all the fancy steps. When time gets really limited, I take a lot of shortcuts. Like this business of dividing eggs and folding them in last, I believe that that's the best way, but it's not essential. It might make a better-textured cake to do it that way, but if you want to dump everything all in together, it's not going to hurt the flavor. A lot of times I've been in such a hurry I didn't even cream the sugar and shortening together; it turns out all right.

• Use common sense if you're substituting one size pan for another. If a recipe calls for an 8-inch round pan, and you insist on pouring it into a 9 × 13-inch tin, be prepared for a skinny, skinny cake. However, if you only have a 9 × 13-inch pan and you're using a recipe for a layer cake, just go ahead and use the 9 × 13-inch tin, bake it, then cut it in two as evenly as possible, plop one half down on the other (rounded tops or straight bottoms together in the middle), put a little filling in between, frost, and you have a layer cake.

• In these recipes, when it calls for a greased pan, it means grease only the bottom; not the sides. The cake needs something to hold onto to get a full rise—how would you like to climb up a greased pole? Also, there's a lot who say "grease and flour, grease and flour," but when you're in a hurry that gets to be an unnecessary mess. However, if you do have more time and patience than we can afford on the farm or in the restaurant and you want to be real fussy, or if you're doing a layer cake for a special occasion, grease the pan, cut wax paper to fit the bottom and sides, pour the batter in, then after the cake has baked and cooled for ten minutes, flip the pan upside down, tap out the cake, and peel the paper away.

• To prevent bubbles from getting in your cake, after you've poured the batter into the pan, take a kitchen knife and draw it back and forth to break up the air pockets. (If you don't do this, and the recipe contains baking powder or baking soda, you'll likely get a cake that looks a lot like the moon.)

• If you're worried about your nutmeats or raisins sinking to the bottom, flour them before adding them to the batter. However, I'm not that fussy, and mine stay afloat.

• It's better to put less time on the dinger (if you're a dinger setter) and to check the cake than to put more time on and wait until the dinger goes off. Check your cakes ahead of time. If a recipe says thirty-five to forty minutes and your oven is different than mine, the cake might be done sooner, and then you're going to have it overbaked. So you're better off setting less time and checking it than going overtime.

• Be sure your rack is in the center of the oven or the cake will come out either too brown on the bottom with a sick-looking top, or too brown on top with a pale bottom.

• If you're getting lopsided cakes, make sure your oven and the shelves are level.

• If you forget to preheat the oven, put the broiler on for a minute to get it up to temperature fast.

• If you're baking, and it consistently takes a longer time to bake a cake than what the recipes prescribe, up your oven the next time by ten degrees. If the baking time is too long, the cake'll get tough and dried out. Likewise if the edges are getting done and the center isn't, raise the oven ten degrees; too long in the oven is going to make the outside edges dry.

• It always takes about five minutes less time to bake just layers than it does whole cakes because of the smaller tins, and if you're particular, when you're baking two layer pans at once, after about fifteen minutes, open the oven and turn the pans a little in order to make sure that the center bakes the same as the outside edge does. (But don't be rough with 'em.) Lorraine, my assistant, always turns them, but if you don't want to monkey with that, do what I do, put 'em in the oven and leave 'em there until they're done.

• When testing for doneness, pull the oven rack out only partway, not all the way if you can help it, so the cake doesn't get too far from the heat. Either stick a toothpick in the center and see if it comes out clean, or touch the middle lightly with your fingertip. If the cake bounces back, it's done; if it leaves a dent, it's not.

• Let the cake sit at least ten minutes before taking it out of the tin. Then run a knife gently around the edges and turn the pan upside down over a pretty plate. (Upside-down cake and jelly roll, of course, have to be removed immediately.)

Cakes

LUCKY FRIDAY'S CARROT CAKE

Like I said, I'd never heard of Jane and Michael Stern when they first came by back then in 1976. I guess they each ate a piece of Sour Cream Raisin Pie in the restaurant, and took this carrot cake along with them because in that first book they wrote, "We ate the two pieces of carrot cake that night in our Minnesota motel room. They were unbelievably moist, spicy, redolent of finely shaved carrots. We dreamt about the Norske Nook that night and occasionally still do—waking up very, very hungry."

This is the same cake I made back then every Friday.

FOR A 9 × 13-INCH CAKE

3 cups grated carrots

2 cups sugar

4 eggs

1½ cups oil

2 teaspoons baking soda

1 teaspoon salt

2 heaping cups all-purpose flour

1 teaspoon ground cinnamon

1 teaspoon vanilla extract

1 generous cup chopped nutmeats

Cream Cheese Frosting (page 190)

1. Preheat the oven to 350° F. Put the carrots, sugar, eggs, and oil in a large mixing bowl, and beat it up. (This will splatter.)

2. Add the baking soda, salt, flour, cinnamon, vanilla, and nutmeats, and beat this well.

3. Pour into a buttered 9 × 13-inch pan, and bake for 50 minutes, until a finger doesn't make a dent. Cool, and frost with Cream Cheese Frosting.

BURNT SUGAR CAKE

FOR A 9 × 13-INCH CAKE

CARAMEL MIXTURE

½ cup sugar

⅓ cup hot water

CAKE

2 cups all-purpose flour

3 teaspoons baking powder

1 teaspoon salt

¾ cup sugar

½ cup (1 stick) butter

2 eggs, unbeaten

1 teaspoon vanilla extract

Sea Foam Frosting (page 192)

1. *To prepare Caramel Mixture:* In a heavy small saucepan, melt the sugar until it turns dark brown. Gradually add the hot water, and stir until it's dissolved. Cool.

2. *To prepare the cake:* Preheat the oven to 350° F. Combine the flour, baking powder, salt, and sugar in a large bowl.

3. Add the butter and 2 tablespoons of the Caramel Mixture, and beat using an electric mixer.

4. Add 1 more tablespoon of the Caramel Mixture, the eggs, and vanilla, and beat well.

5. Pour the batter into a buttered 9 × 13-inch pan, and bake for 30 minutes, until a toothpick comes out dry. Cool, and frost with Sea Foam Frosting.

MAPLE CHIFFON CAKE

FOR 1 ANGEL FOOD–SIZE CAKE

2¼ cups cake flour

¾ cup granulated sugar

3 teaspoons baking powder

½ teaspoon salt

1 cup brown sugar

½ cup Wesson vegetable oil or peanut oil

5 eggs, separated

¾ cup cold water

2 teaspoons maple flavoring

½ teaspoon cream of tartar

1 cup finely chopped pecans

1. Preheat the oven to 350°F. Mix together the flour, granulated sugar, baking powder, salt, and brown sugar. Make a hole or well in this mixture and add the oil, egg yolks, the cold water, and the maple flavoring. Using an electric mixer, beat until smooth.

2. In a large separate bowl, beat the egg whites and cream of tartar together until stiff. Pour the egg yolk mixture over the egg whites and gently fold together, adding pecans as you go.

3. Pour into an ungreased angel food tin and bake for about an hour, or until your finger doesn't leave a print (see Note).

NOTE: This cake needs no frosting, but if you think you'd like one, I'd recommend Basic Powdered Sugar Frosting (page 193) with a little maple flavoring added; I'd thin the frosting to a glaze consistency.

BROWN SUGAR SPICE CAKE

This cake isn't right unless it's made with side pork drippings. What you need to do is, if you're frying up some side pork (page 45) for supper or breakfast, save the grease. For some of you, this will seem like old hat, but if you're new at this, be careful while you're frying so you don't forget and season the pork with pepper or you'll have a peppery cake. Also, allow the drippings to cool and become a solid. (It's best if you let them set overnight.) If you're worried about cholesterol and are determined not to make a meal of the side pork, I still recommend going to a store or a good meat market and buying a half pound to fry just for the drippings; you won't be sorry when you taste the difference it makes in this cake.

FOR A 9 × 13-INCH CAKE

CAKE

1 cup shortening (side pork drippings are best)

2 cups packed brown sugar

2 egg yolks (save whites for topping)

1 teaspoon baking soda

1 teaspoon baking powder

1 teaspoon ground cinnamon

1/4 teaspoon ground cloves

2 1/2 cups all-purpose flour

1 cup buttermilk or sour milk (page 157)

NUT TOPPING

2 egg whites

1 cup packed brown sugar

1/2 cup chopped nuts

1. *To prepare the cake:* Preheat the oven to 350° F. Combine all the ingredients in a large mixing bowl, and mix well, about 2 minutes.

2. Butter the bottom of a 9 × 13-inch pan, and pour in the batter. Set aside.

3. *To prepare the topping:* Beat the egg whites and the brown sugar together until stiff. Spread it on the unbaked cake, and sprinkle the chopped nuts on top.

4. Bake about 45 minutes, until a toothpick comes out dry.

FEATHER NUTMEG CAKE

FOR A 9 × 13-INCH CAKE

½ cup butter

1½ cups sugar

3 eggs, beaten

2¼ cups flour

¼ teaspoon salt

1 teaspoon baking powder

1 teaspoon soda

2 teaspoons nutmeg

1 cup buttermilk

1 teaspoon vanilla

Broiled Coconut Frosting (page 187), or not

1. Preheat the oven to 350° F. Grease a 9 × 13-inch pan.

2. Cream the butter and sugar together. Add the eggs, and beat well.

3. Dump in the remaining ingredients (except frosting), and mix well using an electric beater.

4. Pour into the prepared pan and bake 25 minutes, or until a toothpick comes out clean. If desired, frost the cake while it is still warm.

HARVEST DREAM CAKE

FOR A 9 × 13-INCH CAKE

¾ cup shortening

1⅔ cups packed brown sugar

2½ cups flour

3½ teaspoons baking powder

1 teaspoon salt

1 tablespoon pumpkin pie spice (page 131)

¾ to 1 cup milk

3 eggs

1 teaspoon vanilla

Butter-Cream Frosting (page 186; see Note)

1. Preheat the oven to 350° F. Grease a 9 × 13-inch pan.

2. In a large bowl, stir together the shortening and brown sugar.

3. Add the flour, baking powder, salt, pumpkin pie spice, and milk; mix well using an electric beater.

4. Add the eggs and vanilla. Mix and pour into the prepared pan.

5. Bake for 35 to 40 minutes, until a toothpick comes out dry. Frost when cool.

NOTE: Add a little juice from an orange or a lemon to the frosting.

OATMEAL CAKE

FOR A 9 × 13-INCH CAKE

1 1/4 *cups boiling water*

1 *cup Quaker oats*

1/2 *cup (1 stick) butter*

1 *cup packed brown sugar*

1 *cup white sugar*

1 *teaspoon vanilla extract*

2 *eggs*

1 1/2 *cups all-purpose flour*

1 *teaspoon baking soda*

1/2 *teaspoon ground nutmeg*

1 *teaspoon ground cinnamon*

BROWN SUGAR– COCONUT TOPPING

3/4 *cup packed brown sugar*

1 *cup flaked coconut*

1 *cup chopped nutmeats*

1 *egg*

3 *tablespoons butter*

3 *tablespoons milk*

1. Preheat the oven to 350° F. Pour the boiling water over the oats, and let it stand for 10 minutes.

2. Cream (or beat with a mixer on slow speed) the butter, sugars, vanilla, and eggs together.

3. Add the soaked oats, the flour, baking soda, nutmeg, and cinnamon, and beat well.

4. Pour into a buttered 9 × 13-inch pan, and bake for 45 to 50 minutes, until your finger doesn't leave a dent.

5. *To prepare the topping:* Dump all the ingredients together in a bowl and, using your fingers, mix until crumbly.

6. Sprinkle on the cake, and put under a broiler about 5 minutes, until bubbly.

OUR HIGHNESS'S HOT MILK CAKE

This state of Wisconsin's present cow population is 1,739,000, and a lot of those cows don't live far from the Norske Nook. For years now, even in the toughest of times, we've had more cows and have produced more milk here in the west-central part of Wisconsin than anywhere else in America. Our townships—even some counties—really do have more cows than people. This may seem odd to some, but to us, it's normal.

This cake, with its sweet rich butter and thick hot milk, is named for Our Highness—the cow. It's one of those fast, easy, "hurry up, company's coming" cakes. It hardly ever falls, and though it's usually eaten as fast as it's made, if you're alone, this is a light cake that will stay nice and fresh for days.

FOR A 9 × 13-INCH CAKE

4 *eggs*

2 *cups sugar*

2 *teaspoons vanilla extract*

2 *cups all-purpose flour*

2 *teaspoons baking powder*

1/2 *teaspoon salt*

4 *tablespoons butter melted in 1 cup hot milk*

Broiled Coconut Frosting (page 187)

1. Preheat the oven to 350° F. Beat the eggs, sugar, and vanilla together in a large mixing bowl until it gets thick and lemon colored. Add the flour, baking powder, salt, and butter mixture, and beat all together until well blended (see Note).

2. Pour the batter into a buttered 9 × 13-inch pan, and bake for 45 minutes, until your finger does not leave a print. Remove from the oven, and frost with Broiled Coconut Frosting.

N O T E : Remember, if a small portable mixer is used, use it on high speed. With a KitchenAid, use a medium speed.

O R A N G E · D A T E
C A K E
✵
F O R   A   9 × 1 3 - I N C H   C A K E

1 whole orange rind

1 cup dates

½ cup Butter Flavor Crisco

¾ cup packed brown sugar

¼ cup white sugar

2 well-beaten eggs

1 cup sour cream

1 teaspoon baking soda

 Pinch of salt

2 cups all-purpose flour

O R A N G E · D A T E
T O P P I N G

3 tablespoons butter

4 tablespoons white sugar

5 tablespoons cream

2 tablespoons orange and date mixture (saved in step 3 of the cake)

2 cups powdered sugar

1. Preheat the oven to 350° F. Using a food processor, grind the whole orange rind and the dates together, so they are mixed (see Note). Set aside.

2. In a large bowl, combine the shortening and sugars. Add the eggs, sour cream, baking soda, salt, and flour.

3. Keep back 2 tablespoons of the date mixture, add the rest to the batter, and mix well.

4. Pour into a buttered 9 × 13-inch pan, and bake for 35 minutes, until your finger doesn't leave a dent.

5. *To prepare the topping:* Boil the butter, white sugar, and cream for 2 minutes in a medium saucepan. Add the orange and date mixture and powdered sugar, and beat until smooth.

6. Spread onto the cooled cake.

N O T E : You can use a Cuisinart for this, but don't let the rind and dates get mushy.

OLD-TIME POPPY SEED CAKE

My mother used to like to take this cake to Ladies' Aid. With the tiny black seeds throughout and a layer of lemon or vanilla filling under the frosting, it's the kind of cake that says, "She fussed a little." In fact, in the old days we used to soak the poppy seeds overnight, and any old-timer will still tell you that's what you should do. The seeds swell then, have more taste, and make for a fluffier cake. Nowadays some young folks claim there's a difference in the processing of the seeds and that that makes soaking unnecessary. But back then, if you rushed the soaking of the seeds, they'd sink to the bottom, and you'd get a gummy, heavy cake. Necessary or not, I'm with the old-timers; soak the seeds overnight if possible.

FOR A 9 × 13-INCH CAKE

¹/₃ cup poppy seeds

¹/₂ cup water

1 cup whipping cream

1¹/₂ cups sugar

3 teaspoons baking powder

2 cups all-purpose flour

1 teaspoon vanilla extract

3 egg whites, beaten stiff

1 batch Miss Little's Lemon Pudding (page 152)

Old-Fashioned Seven-Minute Frosting (page 189)

1. Soak the poppy seeds in the water for a while (overnight is better).

2. Preheat the oven to 350° F. In a large bowl, beat the cream until stiff. Add the sugar, baking powder, flour, vanilla, and poppy seeds with the water they were soaked in, and mix using an electric mixer.

3. Fold in the 3 beaten egg whites, and pour into a 9 × 13-inch buttered pan. Bake for 30 minutes, until a toothpick comes out clean.

4. Cool, and top with Miss Little's Lemon Pudding, then frost with Old-Fashioned Seven-Minute Frosting.

Peddler's Quick-and-Easy Crumb Cake

There probably isn't a farm kid around who doesn't remember her mother shooing her up a stairway or into a closet or root cellar to hide from the peddlers. When I was a kid, they'd come through about once a month. They had everything: medicine, kettles, halters, bolts of material, dolls, soap, slingshots, seed corn, spices, hoes, planters. It was exciting for us kids, but depending on your mother's mood and financial condition, you were either home or you weren't; you were either treated to their show or hustled to a hiding place where you had to stand perfectly still, listening to them knock and knock, until they finally gave up and drove away. Sometimes, though, peddlers would hit it off so well when they stopped that through the years they became family friends. For some, when it was getting on toward their time to drop by, we'd even fix their favorite cake.

FOR A 9 × 13-INCH CAKE

2 cups packed brown sugar
2 cups all-purpose flour
Pinch of salt
1/2 teaspoon ground cinnamon
1/2 cup (1 stick) butter
1 egg, well beaten
1 cup sour milk
1 cup ground raisins
1 teaspoon vanilla extract
1 teaspoon baking soda

1. Preheat the oven to 350° F. In a large bowl, using your fingers, mix the sugar, flour, salt, cinnamon, and butter together as you would a pie crust. Save one-quarter of these crumbs for the cake top.

2. To the rest of this, add the well-beaten egg, the sour milk, raisins, vanilla, and baking soda. Mix well using a wooden spoon and pour into a buttered 9 × 13-inch cake pan.

3. Top with the crumbs you saved, and bake for 30 minutes, or until a toothpick comes out dry. This is very good served warm, especially with a dab of whipped cream or a little ice cream on each piece.

WHITE CAKE

This is our basic white cake both on the farm and at the restaurant. We often used it plain with chocolate or white frosting, but if we wanted to get fancy, we'd top it with a batch of Miss Little's Lemon Pudding (page 152) and then Old-Fashioned Seven-Minute Frosting (page 189), or we'd stir chocolate chips or chopped cherries into the cake batter.

FOR TWO 8-INCH LAYERS OR A 9 × 13-INCH CAKE

½ cup (1 stick) butter

1½ cups sugar

1 teaspoon vanilla extract

2¼ cups cake flour (sift before measuring)

3 teaspoons baking powder

Pinch of salt

1 cup milk

4 egg whites

1. Preheat the oven to 350° F. Cream the butter, 1 cup of the sugar, and the vanilla together in a large bowl.

2. Sift the flour, baking powder, and salt together and add alternately with the milk to the butter and sugar mixture.

3. Beat the egg whites until stiff, then beat ½ cup of sugar into them, and fold into the batter. Pour into buttered and wax-papered layer tins, or a buttered 9 × 13-inch pan.

4. If using the layer tins, bake 25 to 30 minutes; for the 9 × 13-inch pan, bake 40 minutes. (These are done when a toothpick comes out dry.)

MARBLE CAKE: Spread two-thirds of the above batter into a buttered cake pan (save one-third of the batter). Melt 1 square of chocolate, and add it to the saved batter. Drop by spoonfuls here and there on top of the batter that's in the cake tin. Take a table knife and run it this way and that, here and there, to get a marble effect.

GARBAGE CAKE

This gets its name because everything except the frosting is dumped in all together. If you have some applesauce and a little molasses left in a jar, this is a good cake to throw together while you clean out your refrigerator.

FOR A 9 × 13-INCH CAKE

2 cups applesauce

2 eggs

½ cup (1 stick) butter

1 cup dates, cut up

1 cup walnuts, chopped

1 teaspoon vanilla extract

½ teaspoon lemon extract

⅓ teaspoon salt

1½ cups sugar

2 teaspoons baking soda

2 cups all-purpose flour

1 teaspoon ground cinnamon

1 teaspoon ground nutmeg

½ teaspoon ground cloves

1 tablespoon molasses

2 cups Fresh Whipped Cream (page 192) or Cream Cheese Frosting (page 190)

1. Preheat the oven to 325° F. Stir all the ingredients except the whipped cream or frosting into a large bowl in the order given. (The butter should be soft but not melted.)

2. Mix slowly by hand at first, then beat on medium speed, using an electric mixer, for about 2 minutes.

3. Pour into a buttered 9 × 13-inch pan, and bake for 1 hour and 20 minutes, until a toothpick comes out dry. Cool, then top with Fresh Whipped Cream or Cream Cheese Frosting.

BRIDE'S WHITE ANGEL FOOD CAKE

✵

This was a fancy cake in the old days, as light and pure as a bride. Anyone, it seemed, could enjoy it, even old folks with poor teeth or people with bad stomachs. But now, as then, cake flour is a must or the cake won't be worth a darn. So go to the store if you don't have any on hand, and when you get home, stand and sift a little more than the amount you need until it's fine. Sift it at least three times because cake flour is heavier than regular flour. I know this seems like a lot of extra effort, but it's worth it.

FOR 1 ANGEL FOOD CAKE

1½ cups egg whites (the whites of about 18 eggs; see Note)

⅓ teaspoon cream of tartar

¼ teaspoon salt

1½ cups sugar

1 cup cake flour

1 teaspoon vanilla extract

1. Preheat the oven to 275° F. Pour the egg whites into a large mixing bowl. Using a wire whisk, beat the egg whites until foamy. Add the cream of tartar and the salt. Beat until stiff, turning the bowl as you whip.

2. Fold in 1 cup of the sugar, a little at a time.

3. Sift the cake flour with ½ cup of the sugar three times, then fold slowly and carefully into the egg white mixture.

4. Carefully add the vanilla, and pour the batter into an ungreased angel food tin. Cut down into the mixture a few times with a table knife to get rid of any big air bubbles.

5. For the first 30 minutes bake at 275° F, then up the oven to 325° F, and bake an additional 30 minutes.

6. Remove the tin from the oven, and tip it upside down to cool. When completely cold, carefully slide a thin, long knife around the edges and around the center ring to loosen the cake from the tin. Invert on a large, pretty plate.

NOTE: You'll have the egg yolks left so you might want to make Custard (page 134) or take a stab at the Golden Angel Food (page 170).

GOLDEN ANGEL FOOD

FOR 1 ANGEL FOOD CAKE

12 egg yolks

3/4 cup boiling water

1 tablespoon grated orange rind

1 tablespoon fresh orange juice

1 3/4 cups cake flour (sift before measuring)

1 1/4 cups sugar

2 teaspoons baking powder

1/2 teaspoon salt

1. Preheat the oven to 350° F. Beat the egg yolks until thick and lemon colored.

2. Add the boiling water and beat 5 minutes, using an electric mixer.

3. Add the orange rind and juice, then fold in the flour, sugar, baking powder, and salt.

4. Pour into an ungreased angel food tin and bake 1 hour. Invert the pan and cool completely before removing the cake.

PEARLY GATE CAKE

FOR A 9 × 13-INCH CAKE

CHOCOLATE-COCONUT FROSTING AND FILLING

1/2 cup semisweet chocolate chips, melted

2 cups flaked coconut

6 tablespoons water

CAKE

3/4 cup Butter Flavor Crisco

2 cups sugar

3 eggs

2 3/4 cups sifted cake flour

2 3/4 teaspoons baking powder

1 teaspoon salt

1 1/3 cups milk

2 teaspoons vanilla extract

1. *To prepare the frosting and filling:* Mix all the ingredients together and set aside.

2. *To prepare the cake:* Preheat the oven to 350° F. Beat the shortening and sugar together in a large bowl, using an electric mixer.

3. Beat in the eggs, flour, baking powder, salt, milk, and vanilla, and beat well.

4. Pour half of this batter into a buttered 9 × 13-inch pan, and using your fingers, sprinkle one-half of the filling mixture over.

5. Add the rest of the batter, and bake for 35 minutes, until a toothpick comes out dry.

6. While the cake is still warm, use your fingers to sprinkle on the remaining filling mixture.

ERNIE'S FAVORITE THREE-LAYER DEVIL'S FOOD CAKE WITH DATE FILLING

This cake took some fussing and cost a little more money because of the amount of sugar and squares of chocolate. It was, and I guess still is, reserved for special occasions. It was carted to Luther League, Ladies' Aid, weddings, and birthday parties. To this day, if I had to put my best foot forward, if someone said, "Choose a cake to serve at the White House," I guess this would be my pick. It's Ernie's favorite.

FOR THREE 8-INCH LAYERS

3/4 cup (1 1/2 sticks) butter

2 1/4 cups sugar

1 1/2 teaspoons vanilla extract

3 eggs

3 ounces unsweetened chocolate, melted

3 cups cake flour (sift before measuring)

1 1/2 teaspoons baking soda

3/4 teaspoon salt

1 1/2 cups ice water

DATE FILLING

1 cup milk

1/2 cup chopped dates

1/2 cup sugar

1 tablespoon all-purpose flour

1 egg, beaten

1/4 cup fresh cream

1 teaspoon vanilla extract

1/2 cup ground walnuts

1. Preheat the oven to 350° F. Cream the butter, sugar, and vanilla together. Add the eggs one at a time, beating well after each addition until light and fluffy.

2. Stir in the chocolate, and add the flour, baking soda, and salt alternately with the ice water.

3. Butter three 8-inch layer tins, divide the batter evenly into each (see Note). Bake for 30 to 35 minutes, until your finger doesn't leave a dent. Remove from the oven, and cool.

4. *To prepare Date Filling:* Heat the milk and dates in a double boiler. In a small bowl, combine the sugar and flour. Add the egg and the cream, and blend until smooth. Slowly add the egg mixture to the hot milk and dates, and cook until thick. When cool, stir in the vanilla and the nuts.

5. Fill the cake layers and frost with the Date Filling.

NOTE: If you don't want to fuss, never mind the layers. Use a 9 × 13-inch pan, and top with the filling when cool.

MOIST BOILED RAISIN CAKE

Sometimes I worry that kids today have so few small pleasures. I'm not sure what it would take—hundred-dollar sneakers, their own cellular phone, a big-screen TV—to make them as happy as a new load of straw for our mattresses made me and my sisters. From one harvest to the next, our weight ground down on that straw padding each night, so by summer, we were left with beds no thicker than pancakes. By July we were waiting as hard for the threshers as we waited for Christmas. When they would finally rumble into our fields with their giant machines, we'd run upstairs and drag our flat bundles down into the sunshine; we'd fight over the knife and just who was going to slit 'em open. Then we'd hurry and scoop out the chaff, wash the ticking, and stand in line for a load of rich, yellow straw. We'd stand and wait for hours as if for a million dollars. But what does this have to do with Moist Boiled Raisin Cake? Well, it's always what Mom made for threshers, and I can't bake it without remembering the fresh smell and cozy satisfaction of those early fall nights—the first on our high, high beds—and how we argued whose mattress was highest, closest to heaven.

FOR A 9 × 13-INCH CAKE OR TWO (9-INCH) ROUND LAYERS

1 cup raisins
2 cups water
1 1/2 cups sugar
1/2 cup shortening
1 capful vanilla extract
2 eggs
1 teaspoon pumpkin pie spice (page 131)
2 1/4 cups all-purpose flour
2 teaspoons baking powder
Pinch of salt
1 cup chopped walnut meats
Basic Powdered Sugar Frosting (page 193) or Caramel Frosting (page 188)

1. Cook the raisins in the water over medium heat for about 10 minutes. Drain, saving 1 cup of the juice. Cool slightly.

2. Cream the sugar, shortening, and vanilla together in a large bowl. Add the eggs, and beat well.

3. Add the pumpkin pie spice, flour, baking powder, salt, and raisin juice. Beat well.

4. Fold in the nuts and pour into a buttered 9 × 13-inch pan or 2 buttered 9-inch round layer tins. Bake the 9 × 13 cake for 45 minutes. Bake the layers for 30 minutes. When your finger does not leave a print, the cake is done.

5. Frost and fill (if layered) with Powdered Sugar Frosting or Caramel Frosting.

CHOCOLATE SAUERKRAUT CAKE

When people first settled here, there was great excitement when new folks arrived, but language was kind of a problem. Most people didn't speak English, and when they did learn, it was heavy with the sound of their homeland. People tended to put up in certain areas around here according to their heritage. There was a Norske Valley, German Valley, Swede Town, a Frenchman's Coulee, all within a few hours' traveling distance by horse and wagon. My mother still talks about these two German women in her Ladies' Aid who brought delicious cakes to church doings, but it was a long time before the Norwegian ladies could get the recipes because they couldn't understand each other. It was a big day I guess, a breakthrough for the community, when the ladies could start communicating and exchanging secrets.

This was one of the recipes those women waited so long to get. It's a nice moist cake, and the sauerkraut tastes like coconut. I had a farm-implement man at the restaurant who loved this cake; he had a piece every day we made it, until he found out it was made with sauerkraut, not coconut. He hated sauerkraut, so that killed it for him.

FOR A 9 × 13-INCH CAKE

2/3 cup butter

1 1/2 cups sugar

3 eggs

2 1/4 cups all-purpose flour

1 teaspoon baking powder

1/4 teaspoon salt

1/2 cup cocoa

1 teaspoon baking soda

1 cup cold water

1/2 cup Homemade Sauerkraut (page 93), drained and lightly chopped (see Note)

1 1/4 teaspoons vanilla extract

Sweet Milk Frosting (page 189)

1. Preheat the oven to 350° F. In a large bowl, blend the butter and sugar until creamy.

2. Add the eggs and stir in the flour, baking powder, salt, cocoa, baking soda, and water.

3. Stir in the sauerkraut and the vanilla. Mix well, and pour into a buttered 9 × 13-inch pan. Bake 40 to 45 minutes, until your finger doesn't leave a dent. Cool.

4. Frost with Sweet Milk Frosting.

NOTE: You can use store-bought kraut for this if you're pressed for time.

WARM GINGERBREAD CAKE AND WHIPPED CREAM

✾

This is good as a dessert. It's also a quick cake for afternoon lunch for guests or a hired man when you're busy with housework or a fussy baby. Eating this warm, rich cake gives even the stone-hearted a cozy feeling. If the whole cake isn't going to go all at once, though, put whipped cream only on the pieces you're going to use or the cake'll get soggy.

FOR AN 8 × 8-INCH CAKE

1/2 cup (1 stick) butter

3/4 cup sugar

1 egg

2/3 cup molasses

2 cups all-purpose flour

1/4 teaspoon baking soda

2 teaspoons baking powder

2 teaspoons ground ginger

1 teaspoon ground cinnamon

1/2 teaspoon salt

3/4 cup buttermilk

2 cups Fresh Whipped Cream (page 192)

1. Preheat the oven to 350° F. In a large bowl, cream the butter, sugar, and egg together well. Beat, and add the molasses.

2. Mix together the flour, baking soda, baking powder, ginger, cinnamon, and salt. Add the dry ingredients alternately with the buttermilk. Beat until smooth, and pour into a buttered 8 × 8-inch pan, and bake for 45 minutes, until a toothpick comes out dry.

3. Serve warm, topped with Fresh Whipped Cream.

SNOWED PEANUT CAKE

✾

FOR A 9 × 13-INCH CAKE PAN

1 cup milk

1 teaspoon butter

2 eggs

1 cup sugar

2 cups all-purpose flour

2 teaspoons baking powder

1 teaspoon vanilla extract

   Basic Powdered Sugar Frosting (page 193)

2 cups ground salted peanuts (see Note)

1. Preheat the oven to 350° F. In a medium saucepan, bring the milk and butter to a boil, and let cool.

2. In a medium bowl, beat the eggs and sugar together well. Add the flour, baking powder, and vanilla. Beat together, add the cooled milk mixture, and blend well with a licker.

3. Pour into a buttered 9 × 13-inch pan, and bake for 30 minutes, until a toothpick comes out dry.

4. Cool, cut into 18 pieces, and roll each piece (all but the bottom of the pieces) in thinned powdered sugar frosting; then roll in ground salted peanuts, let set, and serve.

NOTE: Run the peanuts through a nut grinder once or put the nuts in a plastic bag, and hit 'em with a hammer or a heavy rolling pin.

MOLASSES CAKE

This was one of our old everyday cakes but always a favorite of hired men. There's nothing like it served warm with whipped cream when there's an early winter chill in the air and a hard day's work behind you.

FOR A 9 × 13-INCH CAKE

1 cup white sugar

1 tablespoon lard

2 eggs

1/2 cup molasses

1 cup buttermilk

2 1/4 cups all-purpose flour

1/4 teaspoon salt

1/2 cup raisins (optional)

1/2 teaspoon ground nutmeg

1/2 teaspoon ground ginger

1 teaspoon ground cinnamon

1 1/8 teaspoons baking soda

1/4 cup boiling water

Clever Nellie's Burnt Sugar Frosting (page 187) or Caramel Frosting (page 188)

1. Preheat the oven to 350° F. Cream the sugar and lard together in a large bowl. Beat in the eggs; add the molasses and buttermilk, and mix together.

2. Add the flour, salt, raisins (if desired), nutmeg, ginger, and cinnamon.

3. Dissolve the baking soda in the boiling water, pour into the batter, and mix all together well, but do not overbeat.

4. Pour into a buttered 9 × 13-inch pan, and bake for 45 to 50 minutes, until a toothpick comes out dry or your finger doesn't leave a dent.

5. Frost with Clever Nellie's Burnt Sugar Frosting, Caramel Frosting, or whatever you'd like.

TWOS PINEAPPLE CAKE

This cake requires no shortening. Don't try it either; it doesn't work. It's a moist, delicious cake as is.

FOR A 9 × 13-INCH CAKE

2 cups sugar

2 cups all-purpose flour

1 (20-ounce) can unsweetened crushed pineapple (undrained)

2 eggs

2 teaspoons baking soda

1 cup nutmeats, chopped

Cream Cheese Frosting (page 190)

1. Preheat the oven to 350° F. In a large bowl, combine all the ingredients (except the frosting), and mix well.

2. Butter the bottom of a 9 × 13-inch pan, and pour in the batter. Bake for about 45 minutes, until your finger doesn't leave a dent. Cool.

3. Frost with Cream Cheese Frosting.

FRESH APPLE CAKE

This cake freezes well.

FOR A 9 × 13-INCH CAKE

4 cups peeled, cored, and diced apples (see Note)

2 eggs

2 cups white sugar

2 teaspoons ground cinnamon

1/2 cup salad oil

2 cups all-purpose flour

1 teaspoon salt

1 teaspoon baking soda

3/4 cup chopped walnuts

CINNAMON WALNUT TOPPING

1/4 cup packed brown sugar

1/2 cup white sugar

1/2 teaspoon ground cinnamon

1/4 cup chopped walnuts

1. Preheat the oven to 350° F. In a large bowl, beat the apples and eggs together well.

2. Add the sugar, cinnamon, and salad oil, and mix well.

3. Add the flour, salt, baking soda, and walnuts, and beat again.

4. Butter the bottom only of a 9 × 13-inch pan, pour in the batter, and set aside.

5. *To prepare the topping:* In a small bowl, using your fingers, mix the sugars, cinnamon, and walnuts together, and sprinkle over the top of the cake batter.

6. Bake about 1 hour, but check as it gets close to the end. If a toothpick comes out dry, it's done.

NOTE: Use fresh or water-packed apples.

BLUEBERRY BLUFF CAKE

As kids, if it was near the Fourth of July, and we had permission, we'd grab milk pails and set out for the blueberry bluffs. We'd pick all forenoon and by the time we trotted home, our hands and faces were all purple and our bellies full. We'd charge into the house with almost as many leaves and twigs as berries, but we always believed our mother was pleased. She'd reward us with muffins or this blueberry cake, which is very good as a dessert after dinner.

FOR A 9 × 13-INCH CAKE

1 cup sugar

3 tablespoons butter

1/2 cup milk

2 eggs

2 cups flour

2 teaspoons baking powder

1 pint fresh blueberries

1 more cup sugar and 3 more tablespoons all-purpose flour sifted together

1/2 cup (1 stick) butter, melted

1. Preheat the oven to 375° F. Using an electric mixer, beat the sugar, 3 tablespoons of butter, milk, eggs, flour, and baking powder together for 2 minutes on medium speed.

2. Butter the bottom of a 9 × 13-inch pan, pour in the batter, and cover with a pint of fresh blueberries.

3. Sprinkle the sugar and flour mixture over the berries, and drizzle the 1/2 cup of melted butter over all.

4. Bake about 30 minutes, until the cake bubbles and is browned.

RHUBARB CAKE

❈

FOR A 9 × 13-INCH CAKE

1/2 cup butter

2 cups sugar

2 eggs, beaten

3 cups all-purpose flour

4 teaspoons baking powder

1 cup milk

1 teaspoon vanilla extract

Pinch of salt

4 cups raw (fresh or frozen) rhubarb, cut into 1/2-inch pieces

1 (3-ounce) package strawberry gelatin

1/2 cup sugar

SUGAR TOPPING

1/4 cup flour

1/2 cup sugar

4 tablespoons butter

1 cup Fresh Whipped Cream (page 192)

1. Preheat the oven to 350° F. Mix 1/2 cup butter and 2 cups of sugar together in a large bowl, and add the eggs.

2. Add the flour, baking powder, milk, vanilla, and salt. Mix until it gets to be a smooth, thick batter, and pour into a buttered 9 × 13-inch pan.

3. In a large bowl, mix the rhubarb pieces with the dry gelatin powder and 1/2 cup of sugar, and pour over the batter.

4. *To prepare the topping:* Crumble the flour, sugar, and butter together in a small bowl, and sprinkle over the rhubarb mixture. Bake for 40 to 60 minutes, depending on your oven and the rhubarb (frozen rhubarb takes longer to bake), until a toothpick comes out dry. Serve warm or cool, topped with Fresh Whipped Cream.

GRASSHOPPER CAKE

Whenever I eat this cake, I feel better. If I overdo it and start feeling a little doggy after a big meal, any other cake puts me out, but when this is served as dessert, I perk right up.

FOR A 9 × 13-INCH CAKE

³⁄4 cup (1¹⁄2 sticks) butter

1³⁄4 cups sugar

2³⁄4 cups sifted cake flour

3¹⁄2 teaspoons baking powder

³⁄4 teaspoon salt

1 cup milk

¹⁄3 cup crème de menthe

4 egg whites

2 cups Chocolate Fudge Topping, heated (page 223)

8 ounces Fresh Whipped Cream (page 192; see Note)

¹⁄4 cup crème de menthe

1. Preheat the oven to 350° F. Cream the butter and sugar together in a large bowl, and add the flour, baking powder, and salt with the milk and crème de menthe.

2. In a separate bowl, beat the egg whites until stiff, and fold them into the above mixture.

3. Pour into a buttered 9 × 13-inch pan, and bake for 35 minutes, until your finger does not leave a print. Cool.

4. Cover the cooled cake with the hot fudge, and allow it to set.

5. Fold the whipped cream and crème de menthe together, and spread it over the top.

NOTE: The hot fudge must be hot when added. Do not substitute chocolate syrup; it's completely different. If you're in a rush, you can use store-bought hot fudge and Cool Whip.

COCA-COLA CAKE

This is an old recipe. So old, we even made it when Coke was five cents a bottle. The Coke makes it light.

FOR A 9 × 13-INCH CAKE

¹⁄2 cup butter

1¹⁄2 cups sugar

2 eggs

3 tablespoons cocoa

2 cups all-purpose flour

¹⁄2 teaspoon baking soda

¹⁄2 cup buttermilk

1 teaspoon vanilla extract

1 cup Coca-Cola (Classic)

1¹⁄2 cups miniature marshmallows

Cocoa Coca-Cola Frosting (page 191)

1. Preheat the oven to 350° F. Combine the butter and sugar together in a large mixing bowl. Add the eggs, and mix well.

2. Add the cocoa, flour, baking soda, buttermilk, vanilla, Coca-Cola, and marshmallows, and beat, using an electric mixer.

3. Pour into a greased 9 × 13-inch pan, and bake for 45 minutes. When a toothpick comes out clean, remove the cake from the oven, and cool.

4. Frost with Coca-Cola Frosting.

MAY BASKET JELLY ROLL

Jelly roll was popular all year round, but especially at May Basket time. It calls for a lot of eggs, so if you had a lot of chickens, and the hens were laying good, jelly roll was fast; you could whip one up in nothing flat; kids and adults both loved it, and you didn't have to monkey with frosting because you always had a jar of jelly down in the cellar. Even these days—even if you live in New York and have never seen a chicken—I recommend this simple treat from the past. But if you've never tried it, go with the plain jelly roll first. Chocolate, with Old-Fashioned Seven-Minute Frosting, is more of a fuss, and a little harder to get just right.

FOR A 12 × 15-INCH JELLY ROLL

4 eggs

1 1/3 cups sugar

7 tablespoons water

1 teaspoon vanilla extract

1 1/3 cups all-purpose flour

1 1/3 teaspoons baking powder

3/4 teaspoon salt

   Enough powdered sugar to lightly cover a small dish towel

   Whatever filling or frosting desired (see "For Fillings," at right)

1. Preheat the oven to 375° F. In a large bowl, beat the eggs until thick, then gradually beat in the sugar.

2. Beat in the water and the vanilla all at once. Then add the flour, baking powder, and salt all at once, and beat just until smooth.

3. Prepare the jelly roll pan by lining the sides and bottom with wax paper. Pour the batter into the prepared pan, and bake for 12 to 15 minutes; it should spring back when pressed with your finger.

4. Cover a dish towel with powdered sugar (see Note), and flop the jelly roll from the cookie sheet upside down onto the towel. Quickly peel off the wax paper, spread the cake with the jelly or filling desired, and roll up from the 15-inch side. (If you're unsure of yourself, you can roll this up before spreading with the jelly, then unroll it later to fill.) Fill and frost with any of the suggested variations.

NOTE: You must cover the dish towel with powdered sugar or the cake will stick, and you'll really have a mess.

CHOCOLATE JELLY ROLL: Follow the above recipe, but add 1/2 cup of cocoa to the dry ingredients.

FOR FILLINGS: Use whatever homemade jelly you desire (pages 78 to 81). My favorites are grape, raspberry, and cherry. You can also use puddings (pages 147 to 153). I like the lemon. As a filling for the Chocolate Jelly Roll, I like to use Old-Fashioned Seven-Minute Frosting (page 189) with marshmallows melted in. Be imaginative.

ELECTRIC SKILLET PEACH UPSIDE-DOWN CAKE

FOR AN ELECTRIC SKILLET-SIZE CAKE

1/2 cup white sugar

1/2 cup (1 stick) butter

1 egg

1 1/2 cups all-purpose flour

1 1/2 teaspoons baking powder

1/2 teaspoon salt

1/2 cup milk

1/4 cup (1/2 stick) butter

1 packed cup brown sugar

3 fresh peaches, peeled and sliced (see Note)

1/4 cup pecans (or not)

2 cups Fresh Whipped Cream (page 192), or not

1. Cream the white sugar and 1/2 cup of butter together, using an electric mixer.

2. Add the egg, and beat well.

3. Add the flour, baking powder, salt, and milk, and beat until smooth.

4. Set the heat of the skillet at 275° F. Melt 1/4 cup of butter in the skillet, and stir in the brown sugar.

5. Arrange the peach slices in that mixture, and sprinkle with the pecans, if you're using them.

6. Spread the batter over this, cover, and bake in the skillet 25 to 30 minutes, until a toothpick comes out dry (see Note). (It will not be brown on top; it doesn't get brown in a skillet.) Remove the cover, put a plate on top, and dump the cake upside down. Serve while warm, topped with Fresh Whipped Cream, if desired.

NOTE: You can use home-canned peaches (or store-bought) if you can't get fresh. There's not much difference in the results here because of the brown sugar.

This can be baking while you're enjoying your dinner.

CREAM PUFFS

These are light and wonderful, and they certainly say, "She put her best foot forward." When you're baking them, though, take a brown paper grocery sack, cut it open, and lay it flat on top of your cookie sheet. Bake your puffs on that—the sheet doesn't have to be greased—and you won't have any problems with sticking.

MAKES 9 TO 12 PUFFS

1/2 cup (1 stick) butter

1 cup water

1 cup all-purpose flour

1/2 teaspoon salt

4 eggs

Whatever filling desired (see Note)

1. Preheat the oven to 400° F. Put the butter and the water in a medium saucepan, place over medium heat, and cook until the butter melts.

2. Add the flour and salt, and cook, stirring constantly, until the mixture leaves the sides of the pan. Remove from the heat and add the eggs one at a time, beating after each one.

3. Using a tablespoon, scoop up the batter and drop it a couple of inches apart on the brown paper sack.

4. Bake for 10 minutes at 400° F, then reduce the heat to 350° F, and bake for 25 minutes, or until done (when golden brown and quite firm). Cool.

5. Split 1 inch from the top, and fill with any of the suggested fillings, or something else you like.

NOTE: I like to use Basic Vanilla Pudding (page 150) and then top the cream puffs with a spoon of Fresh Whipped Cream (page 192) and usually some chocolate syrup. You can also use Miss Little's Lemon Pudding (page 152), Basic Chocolate Pudding (page 150), Custard (page 134), Boss's Vanilla Ice Cream (page 218), Chocolate Ice Cream (page 219), or Coffee Ice Cream (page 220). Whipped cream is always good for a topping, but be as creative as you like.

Bars

PUMPKIN BARS

FOR A 12 × 15-INCH PAN

4 eggs

1 cup Wesson oil

2 cups sugar

2 cups pumpkin puree

2 cups all-purpose flour

1/2 teaspoon ground cloves

1/2 teaspoon salt

2 teaspoons baking powder

2 teaspoons ground cinnamon

1 teaspoon salt

1/2 teaspoon ground ginger

1/2 teaspoon ground nutmeg

   Cream Cheese Frosting (page 190)

1. Preheat the oven to 350° F. Mix the eggs, oil, sugar, and pumpkin together, using an electric mixer.

2. Add the flour, cloves, salt, baking powder, cinnamon, salt, ginger, and nutmeg.

3. Pour into a buttered 12 × 15-inch jelly roll pan. Bake for about 45 minutes, until a tooth-pick comes out dry (mustn't underbake). Cool, and frost with Cream Cheese Frosting.

ONE-HOUR BROWNIES

You might think I've lost my mind telling you to bake these an hour, but put them in the oven and walk away. You could wear a hole in the floor going back and forth to the oven to look in; they really do take the full hour to bake. But trust me, it's worth the wait.

FOR A 12 × 15-INCH PAN

1/2 cup (1 stick) butter

2 cups sugar

Pinch of salt

1 teaspoon vanilla extract

4 eggs

1 1/2 cups all-purpose flour

1/2 cup cocoa

1/2 cup milk

1/2 cup chopped nuts

Chocolate frosting

1. Preheat the oven to 300° F. Cream the butter, sugar, salt, and vanilla together in a large bowl until smooth.

2. Add the eggs one at a time, and beat after each one.

3. Sift the flour and cocoa together, and add it with the milk and nuts. Mix well, and pour into a buttered 12 × 15-inch pan.

4. Bake for 1 hour, until a toothpick comes out dry. When cool, spread with any chocolate frosting.

DATE BARS

These are as fundamental on the farm as the tractor.

FOR A 9 × 13-INCH PAN

1 pound dates, cut up

1 cup water

1 cup packed brown sugar

1 cup (2 sticks) butter

2 cups all-purpose flour

2 cups Quaker oats

1 teaspoon baking soda in a little hot water

1. Preheat the oven to 350° F. In a large saucepan, over medium heat, combine the dates and water, and cook until thick. Cool.

2. Meanwhile, using your fingers, lightly mix together the brown sugar and butter (don't overmix).

3. Add the flour, oats and baking soda (in its little hot water), and mix together, using your fingers, until it becomes a well-blended, crumbly mixture.

4. Press a little more than half of this dough into a buttered 9 × 13-inch pan.

5. Spread the cooled date mixture over the top of this, then sprinkle with the rest of the oat dough. Bake about 25 minutes, until lightly brown on top. Cool, and cut into bars.

ESTER'S GLADRAG GINGER BARS

Oh, this is a good old treat; I remember how quickly we stirred them up and the thick, gingery smell of the kitchen as they baked. We usually had most of the ingredients on hand, except maybe the spices we'd have to plan for and get. But flour, we had more than enough of that. In those days we bought it in fifty-pound sacks, and was it pure! Nothing artificial, none of these preservatives. And boy, was buying flour and feed a big thing, because we made dresses and clothes and curtains and sheets from the sacks. Flour sacks were a luxury because we couldn't afford material from those bright-colored, fancy bolts in the store or from the peddler's rack. At first the sacks were white, but then we thought heaven had fallen to earth—the flour and feed companies started to put them out in print! You could go down to the mill and pick out what you wanted—little bluebirds or flowers on a white background, or a bright red, yellow, orange, green, or pink floral mix. They even had border prints you'd cut apart and stitch together so the neck or sleeve of your blouse matched the border of your skirt.

It's funny what one remembers. I'll never forget, for some reason my friend Ester got to go to Rockford, Illinois, and on the way back, she stopped and posed for a picture on the Capitol steps. The outfit she had on was orange, made just from those feed sacks, but it seemed almost sacred back then. Today we look at that photo and kind of chuckle at just how thrilled we were over a little of nothing. (We called our dress-up clothes "gladrags.")

FOR A 9 × 13-INCH PAN

1 cup packed brown sugar

1 egg

2 tablespoons butter

1 teaspoon vanilla extract

1/4 cup molasses

1/4 teaspoon ground cloves

1 cup all-purpose flour

1/2 teaspoon baking soda

1/2 teaspoon salt

1 teaspoon ground ginger

1/2 teaspoon ground cinnamon

1/4 cup milk

1 cup chopped nutmeats (or not; I usually choose not)

Basic Powdered Sugar Frosting (page 193)

1. Preheat the oven to 350° F. Mix the sugar, egg, and butter together in a large bowl, using an electric mixer. Then stir in the vanilla and molasses.

2. Add the cloves, flour, baking soda, salt, ginger, and cinnamon. Add the milk, and mix well. Now stir in the nutmeats, if desired.

3. Pour the batter into a buttered 9 × 13-inch pan, and bake for about 30 minutes, until done (when finger doesn't leave a dent). Cool, and frost with Basic Powdered Sugar Frosting.

BUTTERFINGER BARS

FOR A 9 × 13-INCH PAN

1/2 cup dark corn syrup

2/3 cup butter, melted

1 cup packed brown sugar

1 teaspoon vanilla extract

4 cups oatmeal

PEANUT BUTTER TOPPING

1 small package chocolate chips

1/2 cup peanut butter

1. Preheat the oven to 350° F. Mix the syrup, butter, and sugar together in a large bowl, using a wooden spoon. Add the vanilla and the oatmeal, and mix together, using your fingers. (Don't be alarmed if it's real firm.)

2. Press into a buttered 9 × 13-inch pan, and bake for 15 minutes only. Do not overbake (see Note). Cool only slightly.

3. *To prepare Peanut Butter Topping:* Place the chocolate chips and the peanut butter together in a saucepan over very low heat. Stir, and stand there and watch it until it's melted.

4. Spread onto the slightly cooled bars, and cut into 18 pieces before cold.

NOTE: If you've baked them too long, you'll need a hammer and pickax.

TOFFEE BARS

At the restaurant my workers would always tease me because I liked toffee bars so well we had to have them once a week, and throughout the day I had to sample and sample and sample them to make sure they were just right. They're very rich—a lot like Heath Bars—but you have to watch it because they're easy to overbake. However, I found that if you do, don't worry; unless you burn them, they're always a delight—so much so I stopped making them on a regular basis; I was getting way too heavy.

FOR A 9 × 13-INCH PAN

1 cup packed brown sugar

1/2 pound (2 sticks) butter

Pinch of salt

1 egg yolk

1 capful vanilla extract

1 cup all-purpose flour

1 cup nutmeats

1 cup chocolate chips

1. Preheat the oven to 350° F. Combine the sugar, butter, salt, egg yolk, vanilla, flour, and nutmeats together in a large bowl. Mix well and pour into a buttered 9 × 13-inch pan.

2. Bake for 25 minutes, until light brown on top. Remove from the oven, and sprinkle with chocolate chips. When the chips have softened, spread them around. Cut, and eat.

OH MY! APPLE BARS

FOR A 12 × 15-INCH PAN

2½ *cups all-purpose flour*

1 *tablespoon sugar*

Pinch of salt

½ *pound (2 sticks) butter*

1 *egg*

⅔ *cup milk*

2 *handfuls crushed cornflakes*

Enough fresh or frozen apple slices to cover pan (about 8 to 10 apples, sliced)

1 *heaping cup sugar*

1 *teaspoon ground cinnamon*

Basic Powdered Sugar Frosting (page 193)

1. Preheat the oven to 350° F. Mix the flour, 1 tablespoon sugar, the salt, and butter together in a large bowl, using your fingers, until it gets to be a crumbly mixture like pie crust.

2. Crack the egg into a cup, and add the milk. Beat with a fork until well blended, then add to the crust mixture, and mix, using a fork or your fingers.

3. Divide the dough in half, and on a floured breadboard or a table, roll out one piece into a rectangle to fit a 12 × 15-inch pan. Grease the pan and spread the crust on the bottom and sides of it.

4. Sprinkle the crushed cornflakes over the crust and cover with the apple slices. Sprinkle with 1 heaping cup of sugar and the cinnamon.

5. Roll out the other half of the dough, and place it over the top of this. Flute around the edges of the pan as you would pie, then, using a knife, make a few slits in the top of the crust.

6. Bake about 45 minutes, until the apples have cooked and the crust is lightly browned. Remove from the oven and lightly glaze while warm with Basic Powdered Sugar Frosting.

MINCEMEAT BARS: Prepare the crust as you would above. Use 3 cups of mincemeat, 2 cups of chopped apples, and ¾ cup of sugar for the filling. Mix all together, and pour over the crushed cornflakes. Sprinkle a jigger of brandy and a jigger of rum over all, and dot with butter. Finish steps 5 and 6, as you would for Oh My! Apple Bars. Frost with Basic Powdered Sugar Frosting (page 193) or top with Hot Rum Sauce (page 132).

Hints for Frostings

• Watch the frostings you make with chocolate or brown sugar because they tend to burn easily. You have to keep wiggling and working them in the pan to make them really good. And remember, don't overheat that chocolate or it'll lose some of the flavor or become bitter.

• Do not overstir—just once in a while to prevent the sugar from forming a coating around the edge of the saucepan. And do not scrape down the sides of the kettle when the sugar has formed around the edges.

• To test for the soft- or hard-boiled stage in boiled frostings, drop a few drops of syrup into a little cold water, and using your fingers, gently roll it around. If it's too soft, it will not form a little ball.

• If you want to be fancy, frost a cake using a little butter spreader. For everyday, I just use a kitchen knife or a licker.

• When you're topping a cake with any of the boiled frostings, you certainly don't want it to look smooth. Make little ridges—that looks prettier. If boiled frosting doesn't set up right away (if the syrup hasn't cooked long enough), it gets a glaze on it, and your cake looks like an ice pond, so swirl it around a little. And on chocolate, butterscotch, brown sugar, or caramel, don't be afraid to use a few nutmeats. Or use coconut for a white or gold cake.

• To make a glaze, simply thin out Basic Powdered Sugar Frosting (page 193) with a little half-and-half.

• To color coconut (if not feared), squirt a couple of drops of coloring over it, and either place it in a jar and shake, or use your fingers and mix.

Frostings

BUTTER-CREAM FROSTING

ENOUGH FOR A 9 × 13-INCH CAKE

1 stick (½ cup) butter
½ teaspoon salt
3½ cups powdered sugar
2 egg yolks
1 teaspoon grated lemon or orange rind
2 tablespoons milk

With an electric mixer, beat the butter until soft and creamy. Add the salt, powdered sugar, egg yolks, lemon rind, and milk, and mix until smooth. Spread onto a cooled cake.

CLEVER NELLIE'S BURNT SUGAR FROSTING

This is an old, old frosting that women used when they couldn't afford brown sugar or they didn't have any on hand. It's kind of a poor-man's, makeshift frosting, but it's oh, so good. It was also common during the War when sugar was rationed, and there weren't enough stamps to buy both white and brown sugars. It was tough baking then, especially anything fancy. If a girl had her wedding coming up, her mother and grandmother and aunts and god-mother, even the neighbors, would all save up their stamps so there'd be enough sugar for that wedding cake. Anyway, if you look, you'll notice this recipe and the recipe for Burnt Sugar Cake (page 160) only call for white sugar. Women took what sugar they had and lightly burned it in butter so it tasted and appeared to be brown.

FOR A 9 × 13-INCH CAKE

1 cup white sugar

3 tablespoons butter

1/4 cup fresh cream

A little vanilla extract

1. In a cast-iron skillet, combine the white sugar and about 2 tablespoons of the butter, and place over low heat. Stand at the stove and keep an eye on it, stirring occasionally until the sugar is brown but not really burnt. (If it isn't browning right, add a little more butter.)

2. When the sugar is brown, stir in the fresh cream, then remove from heat, and cool a little.

3. Add 1 more tablespoon of butter and a squirt of vanilla, and beat it by hand. Beat it, and beat it, and beat it until it's the right consistency.

4. Spread onto a cooled, fresh white cake, or any other cake.

BROILED COCONUT FROSTING

This is a farm favorite but is especially good to use on Our Highness's Hot Milk Cake (page 164).

ENOUGH FOR A 9 × 13-INCH CAKE

6 tablespoons melted butter

1/4 cup cream

2/3 cup packed brown sugar

1 teaspoon vanilla

1 cup flaked coconut

1. Combine all the ingredients, and mix together well using a wooden spoon.

2. Spread onto a warm cake and place under the broiler until it's good and bubbly.

CARAMEL FROSTING

This is a delicious, old-time frosting, but you've got to watch it so you don't boil it too hard, or when you set the pan in cold water to cool, then go to stick a spoon in to spread it, the whole works will come up—the spoon, the caramel, and the kettle; in other words, you'll have a sticky mess. However, don't panic; you might be able to fix it by adding a little cream, but it's best to watch closely so you don't ever have to hoe that row.

ENOUGH FOR A 9 × 13-INCH CAKE

> 1 1/2 *cups packed brown sugar*
> 1/2 *cup (1 stick) butter*
> 1/4 *cup milk*
> 1 *capful vanilla extract*

1. Cook the sugar, butter, and milk together in a medium saucepan over medium heat until the mixture forms a soft ball when a few drops are sprinkled into a little cold water.

2. Add the vanilla, cool slightly, then beat and beat and beat until it's thick and a light golden color. Put the pan in cold water to cool, then spread onto a cooled cake.

BLIZZARD WHITE REFRIGERATOR FROSTING

This is an excellent frosting for decorating special-occasion cakes or making fun cakes for the kids. If you're not afraid of food coloring and want to add a few drops to this recipe, you can make red, pink, orange, yellow, green, blue, anything you choose. It's also a perfect, easy, little-mess frosting to use in decorating tubes.

**ENOUGH FOR THREE
9 × 13-INCH CAKES**

> 1 1/2 *cups white shortening*
> 6 *tablespoons cold water*
> *Pinch of salt*
> 2 *pounds powdered sugar*
> 1 *capful white vanilla extract*

1. Using an electric mixer, beat the shortening, water, and salt in a large bowl on low speed until smooth. Gradually add the powdered sugar 1/4 pound at a time. Beat well each time until all of the sugar is used.

2. Add the vanilla, and stir.

3. Spread it immediately on cooled cakes or store in an airtight container in the refrigerator, and use when desired.

OLD-FASHIONED SEVEN-MINUTE FROSTING

When I worked at the minister's, they had some modern, new-fangled equipment I'd never worked with before. What I remember most was this little, tiny electric mixer, and when I first picked it up, I guess I didn't realize what I had in my hand. I was alone and beating this Seven-Minute Frosting, and I must have been marveling at the sound of the motor and how it sped through that mixture, and like a dumbbell I took it up while it was still beating, and frosting flew all over. I'd never seen anything like it—frosting spattered all over the walls, my face, the ceiling, my arms, the cupboards; some even stuck to the Gleaners' picture above the table. I thought, Oh, Lord! But then I had to kind of chuckle too; I looked down at the little electric thing, and I said to myself, "Holy Moses, if it's gonna do that, so much for modern!"

ENOUGH FOR A 9 × 13-INCH CAKE

3/4 cup sugar

1/3 cup white corn syrup

2 egg whites

2 tablespoons water

1/4 teaspoon cream of tartar

Pinch of salt

1 capful vanilla extract

1. Combine all the ingredients except the vanilla in the top of a double boiler.

2. Cook rapidly, beating constantly, using an electric beater until the right consistency for easy spreading. Remove from heat and stir in the vanilla. Spread onto a cooled cake. (It'll be thick and fluffy.)

SWEET MILK FROSTING

ENOUGH FOR A 9 × 13-INCH CAKE

1 cup milk

2 tablespoons cornstarch

1/2 to 3/4 cup Butter Flavor Crisco

1/4 cup sugar

1 teaspoon vanilla extract

1. Heat the milk and cornstarch in a small saucepan over medium heat, cooking until thick (about 10 minutes). Cool.

2. Cream the shortening and sugar together in a medium bowl, and add the cooled milk mixture.

3. Mix in the vanilla, and beat well. Spread on a cooled cake.

COCONUT PECAN FROSTING

ENOUGH FOR A 9 × 13-INCH CAKE

1 cup sugar

1/2 cup (1 stick) butter

3 egg yolks

1 cup evaporated milk

1 cup chopped pecans

1 1/3 cups flaked coconut

1 capful vanilla extract

1. In a medium saucepan, combine the sugar, butter, egg yolks, and milk. Cook over medium heat, stirring constantly, until thickened.

2. Remove from heat, and stir in the pecans, coconut, and vanilla. Spread onto a cooled cake.

CREAM CHEESE FROSTING

In the country, kids learn about work early. It's not uncommon for six- and seven-year-olds to have their own chores feeding calves or chickens, cleaning pens, washing milkers, or even helping to unload hay—boys and girls alike. They also start early in the kitchen, and this no-fail frosting helps many gain confidence as they learn (see Note).

ENOUGH FOR A 9 × 13-INCH CAKE

8 ounces cream cheese

2 1/2 to 3 cups powdered sugar

1/2 cup (1 stick) butter

1 cup nutmeats (or not; I usually choose not)

1. Combine all the ingredients except the nutmeats.

2. Using an electric mixer, beat until smooth and fluffy. Blend in the nutmeats, if desired, and spread onto a cooled cake.

NOTE: This is a good one for Twos Pineapple Cake (page 175) and Lucky Friday's Carrot Cake (page 160).

ORANGE TOPPING FOR ANGEL FOOD CAKE

ENOUGH FOR 1 CAKE

1 tablespoon sugar

1 tablespoon cornstarch

1/2 cup orange juice

1/2 cup water

1 tablespoon butter

1. Mix the sugar and cornstarch together in a small saucepan. Add the orange juice and water, and stir until smooth.

2. Cook over medium heat until thick, stirring constantly. Remove from heat, add the butter, stir, and cool. Drizzle over the cake.

COCOA COCA-COLA FROSTING

ENOUGH FOR A 9 × 13-INCH CAKE

3 cups powdered sugar

1 cup toasted pecans

3 teaspoons cocoa

1/3 cup Coca-Cola (Classic)

1. Mix all together, and beat, using an electric mixer.

2. Spread onto a cooled cake.

NEVER-FAIL CHOCOLATE FROSTING

ENOUGH FOR A 9 × 13-INCH CAKE

1 can sweetened condensed milk

2 squares unsweetened chocolate

1 capful vanilla extract

1 tablespoon hot water

Pinch of salt

1. Cook the milk and chocolate in a small saucepan over low heat, stirring constantly until thick.

2. Add the vanilla, hot water, and salt. Stir together until nice and smooth and creamy.

3. Set aside to cool, then spread onto a cooled cake.

THICK FUDGE FROSTING

This you could fail on, but, oh, it's so good, it's worth the try.

ENOUGH FOR A 9 × 13-INCH CAKE

2 cups sugar

1/2 cup milk

1/4 cup corn syrup

2 squares unsweetened chocolate

Pinch of salt

1/2 cup (1 stick) butter

1 capful vanilla extract

1. Combine the sugar, milk, corn syrup, chocolate, and salt in a medium saucepan, and cook over medium heat until boiling, then boil 1 minute more.

2. Remove from heat, add the butter and vanilla, and let set until lukewarm (see Note).

3. Beat by hand until the right consistency to frost a cake (see Note).

NOTE: Be sure to cool it before you start beating it.

To make this really good, beat until your arms get tired.

FRESH WHIPPED CREAM

❊

On the farm, the goodness of your cream depends on how rich your cows are milking, and how your cows are milking depends, for the most part, on what they eat. My great grandfather and his friends first settled here because of the black soil, the clear water, and the endless unbroken ground. They thought they'd found heaven—"Come," they wrote back to the Old Country, "the grass is so fat it glistens." Today, for us, that grass and hay and corn still make the difference.

**MAKES ABOUT 2 CUPS
(ENOUGH TO COVER
A PIE OR CAKE)**

1 cup fresh cream or whipping cream
1/4 cup sugar
1 squirt vanilla extract

1. Pour a cup of fresh cream into a bowl and, using an electric mixer, beat on high speed until thick. (Don't go too far or you'll end up with butter.)

2. Turn the mixer on low, and gradually fold in the sugar and vanilla. Beat until the cream is fluffy and can stand in soft peaks. (Do not overbeat.)

CHOCOLATE WHIPPED CREAM: Add 1 tablespoon cocoa or 1 tablespoon chocolate syrup when beating in the sugar.

STRAWBERRY WHIPPED CREAM: Fold 2 tablespoons of fresh berries (enough to suit your taste) in with the sugar.

PINEAPPLE WHIPPED CREAM: Fold 2 tablespoons crushed pineapple in with the sugar. If not enough pineapple, add more according to your taste.

SEA FOAM FROSTING

❊

ENOUGH FOR A 9 × 13-INCH CAKE

1 1/2 cups packed brown sugar
1/4 cup milk
3 egg whites
1 capful vanilla extract

1. Cook the brown sugar and milk together in a medium saucepan over medium heat until it forms a soft ball when a few drops are dropped into cold water (see Note).

2. Meanwhile, beat the egg whites until stiff.

3. Slowly pour the hot mixture into the beaten egg whites, beating all the time with an electric mixer on high speed until light and fluffy. Blend in the vanilla, and spread onto the cake.

NOTE: To test for the soft- or hard-boiled stage, spoon a few drops into a little cold water and work with your fingertips to form either a soft- or hard-feeling ball.

BASIC POWDERED SUGAR FROSTING

Powdered sugar frosting most farm women can make in their sleep. But that doesn't mean it's so easy; you have to have sense, because powdered sugar isn't all the same. I don't know whether it's for more profit or what, but a lot of what you get today, there's no weight to it at all. It's like cotton, you take a hold of it and *poouff*. . . . It's so light, it gets sloppy; then, of course, you have to use more of it. So if you ever get a box that's lumpy and packed tight, consider yourself lucky; that's what real powdered sugar should be.

ENOUGH FOR A 9 × 13-INCH CAKE

¼ cup (½ stick) butter
¼ cup milk
2 cups powdered sugar
1 capful vanilla extract

1. Heat the butter and milk together in a small saucepan over medium heat.

2. Put the powdered sugar in a bowl, and pour the hot milk mixture over.

3. Add the vanilla, and beat well to remove all the lumps. If it's too thin, gradually add more powdered sugar.

CHOCOLATE FROSTING: Add 3 tablespoons of cocoa or 1 square of melted semisweet chocolate during step 1.

LEMON FROSTING: Add 1 teaspoon of lemon extract in place of the vanilla.

ALMOND FROSTING: Add ½ teaspoon of almond extract in place of the vanilla.

PEPPERMINT FROSTING: Use the variation above for Chocolate Frosting and add a little peppermint along with the vanilla. (This is very good on chocolate cake.)

MAPLE FROSTING: Add ¾ teaspoon of maple flavoring in place of the vanilla.

ORANGE FROSTING: Use 1 teaspoon of grated orange rind and ¼ cup of orange juice in place of the milk and the vanilla. Add more powdered sugar if not thick enough.

FOR COLORED FROSTING: If not feared, a few drops of food coloring will give you any color.

COOKIES

and

FRY CAKES

Cookies were always the old standby. In older days, there wasn't a farmhouse with a woman in it that didn't have a cookie jar of some kind or other. For a while, fancy store-bought cookie jars got to be the rage. Women scrimped and saved to have at least one bright-colored, clever plaster of paris pig, cow, rooster, carrot, clown, or big red apple. But once we'd satisfied ourselves with those pretty, city jars, we learned they were no good for keeping cookies. We left them empty on our shelves and went back to our earthenware or our old reliable syrup pails with tight tin covers.

Whatever jar we chose, it was never empty. We baked three batches at a time, and a batch was usually three or four dozen. When neighbors would come to visit, we might have to hurry to stir up a cake, but we could always count on being able to dig out a cookie.

Now, in this fast-paced world, even around here, it's hard to find a cookie jar in a kitchen. If people have cookies at all, they buy them and don't bother with a jar—they just leave them in the package they came in. They hardly pay attention to cookies. They buy 'em, and eat 'em, and don't even know if they're tasting the wrapper.

The batch of recipes I've included here are basic, trusty, hand-mixed farm cookies.

Hints for Cookies

• If you're new at this, before you bake the whole batch of cookies, test one first to see whether they're too rich. If you're using chocolate chips or nuts, and you've made the dough too rich, the nuts will stick up and everything else will run away all over the oven. Bake the tester about 10 minutes, but after 5 minutes take a look at it. You can see by that time if it's going to spread all over. If it is, that means you need more flour before you bake the whole batch and have yourself a mess.

• To get the best from a recipe, don't ever think of using an electric mixer; it doesn't work. To get cookies just right, you have to mix them by hand. But watch so you don't forget yourself and mix the daylights out of them or they'll separate and be no good.

• All the sugar here is white sugar unless otherwise specified. The flour is all-purpose flour.

• Don't leave the salt out of the recipes or your cookies will be no good. They'll be flat, and you could just as well not have bothered.

• When rolling and cutting cookies (or fry cakes), the cutter should be dipped into flour each time you cut one, so it won't stick to the dough.

• A lot of experts say "use only flat cookie sheets," but shoot, in the country, ten to twenty miles from town, you can't be that fussy. Lorraine and I, if we're in a pinch, we'll use whatever we have. Many times we've even baked cookies in a cake pan. "Well, then they won't brown right," some experts say, but we've never had any problem. We've made do like that for years, and we've never seen a difference. Just be sure to leave the cookies enough room to expand.

• If you're baking two sheets at a time, when the cookies start to get brown around the outside edges, exchange positions of the sheets. Just put one where the other was and vice versa about halfway (five to seven minutes) through the baking time, and the cookies will bake evenly. And don't have your rack too low, or they'll be brown on the bottom and sick on top. Bake them on the middle shelf.

• The cookie sheet doesn't need to be greased unless that's called for in the recipe.

• The biggest share of these recipes makes about three or four dozen, but, of course, it depends on how big they are when you drop them on the sheet or how big you cut them out, whether you want dainty little antlike things or hefty elephants—whether you're making little bitty ones for a special occasion or feeding hungry kids. Either way, these recipes will seldom yield less than the amount indicated.

• Use a pancake turner to remove the cookies from the sheet.

• Be careful how you store your cookies after they've cooled. I use either a tight gallon glass jar, or a tight metal tin. I don't like anything stored in plastic. With glass or metal, cookies keep as long as a month and so well that when you take off the cover, you can just smell their buttery freshness. Use plastic and you smell and taste the plastic. But if you're going to use metal, when you wash it, be sure to dry the creases around the bottom because if the container's wet and tightly closed, the cookies will absorb whatever liquid is left in there. And be sure the cookies are cooled completely before they're stored or they'll become soft and soggy. Cool them on a chopping block or cutting board, or on a stretch of wax paper. It's also good to line the bottom of the container with wax paper.

• Cookies are done when you touch a finger to them and you don't leave a dent. But if you're after a chewy cookie, watch them closely; you don't want them overbaked. You don't want them hard when you touch your finger to them.

• If the recipe says "flatten slightly," don't press down like a wild heifer or you'll get a hard rock. If a cookie's supposed to melt in your mouth and you flatten it too much, you'll have to bite into it and you might lose your teeth as you do. If it says "slightly," do slightly.

Cookies

WASHBOARD COOKIES

The one big mistake I ever made with cookies, I made with coconut. I hadn't been married long, and I'd hoarded and saved enough to make an old neighbor woman's recipe because I thought it sounded so good. I was nervous about the cost, so I was taking extra pains, but still the paper I'd written on said "2 cups shortening," so like a dummy, I put in two cups of shortening. Those cookies got so rich, I had a hard time getting them off the pan, but once they'd cooled, it was worse; I had to scrape them off the table. They were the richest things, and I felt so bad I could have bawled, but a peddler came along hollering that the cows were in the corn, so there was no time for that. Today, I still always think of those cookies. Now I would know better; you have to use common sense and kind of figure. If you see something like "5 teaspoons baking soda" or "1 tablespoon salt" or "2 cups butter" and not much more flour, you know you're headed for trouble.

MAKES 5 DOZEN

1/2 pound (2 sticks) butter

2 cups packed brown sugar

2 eggs

1/4 cup water

1 teaspoon vanilla extract

4 cups flour

1 1/2 teaspoons baking powder

1/2 teaspoon baking soda

1/2 teaspoon salt

1 cup flaked coconut

1. Preheat the oven to 375° F. Cream the butter and sugar together in a large bowl. Add the eggs and beat a little on the side before mixing in (enough to break the yolks and blend with the whites).

2. Add the water and vanilla, and mix.

3. Dump in the flour, baking powder, baking soda, salt, and coconut, and stir well.

4. Take just enough dough to equal the size of a whole, unshelled walnut, roll lengthwise, and press it down on a cookie sheet with a fork. (Leave the fork marks for a washboard effect.)

5. Bake for 10 to 12 minutes, until lightly brown.

WHITE FILLED FARM COOKIES

This is the classic farm cookie. I'd bet my life that there isn't anyone who grew up on a farm, or for that matter, in rural America, who doesn't remember the white filled cookie. They're white with a gold hue and have soft, fat little bellies that are filled with either dates or raisins. I love them, and they're a good seller at the restaurant.

MAKES 50 OR 60 (SEE NOTE)

2 cups sugar

1/2 pound (2 sticks) butter

1 cup Butter Flavor Crisco

2 eggs, well beaten

2 cups sour cream

2 teaspoons baking soda

1 teaspoon salt

4 cups flour

1 cup flour for rolling out

FILLING FOR COOKIES

2 cups dates

1/2 cup sugar

3 tablespoons flour

1 cup boiling water

1. Preheat the oven to 350° F. Cream the sugar, butter, and shortening together in a large bowl; add the eggs, and mix.

2. Add the sour cream, and stir well.

3. Add the baking soda, salt, and flour, and stir together real good.

4. Pat the dough out on a floured board or table, and roll out to 1/8 inch thick, using a rolling pin (see Note).

5. Cut out with a round cookie cutter, and place on a cookie sheet.

6. *To prepare the filling:* Put the ingredients in a medium saucepan over medium heat, and boil

until thick, being careful not to scorch it. Cool.

7. Take a dab of filling, and drop it in the middle of the cookie. Put another cookie on top, and press the edges together with a fork or your finger to seal. Or like my mother, just fill half the cookie and flop the other half over to cover the filling, and seal around the edges. You get a half cookie.

8. Bake for 12 minutes, until light brown.

NOTE: This makes a larger batch of a softer white cookie than the Brown Sugar Filled Cookies (page 200).

For a chewier cookie, roll the dough to 1/4 inch thick.

WHITE SUGAR COOKIES

❄

You will need a 3½-inch cookie cutter for this recipe.

MAKES 60 COOKIES

3 cups flour

1 cup sugar

1 teaspoon salt

1 cup butter

1 teaspoon baking soda

1 teaspoon cream of tartar

2 eggs

3 tablespoons milk

1 teaspoon vanilla

1. Preheat oven to 375°F. Mix together the flour, sugar, salt, butter, baking soda, and cream of tartar as you would pie crust. Using

→

clean fingers, work until you get a crumbly mixture (don't overmix).

2. Add the eggs, milk, and vanilla. Mix together by hand.

3. Pat the dough down onto a floured table or breadboard. Roll flat with a rolling pin to ⅛ inch thick (for a chewier cookie, roll to ¼ inch thick). Cut with the cookie cutter.

4. Bake for 10 minutes, or until lightly browned.

OLD-FASHIONED HEARTY OATMEAL RAISIN COOKIES

MAKES QUITE A FEW COOKIES, ABOUT 4 DOZEN

> 2 cups raisins
>
> 1 cup water
>
> 1 cup shortening (half butter and half Butter Flavor Crisco)
>
> 2 cups sugar
>
> 1 capful vanilla extract
>
> 3 eggs
>
> 2 cups old-fashioned Quaker oats (not quick cook)
>
> 2 cups flour
>
> 1 teaspoon baking powder
>
> 1 teaspoon baking soda
>
> 1½ teaspoons ground cinnamon
>
> ¼ teaspoon ground nutmeg
>
> ¼ teaspoon ground allspice
>
> ½ teaspoon salt

1. Preheat the oven to 375° F. In a small saucepan, boil the raisins in water for 5 minutes or so, and drain, saving 5 tablespoons of the raisin juice. Let cool.

2. Cream the shortening and sugar together in a large bowl. Add the vanilla, eggs, and cooled raisin juice.

3. In a separate bowl, mix together the oats, flour, baking powder, baking soda, cinnamon, nutmeg, allspice, and salt. Blend with the raisin mixture and drop by rounded teaspoonfuls onto a lightly buttered cookie sheet (see Note).

4. Bake for 12 to 15 minutes, until a finger doesn't leave a dent.

NOTE: These have rounded, not flat, tops.

BROWN SUGAR FILLED COOKIES

MAKES 3 DOZEN

> 1½ cups packed brown sugar
>
> ¾ cup butter or lard
>
> 2 eggs, well beaten
>
> 1 teaspoon baking soda
>
> ¼ cup hot water
>
> 1 teaspoon vanilla extract
>
> 3 teaspoons cream of tartar
>
> 3½ cups flour and a little more for rolling out
>
> Filling for Cookies (page 199)

1. Preheat the oven to 350° F. Cream the sugar and the shortening together in a large bowl, and add the eggs.

2. Dissolve the baking soda in hot water, then dump it into the sugar mixture with the vanilla, and mix.

3. Add the cream of tartar and 3½ cups flour, and stir together well, using a wooden spoon.

4. Pat onto a floured board or table, and roll out with a rolling pin to ⅛ inch thick (see Note).

5. Cut the cookies with a round cookie cutter, and place them on a cookie sheet.

6. Prepare the Filling for Cookies. Take 1 teaspoon of cooled filling, and drop it in the center of one cookie. Put another cookie on top, and press the edges together with a fork or your fingers to seal.

7. Bake for 12 minutes, until light brown.

N O T E : For a chewier cookie, roll the dough to ¼ inch thick.

OLD-TIME CHUNKY CHOCOLATE CHIP COOKIES

It's hard to imagine, as basic as chocolate chip cookies are now, what a rarity they were to farm folks. Way back, women seldom made any cookies but white, rolled molasses, honey, or ammonia. They were the four we relied on, because they didn't require what was considered delicacies—no fancy nuts or even dates. Unless we'd been saving and saving, we stuck to basics. At home, my mom and dad would sometimes splurge and buy peppermint sticks, or coconut, or chocolate, or nutmeats—and at the minister's there were even maraschino cherries—but after I was married, I found out where money came from. Those items weren't only delicacies but the stuff of dreams. With what little time I had for indulgence or fancy, I longed to make these cookies.

M A K E S 3½ D O Z E N

½ pound (2 sticks) butter

¾ cup packed brown sugar

¾ cup white sugar

2 beaten eggs

1 teaspoon baking soda in 1 teaspoon hot water

2¼ cups flour

1 teaspoon salt

1 cup chopped nuts

1 (7-ounce) bar semisweet chocolate, cut up into small pieces

1 teaspoon vanilla extract

1. Preheat the oven to 375° F. Cream the butter and sugars together.

2. Add the eggs and baking soda and water, and mix well.

3. Add the flour, salt, nuts, chocolate pieces, and vanilla.

4. Drop by teaspoonfuls onto a cookie sheet, and bake 12 to 15 minutes, until a finger doesn't leave a dent.

HONEY COOKIES

MAKES ABOUT 90

2 cups sugar

2 cups honey

5 eggs

2 tablespoons cream of tartar

2 tablespoons baking soda

Flour for kneading

Basic Powdered Sugar Frosting (page 193)

1. Preheat the oven to 350° F. Stir the sugar, honey, and eggs together in a large bowl, and add the cream of tartar and baking soda.

2. Add enough flour to knead. Then knead and put into the refrigerator overnight; the next day, roll out ¼ inch thick.

3. Cut with a doughnut cutter (see Note). Bake about 15 minutes, until a finger doesn't leave a dent. Cool, and frost with Basic Powdered Sugar Frosting, as needed.

NOTE: If you don't have a doughnut cutter, use either a water glass or a cookie cutter, then cut the center hole with a thimble. The hole in these does not have to be stretched. It doesn't matter if it closes.

SUPERDUPER CRISPY GINGERSNAPS

If done right, these cookies snap when you break 'em; if they don't, they're no good. But sad to say, today they never get quite as good with vegetable shortening as they did with home-rendered lard. Butter Flavor Crisco is the closest you can come to that now in flavor, but you mustn't forget the salt.

MAKES 3½ DOZEN

¾ cup Butter Flavor Crisco or good-tasting lard

1 cup sugar

½ cup molasses

1 egg, well beaten

2 cups flour

½ teaspoon salt

2 teaspoons baking soda

1 teaspoon ground cinnamon

1 teaspoon ground cloves

1 teaspoon ground ginger

Sugar for rolling

1. Preheat the oven to 375° F. Cream the shortening and sugar together in a large bowl, add the molasses and well-beaten egg.

2. Using a wooden spoon, work in the flour, salt, baking soda, cinnamon, cloves, and ginger, and then mix well, using your hands.

3. Roll into 1-inch balls, dip one side in sugar, put on a buttered cookie sheet, and bake for 15 minutes, until they have little cracks like creeks running through them.

KROT (PORK RIND) COOKIES

For this recipe, take krot from Home-Rendered Lard (page 257) and grind enough to fill one cup.

MAKES 3½ DOZEN OR SO

1 cup krot
1½ cups sugar
2 eggs
1 cup sweet milk
1 teaspoon vanilla or lemon extract
3 cups flour
1 teaspoon baking powder
1 teaspoon baking soda

1. Preheat the oven to 375° F. Combine the krot, sugar, eggs, milk, and extract in a large bowl, and mix well, using a spoon.

2. Add the flour, baking powder, and baking soda. Stir together thoroughly, and form into balls. Drop onto a cookie sheet, and flatten slightly. Bake for 10 minutes, until lightly browned.

AMMONIA COOKIES

Talk about Old Faithful, this was one of those basic standbys every farm lady made. Now hardly anyone's heard of such a thing—"Ammonia cookies? Yuk!" today's young ones say. But for us, they were a treat. They're dandy cookies. Just be sure you get baking ammonia and not the cleaning agent ammonia or you'll have a problem on your hands (you must go to a drugstore and get the baking ammonia and oil of lemon).

**MAKES QUITE A LARGE BATCH
(ABOUT 5 OR 6 DOZEN
DEPENDING ON SIZE)**

2 cups sugar
1 cup lard
3 eggs
3 tablespoons baking ammonia
1¼ cups milk
1 teaspoon oil of lemon
Flour to make plenty hard

1. Preheat the oven to 350° F. Mix the sugar and lard together in a large bowl. Add the eggs, baking ammonia, milk, and oil of lemon. Add the flour until plenty thick and firm. Knead into a ball, and roll out quite thick (¼ to ½ inch). Roll the dough oblong, and cut it with a knife (you do not use a cookie cutter) to make 3-inch squares. Poke holes with a fork to make a design on top.

2. Bake at least 15 minutes, until brown.

DARK ROLLED MOLASSES COOKIES

MAKES 50

3/4 cup shortening

1 1/2 cups sugar

3/4 cup molasses

2 eggs

3 teaspoons baking soda

1/4 cup hot water

1 teaspoon ground ginger

1 teaspoon ground cinnamon

4 cups flour

Sugar to sprinkle over

1. Preheat the oven to 375° F. Cream the shortening and sugar together in a large bowl, add the molasses, and mix.

2. Push the dough to the side of the bowl; add the eggs and slightly beat them with a whisk before mixing in.

3. Dissolve the baking soda in the hot water, add it to the dough, and blend well.

4. Dump in the ginger, cinnamon, and flour, and work in well using a wooden spoon. Chill the dough for a while, then pat it onto a floured board or table, roll out with a rolling pin, and cut with a cookie cutter.

5. Place on a cookie sheet, sprinkle with sugar, and bake for 10 minutes, until done (this will depend on how thick you've rolled them). And remember, all of them will not be done at once unless you're awfully darn perfect, so put the thicker ones back in the oven until a finger leaves no dent.

SISTER SALLY ANN COOKIES

When I was a kid, we'd wait to go to town to trail after Mom into the grocery store. That was a paradise to us. All the shiny colors and sweet smells, and a clerk who paid us kind attention. Most remarkable, though, was that they sold cookies and candy in bulk. There were Sally Anns, washboards, gingersnaps, and chocolate salerno, all in big boxes with glass covers. These "town cookies" were an extravagance to country folks. We didn't get them except maybe around Christmas or the Fourth of July when Mom or Dad were in a rare mood, but if your family bought a large order of groceries, sometimes the clerk would come around the counter, reach into one of the boxes, and hold out his hand offering what we thought was too good to be true. I suppose nowadays city people would think it awful unsanitary or be afraid of poisoning—cyanide, strychnine, razor blades, slivered glass—but back then, clerks kept their eye out and doing harm like that would never occur to anyone.

I have moments when I wish those days were back. I'd rather go into a little store and go on this side and get my dry goods, and go down there and get my groceries, and go over here and get my shoes, and go home. Back then, the local Farmers' Store had it all: our fabric, bedding, groceries, appliances, cologne, work shoes, dress shoes, and men's overalls—sizes 13 to 52. Going to these modern stores today and walking your darn feet off to go get stuff, it's crazy. You go in one end of the mall and come out the other, and what've you got? You look at the stuff, and you think, "Ah, I don't want that, and I don't want that." I'd rather have less to choose from and have quality and friendliness you can count on. And maybe even one of these old-fashioned Sally Ann Cookies, with thick, soft white frosting, from a clerk who thinks I look like a nice girl.

MAKES 45

1 cup Butter Flavor Crisco

1 cup sugar

2 eggs

1 cup molasses

2 teaspoons baking soda

1 tablespoon hot water (approximately)

5 1/2 to 6 cups flour (depends on your flour)

2 teaspoons ground cinnamon

1/4 teaspoon ground cloves

1 teaspoon ground ginger

Pinch of salt

1/2 cup hot coffee

GELATIN FROSTING

1 envelope Knox gelatin

1 cup cold water

1 cup white sugar

2 cups powdered sugar

1/2 teaspoon baking powder

1 teaspoon vanilla extract

1. Preheat the oven to 350° F. Cream the shortening together with the sugar in a large bowl.

2. Push the dough to the side of the bowl, break the eggs into the bowl, beat them with a whisk, and add the molasses. Combine with the sugar and the shortening mixture.

3. Dissolve the baking soda in the hot water and add it with 5 1/2 cups of flour, cinnamon, cloves, ginger, salt, and hot coffee. Mix well, using a wooden spoon. (Add more flour if the dough is too soft; the dough should be smooth and not real sticky.)

4. Put onto a floured board or table, and roll out with a rolling pin to 1/4 inch thick. Cut these cookies out with an empty Spam can (see Note). Bake for 10 to 12 minutes, until a finger doesn't leave a dent.

5. *To prepare the frosting:* Dissolve the gelatin in the cold water, then put it in a small saucepan and add the white sugar. Bring to a boil on medium heat, and cook slowly for 10 minutes (or a little less; see Note).

6. While this is cooking, combine the powdered sugar, baking powder, and vanilla in a medium bowl.

7. Remove the gelatin mixture from heat, pour it over the powdered sugar mixture, and beat with an electric mixer until the frosting gets like stiffly beaten egg whites. (Be patient; it will take a while, 10 minutes or longer.)

8. When the cookies have cooled, flip them upside down, and frost lavishly using a table knife or butter spreader.

NOTE: Don't worry if these are not uniform; unevenness is what makes them "homemade."

This frosting is supposed to be thick, and it takes forever to whip it up, but don't cook it too long—err under rather than over in the cooking or it'll get hard and crunchy.

ORANGE PECAN JUMBLES

"I pledge my head to clearer thinking, my heart to greater loyalty, my hands to larger service, my health to better living, for my club, my community, my country, and my world." That's the 4-H pledge, and I can't tell you how many tiny farm kids struggle to learn it. 4-H is a big thing here; it gives parents and kids alike a chance to get together and breaks up the routine of outdoor chores. In summer, there's always a fair and each child has at least one project that's entered and judged in a cattle ring or large tent. They might raise and train a calf or a goat or lamb or pig or rabbit, or grow vegetables, or bake a cake or cookies. When my kids were young, they were always convinced that the judges for baking were city folks who cared more about the way the cookies looked than how they tasted. In our old country kitchens, we never fussed—if the cookies weren't uniform—if one got a little oblong or square, or one was a little browner than another—we didn't think anything of it as long as it tasted all right and the family had something to chew on and dunk in its milk or coffee. But getting ready for that fair was different. The kids worked to find four or five cookies exactly alike, then practically wore them out rearranging them on the prettiest plate they could find. Many a judge tasted these orange pecan jumbles. In fact, my grandchildren are still entering them, and they're still a favorite.

MAKES 2½ DOZEN

½ cup sugar

½ cup (1 stick) butter

1 egg

1¼ cups flour

¼ teaspoon baking soda

1 teaspoon vanilla extract

½ teaspoon salt

2 teaspoons grated orange rind

½ cup pecan halves

1. Preheat the oven to 350° F. Cream the sugar and butter together in a large bowl, add the egg, and mix until fluffy.

2. Add the flour, baking soda, vanilla, salt, and orange rind, and mix well, using a wooden spoon.

3. Drop from a teaspoon onto a cookie sheet, and place a pecan half on each cookie. Bake for 12 to 15 minutes, until a finger doesn't leave a dent.

DATE DROP COOKIES: Add 1 cup of cut-up dates (wet scissors work well) to the above recipe.

LEMON DROP COOKIES

MAKES 3 DOZEN

1/2 cup (1 stick) butter

3/4 cup sugar

1 egg

2 cups flour

1/2 teaspoon baking soda

1 teaspoon baking powder

1/2 teaspoon cream of tartar

1 cup crushed lemon drops (see Note)

Sugar for dipping

1. Preheat the oven to 350° F. Cream the butter and the sugar together in a large bowl, push it to the side of the bowl, drop in the egg, and beat it slightly with a whisk. Then mix all together.

2. Stir in the flour, baking soda, baking powder, cream of tartar, and crushed lemon drops, and keep stirring until well mixed.

3. Make a ball the size of a whole unshelled walnut, and flatten it, using a water glass dipped in sugar.

4. Bake 10 to 12 minutes, until lightly browned.

NOTE: To crush the lemon drops, put them into a plastic bag and smash with a hammer.

ICEBOX COOKIES

MAKES ABOUT 48

1 cup white sugar

1 cup packed brown sugar

1 cup shortening

3 eggs, well beaten

1 pound peanuts, chopped

2 teaspoons baking soda

1 tablespoon ground cinnamon

5 cups flour

1. Preheat the oven to 375° F. Cream the sugars and shortening together in a large bowl, and add the eggs and peanuts.

2. Stir in the baking soda, cinnamon, and flour, and mix well, using your fingers.

3. Divide the dough into 4 portions, shape into rolls about 2 inches in diameter, wrap in wax paper, and put in the refrigerator overnight.

4. When you are ready to bake, remove them from the refrigerator, slice the rolls 1/4 inch thick, and bake about 10 minutes, until your finger doesn't leave a dent.

CHOCOLATE SANDWICH COOKIES

❈

Oh, these were good! They have a better flavor, but these were our Oreo cookies before we'd ever heard the word *Oreo*. We rolled them all out and baked them, frosted one, and plopped on another. It was a lot of fussing, but we looked forward to it as something very, very special.

MAKES 36

½ cup (1 stick) butter

1 cup sugar

2 eggs, well beaten

1 tablespoon thin cream

3 squares unsweetened chocolate, melted

2¼ cups flour

⅓ teaspoon ground cinnamon

1½ teaspoons baking powder

¼ teaspoon baking soda

Basic Powdered Sugar Frosting (page 193)

1. Preheat the oven to 375° F. Cream the butter and sugar together in a large bowl. Add the eggs, cream, and chocolate, and mix well.

2. Stir in the flour, cinnamon, baking powder, and baking soda, and work well.

3. Pat onto a floured board or table, roll out (about ⅛ inch thick), and cut with a small cookie cutter or a fruit glass.

4. Bake for 10 minutes, until a finger doesn't leave a dent.

5. Make the Basic Powdered Sugar Frosting, and spread between two baked cookies.

PINWHEELS

❈

MAKES 4 DOZEN OR SO

1 cup shortening (Butter Flavor Crisco is best here)

2 cups packed brown sugar

3 eggs

1 teaspoon vanilla extract

1 teaspoon baking soda

1 teaspoon cream of tartar

4 cups flour

¼ teaspoon salt

PINWHEEL FILLING

1 cup dates, cut fine

½ cup sugar

½ cup water

1. Preheat the oven to 375° F. Cream the shortening and sugar together in a large bowl. Add the eggs and vanilla, and mix until fluffy.

2. Stir in the baking soda, cream of tartar, flour, and salt, using a wooden spoon, and keep stirring until well mixed.

3. Pat the dough onto a floured board or table, and roll out oblong, to about ¼ inch thick. (If it is too much dough to handle easily, divide the dough in half before you roll it.)

4. *To prepare the filling:* Mix all filling ingredients in a small saucepan. Boil until thick. Cool.

5. Spread the filling over the dough, then roll up as you would a jelly roll (page 179).

6. Chill until firm, and slice ¼ inch thick.

7. Bake until light brown (12 to 15 minutes).

STURDY WHEAT COOKIES

We made these cookies during World War II. Stores started carrying this hearty, grainy cereal, and women put their heads together on how to stretch it beyond breakfast. We came up with this recipe, only we used lard. The men went for this new concoction, and we were proud of ourselves, of course.

MAKES 4 DOZEN

1/2 cup shortening

1 cup packed brown sugar

1/2 cup white sugar

2 eggs, beaten

2 tablespoons sour milk

1 teaspoon vanilla extract

1/2 teaspoon salt

1 teaspoon baking soda

1 teaspoon baking powder

2 cups flour

1 cup Sturdy Wheat cereal (see Note)

2/3 cup chopped peanuts or 2/3 cup shredded coconut

1. Preheat the oven to 375° F. Cream the shortening and sugars together in a large bowl. Add the eggs, milk, vanilla, and salt, and beat a few minutes, using a wooden spoon.

2. Add the baking soda, baking powder, flour, Sturdy Wheat, and peanuts or coconut. Mix lightly, and drop by rounded teaspoonfuls onto a buttered cookie sheet.

3. Bake for 10 to 12 minutes, until lightly browned.

NOTE: If Sturdy Wheat is not available, use any coarsely ground wheat cereal such as Elam's Cracked Wheat. In a pinch, you might even try Malto-Meal.

ROOSEVELT COOKIES

Why these are called Roosevelt Cookies I don't know. I've been making these since I was ten years old; he was president then, so I suppose it was a tribute.

MAKES 2½ DOZEN

1 cup powdered sugar

2½ cups flour

1/4 teaspoon baking soda

1/2 teaspoon salt

1 scant cup butter

1 teaspoon vanilla extract

1 egg

1/2 cup chopped nutmeats (or not)

1. Preheat the oven to 375° F. Mix the powdered sugar, flour, baking soda, and salt together in a large bowl. Add the butter, and mix, using your fingers.

2. Using a wooden spoon, stir in the vanilla and egg, and mix well. Stir in the chopped nutmeats, if desired.

3. Make 1-inch balls, and press them onto a cookie sheet.

4. Bake 12 minutes, until lightly browned.

THRILL-ME DATE COOKIES

These cookies, with their name, always remind me of one of my best friends from country school. At sixteen, we hadn't been out much; and things were different then—we didn't know so much about the world at such a young age. Anyway, there were dances at the city hall in Osseo, and this city boy, Chester Fiedler, who always got to drive his father's shiny green Overland, asked my friend to go for a ride. All the girls were crazy about Chester, so she left me and went, but it didn't last long. They didn't drive far before he stopped and said, "How would you like to get in the backseat?"

"No. That's okay," she said. "If you don't mind, I'll just sit up here with you."

MAKES ABOUT 4 DOZEN

FILLING

2 cups chopped dates

1 cup water

1/2 cup sugar

COOKIES

1 cup Butter Flavor Crisco

1 cup sugar

1/2 cup sour milk

3 cups Quaker oats (or quick-cooking oats)

1 teaspoon baking soda

2 cups flour

Dash of ground nutmeg

1. *To prepare the filling:* Combine the ingredients in a medium saucepan on medium heat, and cook until thick. (Be careful not to burn it. Watch closely, and stir.) Remove from heat, and cool (see Note).

2. *To prepare the cookies:* Preheat the oven to 375° F. Cream the shortening and sugar together in a large bowl. Add the sour milk, and mix.

3. Add the oats, baking soda, flour, and nutmeg, and mix well, using your fingers. Roll out very thin on a floured board or table, and cut with a round cutter. Bake 8 to 10 minutes, until lightly browned. Cool.

4. Spread the cooled filling between 2 cooled cookies, and press together.

NOTE: For these cookies, do the filling first. If you wish, the filling can be kept in a tightly covered container in the refrigerator and spread on when serving.

RUSSIAN TEA CAKES

I learned to make these at the minister's. They're a lot of monkey work, but you can't beat 'em for goodness. They're a special-occasion cookie; we made them for baptisms or weddings, or when someone was coming in to get advice from the preacher. Use them today too when you entertain; they'll go over just as good.

**MAKES QUITE A FEW; FOR A
10 × 15-INCH JELLY ROLL PAN**

½ *pound (2 sticks) butter*

2 *cups sugar*

4 *eggs*

1 *cup chopped almonds*

1 *teaspoon almond flavoring*

4 *cups flour*

1 *teaspoon baking powder*

½ *teaspoon salt*

1. Preheat the oven to 350° F. Cream the butter and sugar together in a large bowl.

2. Add the eggs one at a time, beating after each addition, using a wooden spoon.

3. Stir in the almonds and the flavoring, then the flour, baking powder, and salt, and mix well.

4. Pour into a 12 × 15-inch jelly roll pan, and bake for 30 minutes, or until a toothpick comes out dry.

5. Take the pan out of the oven, let set a few minutes, then, using a knife, cut into finger-shaped pieces the length of a finger. Place onto another jelly roll pan, leaving space between the pieces, and bake again in the oven. Turn, using a fork and your fingers, until the cookies are toasted and lightly browned. (Be sure to toast on both sides.)

Hints for Fry Cakes

• You can't stir up fry cakes and then let them stand before you roll them out and fry them, or they'll fall. When you roll one out and put it in hot grease, it should pop up so it gets nice and thick. When they're left to stand, they won't do that; they get skinny because they don't have much raising left in 'em—they've raised already in the bowl so maybe the bottom will be flat and just the top will raise. So stir them up, roll 'em out, and fry 'em right away. If, though, for some reason, you get interrupted and just have to stop, stick the batter in the refrigerator; that will help.

• Be careful with fry cakes so you don't put in much extra flour when you roll them out. You have to knead in a little, but don't mix in too much or they'll become firm, and you'll ruin your good dough.

• After you've cut the fry cakes (making sure to dip the cutter and thimble in flour each time you cut), be careful with the first batch because they're very soft and tender when you put them into the grease. Handle them deftly so they don't stretch all out. The second rolling they have more flour in so you have to stretch them, but the first time, watch, or you'll have Gumby. Pick them up gently off the board—

underneath—with your fingers, and lay them into the grease. (If you drop them, they'll splatter.) Get as close to the grease as you can without putting your fingers into it. Go slowly at first; you'll get the hang of it and eventually you'll probably be able to do three or four in one reach.

• How thick you roll and cut them doesn't have anything to do with the flavor, but you want 'em to look nice. If you roll 'em too thin, they're going to get skinny. If you want a thick doughnut, roll 'em a little thicker. If you're new at this, experiment. I find one-half inch (before frying) is ideal.

• To make sure the grease is hot enough before frying, take a little ball of dough (the hole will do), and gently lay it into the grease, and see if it comes right back up to the top. If it does, the grease is ready. If it lays in the bottom, wait, or you're going to get some soggy, grease-soaked doughnuts.

• A big, black cast-iron pan is the best for fry cakes—the bigger, the better. Ours at the restaurant fries eighteen cakes at a time. Whatever you use, be sure it's heavy. Some substitute a deep well cooker or French fryer, but to make these look and taste right, try cast iron.

• By the time you get the last ones into the hot grease, the first ones are ready to turn. The sooner you turn 'em, the fluffier they'll get; they won't get flat on the bottom. When you drop 'em in, they'll sink, but turn 'em over the minute they come to the top. It's a busy job keeping up.

• You can't beat home-rendered lard for fry cakes, but as I say, don't use store-bought lard. Unless you find an old-time meat market or render the lard yourself, the only substitute to use these days for fry cakes is peanut oil. (Vegetable oils can have a sweet flavor to them and give fry cakes an off-taste.)

• To turn the fry cakes over, we use two wooden spoon handles—one in each hand. Then when you take the cakes out, you put one handle in the hole and the other against the outside. When you have them out of the grease, you can pile so many on the one handle and let them drain and then shake off the excess oil before laying them down on paper towels.

• Doughnut cutters tend to be flat these days, so keep your eye out for an old-time, good one—the thicker (deeper), the better. But whatever you can come up with will do.

• I eat a couple of fry cakes while I'm making 'em because that's the best time. Fry cakes are great to serve warm; there's nothing like it, so treat yourself. The holes are good too.

• Fry cakes freeze beautifully if you freeze them as soon as they've cooled. Seal them in tight, plastic bags and put them in the freezer. You'll be surprised how fresh they'll keep. But when you take the bag out of the freezer, don't go setting the doughnuts out on a plate right away. Leave the bag sealed, throw it on the counter, and forget about it until it's thawed. Always thaw fry cakes in the container they've been frozen in, and they won't dry out as easily; they'll stay moist.

Fry Cakes

Fry cakes are the old-fashioned doughnuts made from nonyeast dough. My mother made fry cakes with a Calumet baking powder can to cut them out, and her sewing thimble to make the hole. They rose from flat dough as they fried, and filled the kitchen with a sweet aroma.

(For Raised Doughnuts, see page 11.)

FRY CAKE BATTER
❈

BIG·BATCH RECIPE (6 DOZEN)

Enough lard or peanut oil to fill a pan ¹/₂ inch from the top

2 cups sugar

1 teaspoon salt

¹/₂ teaspoon ground nutmeg

1 teaspoon ground mace

6 eggs

6 tablespoons melted butter

2 cups buttermilk

1 tablespoon baking soda

2 teaspoons baking powder

1 teaspoon vanilla extract

6 cups flour

SMALL·BATCH RECIPE (3 DOZEN)

Enough lard or peanut oil to fill a pan ¹/₂ inch from the top

1 cup sugar

1 teaspoon salt

¹/₄ teaspoon ground nutmeg

¹/₂ teaspoon ground mace

2 eggs

3 tablespoons melted butter

1 cup buttermilk

1 teaspoon baking soda

1 teaspoon baking powder

1 teaspoon vanilla extract

3¹/₂ cups flour (no more)

1. Fill an old cast-iron fry pan with home-rendered lard or peanut oil to ¹/₂ inch from the top. Heat, so later when a doughnut hole is dropped in, it will quickly turn brown.

2. Using your fingers, mix the sugar, salt, nutmeg, and mace together in a small bowl. Add the eggs, and beat well. Add the melted butter, and mix. Add the buttermilk, and mix thoroughly. Then add the baking soda, baking powder, vanilla, and flour; stir again.

3. Pour the dough onto a well-floured table (you may have to work extra flour in before you can roll). Roll to ¹/₂ inch thick, then cut with a doughnut cutter (see Note). Carefully place into the hot grease, and fry until the cake comes to the top. Turn over and brown the other side. Turn again when brown, and fry until golden brown.

NOTE: When rerolling dough, stretch the doughnut holes a little before frying.

CHOCOLATE FRY CAKES

MAKES 4 DOZEN CAKES

3 eggs, well beaten

1¼ cups sugar

3 squares unsweetened chocolate, melted

1 teaspoon vanilla

1 cup milk

4 cups flour

1 teaspoon salt

4 teaspoons baking powder

1. Prepare the grease as for fry cakes (page 213).

2. To the beaten eggs, add the sugar; beat thoroughly. Stir in the melted chocolate and the vanilla, and blend well.

3. Add the milk, flour, salt, and baking powder, and keep stirring until thoroughly blended. Chill the dough for 1 hour.

4. Cut and fry (chocolate burns easily, so be careful not to overcook the mixture).

Fry Cake Frostings

and Toppings

BASIC VANILLA FROSTING

FOR 2 DOZEN DOUGHNUTS

¼ cup rich whole milk or half-and-half

1 tablespoon butter

2 cups powdered sugar

1 capful vanilla extract

1. Heat the milk and butter in a small saucepan, pour it over the powdered sugar in a mixing bowl, and add the vanilla.

2. Stir like you've never stirred before, until it's like heavy whipped cream. If too thick, add a few drops of cream.

CHOCOLATE FROSTING: Melt ½ square of unsweetened chocolate, and mix it into the Basic Vanilla Frosting in step 1. Whip until well blended.

LEMON FROSTING: Grate 1 teaspoon of lemon rind, and mix it into the Basic Vanilla Frosting with a drop or two of yellow food coloring (if not feared) in step 1. Whip well.

ORANGE FROSTING: Grate 1 teaspoon of orange rind, and mix it into the Basic Vanilla Frosting recipe in step 1, and whip well.

PEANUT TOPPING: Spread ¾ cup of finely chopped peanuts out on a plate. Frost the cakes with the Basic Vanilla Frosting, and dip the frosted side into the chopped nuts.

COCONUT TOPPING: Frost the fry cakes with the Basic Vanilla Frosting. Spread flaked coconut out on a plate, and dip the frosted side in the coconut.

CHOCOLATE-WALNUT TOPPING: Frost the fry cakes with the Chocolate Frosting variation. Spread ¼ cup of finely chopped walnuts out on a plate and dip the frosted side in the nuts.

POWDERED SUGAR FRY CAKES: Dump 1 cup of powdered sugar into a paper sack. Drop 3 fry cakes in the sack at a time, twirl the top of the sack so it's tight, and shake gently (not too hard or you'll break the cakes all to pieces).

WHITE SUGAR FRY CAKES: Dump 1 cup of white sugar into a paper sack, drop in 3 fry cakes at a time, twist the top of the sack so it's tight, and shake gently.

WHITE SUGAR AND CINNAMON FRY CAKES: Dump 1 cup white sugar and ½ teaspoon ground cinnamon into a paper sack, drop in 3 fry cakes at a time, twist the top of the sack so it's tight, and shake gently.

FOR DOUGHNUT MAKER

MAKES 4 DOZEN

Enough lard or peanut oil to fill a pan ½ inch from the top

2 *whole eggs*

3 *egg yolks*

1¾ *cups sugar*

1 *teaspoon salt*

2 *cups buttermilk*

4 *cups flour*

1 *teaspoon baking soda*

3 *teaspoons baking powder*

Dash of ground nutmeg

¾ *teaspoon ground mace*

1 *teaspoon vanilla extract*

1. Fill an old cast-iron fry pan with home-rendered lard or peanut oil to ½ inch from the top of the pan. Heat until a doughnut hole or a crust of bread thrown in turns brown.

2. Mix the whole eggs, egg yolks, sugar, and salt in a large bowl. Whip with a whisk.

3. Stir in the buttermilk. Add the flour, baking soda, baking powder, nutmeg, mace, and vanilla, and mix well.

4. Spoon into a doughnut maker, and fry until the doughnut comes to the top (see Note). Turn over and brown on the other side. Turn again when brown, and fry until both sides are golden.

NOTE: Hold the doughnut maker close to the oil when dropping the batter in, so the doughnuts don't get drip points.

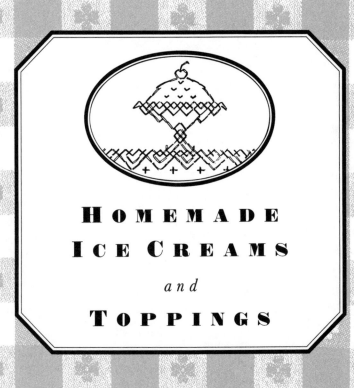

HOMEMADE ICE CREAMS
and
TOPPINGS

Ice was a precious commodity in the days before refrigerators. There were a few refrigerators available, but they were either gas or they ran on a generator and cost just about what they do now, only back then, in these parts, a dollar was two days' wages for a grown man. But almost every community had what we called an "ice shack." In the winter months, men would go out on the lake with a handsaw or some machine they'd rigged up, and they'd cut and cut and cut 16-inch square blocks all day long. Someone would pile them up, and when the stack got so high, it was hauled away to the icehouse. There the blocks were packed in sawdust so thick, it's hard to believe, but that ice lasted through even the dog days of August. In town you got regular ice deliveries from the ice wagon, but country folks had to go in to town to the icehouse and pick it up. We'd have to keep the sawdust around it, then give it a good washing at the pump when we got it home. We'd tote it down to the cellar with us, and we'd sit there and make ice cream where it was cool. We'd make three or four batches because we were usually so excited we invited the neighbors. We were always ready to gobble it down before it was made, but we had to sit there and crank and crank at a steady pace till our arms were ready to drop off.

The old ice cream makers with the wooden paddles are hard to beat, but there are a few good new models available now that make the job a lot easier (page 261). Most of these recipes will work in today's machines, but use your sense in making any adjustments necessary for your brand or model. But there are also recipes here that don't require a machine because there were a lot of folks even in my day who didn't have them.

Ice Creams

BOSS'S VANILLA ICE CREAM

We lived on a forty-acre farm when I was little, and my dad bought another farm a little ways down the road, but it didn't have a barn on it so we chased the cows back and forth to our home place for milking. About four in the afternoon, one or two of us kids would go down to the new pasture to get them. "Come Boss! Come Boss!" (pronounced *B-ah-s*, that's how you call a cow). We'd yell till our throats tickled. But our job wasn't too tough. They all stood waiting at the gate, and Buttercup, the lead cow, would head them up the road. In the morning after milking, they'd wait at the gate by the barn for the trip back down. They had to make a couple of turns, but they always seemed to go right along without any coaxing—better than cars sometimes these days.

MAKES ABOUT 1 QUART

1 *pint and 2 tablespoons milk*

2 *tablespoons flour*

3/4 *cup sugar*

2 *egg yolks, beaten*

1 *cup heavy cream*

1 *teaspoon vanilla extract*

1. Scald the pint of milk, stirring constantly.

2. Mix the flour and 2 tablespoons of milk into a smooth paste. Add it slowly to the hot milk, and continue stirring.

3. When thick, add the sugar and beaten egg yolks. Cook 2 minutes more, and cool.

4. When cool, add the cream and vanilla, and put into the ice cream freezer. Either crank and crank until your arms drop off, or follow the instructions on your new model.

CHOCOLATE ICE CREAM: Use the same recipe, but add 1½ squares melted, unsweetened chocolate to the milk when scalding.

STRAWBERRY ICE CREAM: Follow the recipe for Boss's Vanilla, but add 1 cup of fresh crushed strawberries after you add the vanilla.

PEACH ICE CREAM: Follow the recipe for Boss's Vanilla, but add 1 cup of fresh crushed peaches after you add the vanilla.

COCONUT ICE CREAM: Follow the recipe for Boss's Vanilla, but add 1 cup of flaked coconut.

OLD-FASHIONED BUTTER BRICKLE ICE CREAM: Follow the recipe for Boss's Vanilla, but add ½ cup of hammered Ragged Brown Sugar Lumps (page 231) after you add the vanilla.

RASPBERRY ICE CREAM: Follow the recipe for Boss's Vanilla, but add 1 cup of fresh crushed raspberries after you add the vanilla.

ANY NUMBER OF VARIATIONS: Swirl in some prepared homemade preserves (pages 78 to 81).

A GOOD MALTED: Shake up 1 pint of any of these homemade ice creams, 1 teaspoon malt powder, and ¼ cup syrup or fruit together in a blender, or use Hamilton Beach's Drinkmaster. (It's interesting that Chester Beach and Louis Hamilton started up in Racine, Wisconsin, in 1911, and in 1991 the company [now based in Virginia] held a nationwide "oldest running appliance contest," and an old retiree from Green Bay, Wisconsin, won with a Hamilton Beach, circa 1911, "Cyclone" Drinkmaster.)

COTTAGE CHEESE ICE CREAM

MAKES ABOUT 1 QUART

This tastes a lot like yogurt.

>   *2 egg yolks, beaten*
>   *1 cup sugar*
>   *2 cups scalded milk*
>   *1 cup fine-curd cottage cheese*
>   *2 cups rich milk or half-and-half*
>   *½ teaspoon vanilla extract*

1. Combine the egg yolks, sugar, and scalded milk, and cook in a double boiler until it coats a spoon. Cool immediately.

2. Put the cottage cheese through a fine sieve.

3. Combine the cottage cheese and the rich milk. Add the vanilla, and combine with the egg yolk mixture. Put it into the ice cream freezer and either crank and crank, or follow the instructions on your new model.

COFFEE ICE CREAM

**MAKES A LITTLE MORE THAN
1½ QUARTS**

1 pint milk

3 pints heavy cream

½ cup very strong black coffee

2 cups sugar

1. Heat the milk and half of the cream in a double boiler. Add the coffee and sugar, and stir until dissolved.

2. Remove from heat. When cool, add the remaining cream. Put the mixture in an ice cream freezer. Crank or follow the model instructions.

COFFEE CUSTARD ICE CREAM

MAKES ABOUT 1 QUART

1 pint milk

4 eggs

1 cup sugar

½ pint heavy cream

½ pint strong black coffee

1. In a heavy saucepan, scald the milk. Beat the eggs and the sugar together until well blended, and add to the hot milk. Cook over medium heat until thick (about 5 minutes), then take from the heat.

2. Add the cream and coffee, and stir. Cool, and put it in the ice cream freezer. Either crank or follow the model instructions.

PUMPKIN ICE CREAM

**MAKES 1 LARGE OR 2 SMALL
FREEZER TRAYS**

1¾ cups milk

1½ cups sugar

2 tablespoons cornstarch

1 teaspoon ground cinnamon

¼ teaspoon ground nutmeg

½ teaspoon salt

1½ cups pumpkin puree

2 teaspoons gelatin

⅔ cup cold water

4 egg yolks, beaten

2 tablespoons grated orange peel

1 cup Fresh Whipped Cream (page 192)

1. In a heavy medium saucepan, scald the milk.

2. Combine the sugar, cornstarch, cinnamon, nutmeg, salt, and pumpkin, and add it to the scalded milk. Remove from heat.

3. Dissolve the gelatin in the cold water, add it to the scalded milk mixture, and stir well.

4. Add the egg yolks and orange peel. Blend well, and cool.

5. Fold the whipped cream into the mixture, and pour the mixture into one large or two small freezer trays (without the cube inserts), stir once or twice, and freeze.

CHOCOLATE MINT ICE CREAM

MAKES ABOUT 2 QUARTS

4 cups milk

1 tablespoon gelatin

2 squares unsweetened chocolate

1½ cups sugar

1 tablespoon flour

Pinch of salt

3 egg yolks, slightly beaten

3 egg whites, stiffly beaten

2 cups Fresh Whipped Cream (page 192)

1 tablespoon vanilla extract

1 tablespoon mint extract or crème de menthe

1. In a heavy medium saucepan, scald the milk with the gelatin and the chocolate.

2. In a bowl, mix the sugar, flour, and salt together, and add it to the milk and chocolate mixture, stirring frequently, until it begins to thicken.

3. Add part of this mixture to the egg yolks, stir, then add all to the hot milk mixture. Cook 1 minute over medium heat (careful not to scorch).

4. Chill until thickened, then beat until light and fluffy.

5. Now add the egg whites, whipped cream, vanilla, and mint extract, and pour into freezer trays (without the cube inserts). Freeze about 45 minutes to 1 hour.

6. Remove from the freezer trays, and beat until smooth and silky. Pour into containers and place in the freezer. This is a good after-dinner dessert and stomach settler.

CHOCOLATE-MARSHMALLOW ICE CREAM

MAKES 1 LARGE OR 2 SMALL FREEZER TRAYS

18 marshmallows

1 cup milk

1 square chocolate, grated

½ teaspoon vanilla extract

½ cup freshly whipped cream

1. Combine the marshmallows, milk, and chocolate in a medium saucepan. Melt over a low flame. Cool, and add the vanilla (see Note).

2. Fold in the whipped cream, and freeze in freezer trays. Stir two or three times.

NOTE: For a crunchy treat, add ½ cup of chopped almonds.

CHILD'S PLAY ICE CREAM

MAKES ABOUT 1 QUART

This is great fun for kids, and it tastes pretty good, too.

> 1 cup milk
> 1 cup heavy cream
> 1 cup sugar
> 1 teaspoon vanilla extract
> 1 cup nuts and/or fruit (if desired)
> 1 (1-pound) coffee can (with lid)
> 1 (3-pound) coffee can (with lid)
> Ice
> Rock salt

1. Place the milk, cream, sugar, and vanilla (and nuts and fruit, if desired) in a 1-pound coffee can. Stir well, and place a tight lid on the can.

2. Place the 1-pound can into the 3-pound can. Around the 1-pound can, place the ice and the salt. Put a tight lid on the 3-pound can. Have your kids roll the can back and forth on the floor or driveway for 10 or 15 minutes.

3. Open the cans and check to see if the ice cream is freezing. Stir again, and put the lids back on. The kids can roll the cans again until it is ice cream (about 5 or 10 more minutes).

LEMON SHERBET

SERVES 6

> 1 cup water
> 3/4 cup sugar
> Pinch of salt
> 1/2 cup half-and-half
> 1/2 cup lemon juice
> 1/4 cup sugar
> 2 egg whites, stiffly beaten

1. Combine the water, 3/4 cup sugar, and the salt. Cook about 5 minutes in a heavy medium saucepan over medium heat, and cool.

2. Add the half-and-half and lemon juice. Pour into freezer trays (without the cube inserts). Freeze until real firm.

3. Gradually add the remaining 1/4 cup sugar to the beaten egg whites, and beat until stiff.

4. Dump the frozen mixture into a large mixing bowl. (You may want to break it up a little to mix it easier.) Beat until smooth. Fold the beaten egg whites into the frozen mixture, put the mixture back into the cold freezer tray, and freeze again.

Toppings

B U T T E R S C O T C H
T O P P I N G

M A K E S   A B O U T   1 1/2   C U P S

2 cups packed brown sugar

1/3 cup corn syrup

1/4 cup heavy cream

1/4 cup butter

Mix all the ingredients together, and cook over medium heat in a heavy medium kettle until a few drops dropped into a little cold water form a very soft ball (it just barely forms). Cool. Pour into a container that has a tight lid. Refrigerate. This is good cold or warm.

For ice cream toppings you can also use fresh homemade jams (pages 78 to 81): strawberry, peach, raspberry, blueberry, and blackberry are always good on ice cream.

C H O C O L A T E   F U D G E
T O P P I N G

You can also use this syrup for a quick chocolate milk drink. Just stir 1 tablespoon into your milk glass.

M A K E S   A B O U T   1   P I N T

3 cups sugar

4 squares unsweetened Hershey's chocolate

1/3 cup corn syrup

1/2 cup butter

1 cup evaporated milk

In a heavy medium kettle, over medium heat, combine all the ingredients, stirring well, until the chocolate is melted. Continue stirring until the syrup cooks to a smooth, silky substance. (Be careful not to have too hot of a flame because it'll scorch easily.) Cool, and store in a tight covered container in the refrigerator. Serve cold, or heated slightly.

P I N E A P P L E
T O P P I N G

M A K E S   A B O U T   1 1/2   C U P S

3/4 cup unsweetened pineapple juice

1/2 cup orange juice

2 tablespoons lemon juice

3 tablespoons cold water

1 egg, slightly beaten

3 tablespoons sugar

1 tablespoon flour

Heat the pineapple, orange, and lemon juice in a medium saucepan. Mix the water, egg, sugar, and flour together, and slowly add them to the juices. Cook over a low flame in a heavy kettle until thick. Cool, and store in the refrigerator.

OLD-FASHIONED BEVERAGES

BEVERAGES

and

NEW-FANGLED PUNCHES

When I was a girl, Nig's grocery carried soda pop for just a few cents a bottle, but that was an extravagance for us kids, so we never had that, and there was no Kool-Aid. Instead, peddlers would come by with something called Nectar; you had to shake it up and add water, and boy, did we think the world of that.

Day to day, though, we drank good fresh cow's milk, and of course, there was coffee, although in the morning, even that was no fuss—just water and grounds set in a basin on the wood stove so it'd heat quickly before we went to the barn. If you couldn't find the strainer, you had to pour carefully so the grounds wouldn't get into your cup, but kids didn't mind; we were told that meant you would be rich. We even chewed on them for flavor.

What I've included here were our true treats—any of these recipes, however simple, made any old humdrum afternoon or night a special occasion.

NOTE: Some of these recipes call for fresh, cold spring water. Most farms had springs, because people tended to settle where they could easily tap clear spring water. Although it's not quite the same as our fresh gurgling springs, if you're in the city and want to try these recipes, I suggest you use bottled spring water.

LEMONADE IN THE MILK CAN

7 GALLONS, FOR PICNICS OR FAMILY GATHERINGS

2 dozen oranges

1 1/2 dozen lemons

10 cups sugar

Spring water to fill two-thirds of the milk can (see Note)

1. Roll the oranges and lemons back and forth on a hard surface to break down the fibers, squeeze the juice and pulp out of the fruit, and pour the juice and pulp into a milk can. (Save some of the rinds.)

2. Add the sugar, and stir until it's dissolved.

3. Add the cold spring water to fill the milk can to two-thirds.

4. Stir real good. Put some of the lemon and orange rinds in the can to bring out more flavor. Serve.

NOTE: Our milk cans hold 10 gallons.

LEMONADE AT HOME

On hot summer nights the breeze through the big maple was our air-conditioning. Our house was so warm my mother put her ironing board outside on the sidewalk. It set on two wooden chairs and acted as our picnic table. She made sandwiches and this lemonade, and we sat there in the yard trying to keep cool.

2 QUARTS, FOR YOUR OWN FAMILY

4 lemons

1 cup sugar

Enough cold water to fill a 2-quart pitcher

1. Roll the lemons on a hard surface so you can get more juice out, and squeeze the juice into a 2-quart pitcher.

2. Add the sugar, stir, and fill the pitcher with cold water. (Pump a little water out of the pump or run the faucet so the water gets cold before you fill up your pitcher.) Or use fresh spring water.

ROOT BEER IN THE FRUIT JAR

I remember it was so terrible to wait and wait for this as a kid. It was set in a dark corner in the cellar, and we couldn't touch it, but we'd go down and look at it once in a while. Toward the end of the two weeks of hard waiting, we even had dreams about it.

MAKES 1 GALLON

1/8 teaspoon caked or dry yeast (see Note)

1/2 cup lukewarm water

1 gallon water

1 tablespoon root beer extract

2 cups sugar

1. Dissolve the yeast in 1/2 cup of lukewarm water.

2. Put about 1/3 of the gallon of water into a pail or a large kettle (see Note). Shake the extract bottle well, and combine the extract and the sugar in the pail with the 1/3 gallon of water. Stir until the sugar is dissolved.

3. Add the yeast mixture and the rest of the water. Taste it; if it doesn't seem strong enough, add more extract.

4. Pour into 1- or 2-quart fruit jars (see Note). Fill to 1/2 inch from the top, seal real good, and lay the jar on its side to see if it leaks. Leave in room temperature for 2 to 4 days, then store in a cool, dark place for 1 to 2 weeks. It should be so bubbly the fizz will tickle your nose.

NOTE: This takes very little yeast, just a pinch.

You can mix this in anything but cheap aluminum.

This is my old, old recipe from back when we made it in a fruit jar. We had to use jars with zinc covers and rubber rings, nothing else. And we had to heat the rubber rings in hot water so they softened up and sealed better. Today I recommend using glass soda pop bottles. You can buy bottle cappers and cap according to the manufacturer's instructions.

SUN TEA

Talk, talk, talk about the weather, that's what we do in farm towns, because the crops—and so our lives—depend on it. Rain and sunshine are as important as air, and I like to think that the sun gives this tea all it gives the tiny seeds that become our high waving fields of alfalfa, wheat, and corn.

MAKES 1 GALLON

Enough cold spring water to fill a 1-gallon glass jar

6 to 8 homemade or regular tea bags or 6 to 8 teaspoons of bulk tea (see Note)

1. Fill a glass gallon jug with cold spring water, and add the tea bags.

2. Put the jar in a place where the sun will shine on it all day. In the evening, bring in the jar and remove the tea bags. The tea is ready with all that good energy from the sun.

NOTE: If you're making this from bulk tea as we did, take a square piece of thin white cloth from an old worn dish towel, put the tea in the middle, take up the corners, and tie together with a string.

HOT SPICY SWINDLER'S TEA

If you want to butter someone up on a cold December night, this is your tea.

MAKES ABOUT 4 CUPS

1 cup strong tea (see Note)

2 cups fresh orange juice

3 cups sugar

1/2 teaspoon ground cloves

1/2 teaspoon ground allspice

1 teaspoon ground cinnamon

1 teaspoon lemon juice (see Note)

1. Mix all the ingredients together, and stir, using a wooden spoon.

2. Heat, strain, and serve.

NOTE: If you'd like to take a shortcut, omit the tea and the lemon juice from the above recipe, and use 1 cup of instant lemon tea.

DECEMBER HOT COCOA

When your toes have been nipped and burn like fireweed, this and the proper first-aid make life good again.

MAKES 6 CUPS

6 *tablespoons cocoa*

7 *tablespoons sugar*

²⁄₃ *cup water*

4 *cups milk*

1. In a stainless steel medium kettle, mix the cocoa and sugar together, add the water and place the kettle over low heat until it cooks good for 2 minutes (see Note).

2. Add the milk and heat until boiling. Be careful not to scorch.

NOTE: Do not use a metal or tin pan or you'll ruin the taste.

OLDEN-DAYS COCOA IN A CUP

When I was just little, I'd trot home from school and stir this up in Dad's coffee mug. With a slice of fresh baked bread bathed in butter and brown sugar, I'd sit at the table day after day, paying no mind to my wide chocolate mustache.

MAKES ENOUGH FOR 1 COFFEE MUG

1 *teaspoon cocoa*

2 *teaspoons sugar (heaping if you like it real sweet)*

Hot water until mug is two-thirds full

Milk to fill rest of cup

1. Put the cocoa and sugar in a mug, and add hot water from the teakettle until the mug is two-thirds full. Stir together.

2. Add the milk to fill the rest of the cup, stir again, and drink while hot.

CHOCOLATE SYRUP

I always made this up to have on hand for mixing the kids a quick after-school treat.

MAKES ENOUGH FOR 1 PINT BOTTLE OR FRUIT JAR

2 *ounces bitter chocolate*

2 *cups boiling water*

4 *cups sugar*

2 *tablespoons vanilla extract*

1. Slowly melt the chocolate in a heavy medium kettle, stirring a little until melted.

2. Gradually add the water and sugar, then the vanilla. Heat thoroughly.

3. Bottle, or put into a pint jar, and seal.

4. *To use:* Put 1 tablespoon of syrup in each glass of cold or hot milk.

EGG COFFEE FOR LADIES' AID OR COMPANY

No matter what the fancy brew, there's no better way to make coffee. My mother taught me how because years ago, when you had company you always used egg, and for threshers and Ladies' Aid and Luther League, it was always Egg Coffee.

One summer during a storm when the lights were off at the restaurant and we had to cook coffee on the gas stove, I took a stainless steel kettle and cooked Egg Coffee that whole day. Oh, it was wonderful coffee, golden brown and clear as a bell; everybody bragged about that coffee. They thought it was something foreign from South America or Turkey. But don't try Egg Coffee in a coffee maker—it doesn't work.

**MAKES ENOUGH FOR
A LARGE GROUP**

Enough water to fill a 2-gallon granite coffeepot two-thirds full (see Note)

1 egg

2 cups regular-grind coffee

1 more quart water

1. Put the water into the coffeepot until two-thirds full, and place over medium heat to boil.

2. Break the egg into a bowl, and mix the coffee and the egg together until all the grounds are moist. (You may have to add a little water to moisten completely.)

3. When the water is at a full boil, add the coffee mixture, and stir constantly so it won't boil over onto the stove or you'll have a mess. Boil about 5 minutes, then set aside to let settle. (Add 1 quart of cold water to help make it settle faster.)

4. Strain into another pot, and discard the grounds. It's now ready to serve nice and clear and smooth.

NOTE: My favorite brand of coffee is Hills Brothers. That's what I use both at home and at the restaurant.

EGG COFFEE IN A HOME-SIZE POT

MAKES ENOUGH FOR YOUR FAMILY

Enough water to fill an 8-cup coffeepot two-thirds full

1 small egg (a pullet egg is good)

¼ cup regular-grind coffee

1 more cup cold water

1. Put enough water in a coffeepot until two-thirds full, and heat to a full boil.

2. Mix the egg and the coffee until moistened as above, and add to the boiling water, stirring all the while to keep from boiling over. Boil about 2 to 3 minutes.

3. Remove from heat, and let steep. (Add 1 cup of cold water to help settle the grounds.)

4. Strain as you serve.

RAGGED BROWN SUGAR LUMPS

This was our loaf sugar. My mother made them two or three times a week. They were cheaper and always tasted better than what you bought at the store. Some folks dropped the lumps in their cups as sweetener, others used them as candy, but mostly they were used to dunk in our coffee and slurp. I've been doing that and slurping and drinking coffee since I was five years old.

MAKES ABOUT 20 (½-INCH TO ¾-INCH) PIECES

2 cups packed brown sugar

¼ cup water

1. Put the brown sugar and the water into a medium saucepan and cook for 5 minutes over medium heat, watching closely so it doesn't scorch.

2. Test a few drops of this mixture in cold water. It should be hard when pressed with your fingers.

3. Pour at once into a well-buttered pie tin. When cold and set to about the consistency of fudge, only grainy, break into bite-size pieces (see Note). It doesn't matter if they aren't all the same size or shape; this is homemade.

NOTE: Many broke these up with pliers. You don't have to be too fussy. Also, don't worry if they're a little gummy around the edges.

BEET WINE

MAKES ABOUT 4 GALLONS

5 pounds unpeeled beets, washed

Enough water to cover beets and then enough to make 1 gallon when added to beet juice

3 pounds sugar

1 lemon, sliced

1 orange, sliced

1 pound raisins

1 1/3 ounces caked yeast or 1 package dry yeast

1. Cover the beets with water, and boil until tender. Remove the beets and add enough water to the beet juice to make 1 gallon.

2. Put in a large jar and add the sugar, lemon, orange, raisins, and yeast. Let the solution stand 28 days. Stir every other day.

3. Strain and let the juice set 4 or 5 more days to settle. Put into jugs or wine bottles (see Note).

NOTE: There may be a sediment on the bottom after the wine has been allowed to settle. Be careful when you bottle it so as not to get the sediment into your bottles or your wine will not be clear.

BLACKBERRY WINE

MAKES 2 GALLONS IN A STONEWARE CROCK

1 quart crushed blackberries

8 cups white sugar

3 cups spring water

1. Place all the ingredients in the crock, and stir every morning for 10 days.

2. On the tenth day, strain it, and pour it into clean, scalded glass fruit jars, but do not tighten the covers.

3. Let this stand for 2 months before you tighten the covers completely. If the covers are too tight while the juice is working, you'll wake up in the night thinking the militia is invading.

ELDERBERRY WINE: Follow the same recipe using elderberries.

GRAPE WINE

It's fun to say "I made it myself."

MAKES ABOUT 8 QUARTS

20 pounds Concord grapes

6 quarts boiling water

10 pounds sugar

1. Put the grapes in the boiling water, and let stand. When cool, squeeze the grapes through a fine-mesh sieve or place them in a flour-sack dish towel, and let them drip into a kettle. Discard the pulp, but be sure and squeeze out all the juice.

2. Add the sugar to the juice and let it stand for 10 days in a large glass or granite container (a crock is best if you have one). Stir daily, then after 10 days, bottle it. If it's too thick, add a little warm water.

3. Pour into clean, scalded glass fruit jars. Do not seal tight until you're sure it is done working or—bang!

NORM'S DANDELION WINE

There's a swell old character north of town here who won two silver stars during World War II. Everybody raves about his dandelion wine. This is his recipe.

MAKES A 5-GALLON CROCK

> 5 cups dandelion heads (just the flowers)
> 4 ounces caked yeast
> 2 or 3 cups sugar
> 5 gallons water

1. Pick some bright yellow dandelions, and snap off the heads (the more flowers you pick, the stronger the wine). Forget about the stems.

2. Put the dandelions in a large crock with the cake of yeast, the sugar, and the water. Cover the crock so the flies don't get into it, and let the mixture stand 3 weeks, but be sure to stir it every 2 or 3 days.

3. After 3 weeks, when ready, strain, and put into clean, scalded glass bottles or jugs.

BRANDY SLUSH

MAKES 5 QUARTS

> 9 cups water
> 2 cups sugar
> 4 tea bags black tea
> 12 ounces frozen orange juice
> 12 ounces frozen lemonade
> 2 cups brandy
> 7Up or Squirt (to fill glasses)

1. In a large saucepan, boil 7 cups of the water and the sugar until dissolved, then remove from heat.

2. In another saucepan, bring to a boil the remaining 2 cups of water and the tea bags. Set aside, and let the bags stand a while in the water.

3. Remove the bags from the water, and discard if spent. Now mix the sugar mixture, the tea, the orange juice, lemonade, and brandy together in a large bowl or kettle.

4. Pour into a 5-quart plastic pail, place the cover on, and put into the freezer (see Note).

5. When it comes to serving this, stir well, then fill a glass two-thirds full of this mixture and top off with 7Up or Squirt.

NOTE: This will not freeze hard. It will always be icy, slushy.

DANIEL'S EGG NOG

Farm work and alcohol don't mix too well, but even in the old days people liked an occasional swig. Egg nog and homemade wine were always popular on a winter's Sunday afternoon, especially during the Christmas season when the celebrating lasted twenty-one days. Whenever my late brother-in-law, Daniel, would come home from the East for the holidays, he'd make this as a treat for the workers in the back room of the Nook.

MAKES A LARGE BATCH

1 dozen eggs

2 cups sugar

1 quart liquor (vodka is best because it is smooth and does not intrude)

1 quart milk

1 pint whipping cream

Shake of ground nutmeg on top of each serving (if you like)

1. Separate the egg whites from the yolks, add the sugar to the yolks (save the whites), and beat until light in color (see Note).

2. Add the liquor a little at a time, beating all the while. Add the milk the same way.

3. Beat the egg whites until they can stand in stiff peaks, then set aside.

4. Beat the whipping cream until stiff, then fold the egg whites and whipping cream into the liquor and milk mixture, using a rubber licker.

5. Serve with a shake of nutmeg on top of each serving, if you like.

NOTE: This was good in the old days when we mixed it all by hand, but it's even better now if you use a KitchenAid mixer, or a high-powered blender (page 260).

ICE MOLDS FOR PUNCH

Around these parts, punch isn't anything unless it's in a pretty bowl with pretty ice. Use your imagination and you can come up with any number of ideas. If you're stumped, this is what we do:

Fill the ice trays with water and put a petal from a flower in each cube. Or take a gelatin mold and freeze any color of Kool-Aid that goes with or highlights your punch. For strawberry punch, arrange a few whole strawberries and freeze them in with the water or use a good shade of Kool-Aid in a Jell-O mold. Mint leaves look nice too. Or just freeze water into unusual shapes (such as in *sandbakkel* tins).

SUNSET PUNCH

MAKES ABOUT 50 (4-OUNCE) SERVINGS

3 quarts strawberries, crushed

1 cup sugar

4 liters rosé wine

1 cup lemon juice

2 (1-quart) bottles carbonated water

1. Combine the strawberries, sugar, and 1 of the bottles of wine. Let stand for 1 hour, then strain, and discard the strawberry pulp.

2. Combine this liquid with the lemon juice, then add the carbonated water and the rest of the wine. Chill, and serve.

PUNCH WITH A PUNCH

MAKES A LARGE BATCH, ABOUT 50 (4-OUNCE) CUPS

6 quarts 7Up

12 ounces lemon juice

12 ounces orange juice

2 (6-ounce) jars homemade (or frozen) lemonade

1 fifth Southern Comfort

1. Mix all the ingredients together, the Southern Comfort last.

2. Serve as is.

FRESH CRANBERRY PUNCH

MAKES QUITE A BIT

4 cups cranberries

4 cups water

2/3 to 1 cup sugar

2 liters cold 7Up

1 pint fresh, cold orange juice

1. Cook the cranberries in the water until their skins burst. Strain through a fine sieve, making sure to remove the skins and seeds.

2. Heat the cranberry juice over medium heat, add the sugar, and boil 2 to 3 minutes. Chill.

3. Before serving, add the cold 7Up and the orange juice. (Add or decrease the 7Up to taste or to stretch or to make a lesser amount.) Serve chilled.

SCANDINAVIAN
SPECIALTIES

Like most farm women in this Scandinavian community, I always made a ritual out of baking for the holidays. I worked late into the night to make big batches to last through our twenty-one days of Christmas; it was an unwritten rule any woman worth her salt had at least seven kinds of Christmas baking. Starting after Thanksgiving, I'd keep on with these delicacies, taking special care to store the fragile goodies in tight metal containers in a cool room away from the kids until the week of Christmas.

Out here, it's a year-long thing to worry about the weather, or a husband or child alongside the big machinery, but at Christmas I don't think there's a Scandinavian farm woman my age who still isn't accustomed to worrying about breaking the teeth off the *sandbakkels* or the petals off the rosettes. After all those long hours, tip the container upside down, you have nothing but crumbs, and a big heartache.

There's more to this section than baking; there's meats and cheeses and other specialties, but every one of these recipes was made with that same care and feeling we had for our holiday baking. How each of these looked and tasted was who we were, and oh, how we wanted to please—*Var Sa Gud* (help yourself), enjoy these recipes.

BLOD KLUB
(BLOOD DUMPLINGS)

I doubt there's a person in Osseo, Wisconsin, who was alive back in the 1950s who doesn't remember when the butcher at Nig's had his car accident. He'd been out butchering at the slaughterhouse just outside of town, and on the way back to the market, toward evening, he had a mishap and rolled his car over. Everyone was sure he was dead; you couldn't see him for the blood, blood everywhere. Word traveled through town, "Rushed to the hospital," "Way he looked, he's not long for this world," "Wasn't a drop a blood left in him." No one stopped to remember it was klub season. The whole town was sad and praying, until there he was the next day walking around without a scratch, just minus the pork blood he'd been hauling back to Nig's market.

MAKES 2 (12 × 5-INCH) SACKS

3 quarts blood (see Note)

1 cup water

1 tablespoon salt

4 to 5 cups flour

Enough cream to cover (or not)

Side pork, fried crisp (or not)

1. Strain the blood through a cloth, then add the water, salt, and flour; mix well (this must be real thick, thicker than pancake batter).

2. Sew some good linen or other white cloth to make a sack 12 inches long and 5 inches wide. With rough seams to the outside, fill the sack with batter to three-quarters full. Tie securely, and place it in a large kettle of slightly salted boiling water. Boil 2½ hours, or until done (when a fork comes out dry).

3. Remove the klub from the sack when ready to serve. Slice, and serve it hot with butter, or cut it into pieces, and place them in a heavy skillet.

4. Pour in the cream, and stir over medium heat until the cream forms a gravy.

5. Serve as is or with crisply fried side pork. (If stored in the refrigerator, this will keep for several days; see Note.)

NOTE: Pork blood is best.

Klub can be frozen, but slice or cube it before you store in freezer bags or else it will be impossible to cut when frozen.

VARIATIONS: Partially cooked barley or plain rice may be added before the flour, or you can add diced pork while filling the sacks. If you prefer, the batter can be made into dumplings by dropping large balls the size of a mixing spoon into boiling salted water. Cook ½ hour, and test by breaking one in two; it should not be doughy.

RULLEPØLSE (NORWEGIAN MEAT ROLL)

MAKES 1 (12- TO 16-INCH) LONG ROLL

1 flank beef
Salt to sprinkle over
Pepper to taste
As much minced onion as you like
A little ground ginger

1. Wash the flank, and spread it onto a board or a table. Sprinkle with salt and pepper, the minced onion, and a little ginger.

2. Roll lengthwise and sew it with a heavy cord (sew the outer skin very tightly so it holds its shape; see Note). It will look like a large stick of summer sausage.

3. After sewing it together, wrap heavy cord around and around the meat, so it won't come apart when boiling.

4. Place in a large kettle, cover completely with water, and cook on top of the stove slowly over medium heat for about 2 hours.

5. Remove from the water, place on a board or a cake pan, and weight the roll down with something heavy like a breadboard or a wooden block. (This will flatten the roll and press it together.)

6. When cold, slice thin, and eat as is or make sandwiches. (Don't forget to remove the cord before slicing.)

NOTE: A little fresh pork roast may be put inside the *pølse* before rolling, if desired.

SYLTE
(HEAD CHEESE)

✳

When you start looking at this, you might say, "Good Lord, what does she fix?" But years ago when we butchered, we never let anything go to waste. We saved the liver; we saved the heart, everyone did. The heart and tongue we sometimes ground up for mincemeat (page 93). But as for head cheese—you go to the store today, what you get in those packages is not head cheese. This is head cheese.

MAKES A CHUNK 12 INCHES ROUND AND 2 INCHES THICK

1 pig head (svine huget)

Salt, pepper, and ground ginger to taste

2 cups vinegar (or not)

1. Get a pig head at a locker plant or a good meat market. (You might have them cut it in half with one of their meat saws, otherwise take an ax and split it so it will fit in a large boiler. Make sure it has been shaved so the hair is off. If not, scald and scrape the hair off with a sharp knife. Be sure the eyes are removed.)

2. Half-fill a large boiler with water. Drop in the head, and add more water if necessary to cover. Put on a lid, and boil about 2 hours, until it's cooked through, depending on the size of the head. (The meat should fall away from the bone.)

3. Put a cookie sheet on the table beside a clean kettle. On the other side of the kettle, spread a large dish towel. Remove the head from the boiler, and place it on the cookie sheet. While still so hot you can barely touch it, find the tongue and peel off the skin. Put the

tongue into the kettle (it will help make a leaner head cheese). Pick through the rest of the head quickly but carefully, placing all the meat in a large bowl, except the skin, bone, gristle, and two or three little gray oysterlike balls we call "etler." Discard those. Toss everything else into the bowl. Season with salt, pepper, and ginger to taste (the amount will depend on how large or old the pig).

4. Quickly take the meat from the bowl while still very hot, and place it in the middle of the dish towel (see Note). Taste, and season if necessary. When the flavor is what you want, bring the corners of the dish towel together up over the meat and tie tightly. Put something heavy on top—a rock, brick, or board—and press down. Leave overnight.

5. The next morning, when it has set, remove the towel. Cut up the head cheese.

6. Combine the vinegar with 2 cups water in a bowl, if desired. Place the cheese in the brine, if desired. Salt and pepper to taste, slice, and serve with homemade bread and butter. (I like to spread a little mustard on mine.)

7. Wrap the remainder in wax paper or plastic wrap, and store in the refrigerator or refrigerate in a covered glass dish with vinegar brine.

NOTE: It's important that the meat be put into a towel when very, very hot so when weighted overnight, the fat will melt and press out into the towel, leaving you with a leaner, better-tasting head cheese. (Before we had refrigerators, we cut the head cheese up and put it in an earthen crock in vinegar brine; that's why country folks today insist on vinegar with their head cheese.)

SYLTELABBER (PICKLED PIG'S FEET)

MAKES ABOUT 2 TO 3 QUARTS DEPENDING ON SIZE OF FEET

The feet of 1 pig
4 quarts water
2 ounces salt

1. Clean and scrape the pig's feet thoroughly. Cut in half lengthwise, then into 3 or 4 pieces.

2. Pour the water and the salt into a large kettle, add the pig's feet, bring them to a boil over medium heat, and cook until tender (about 1 hour).

3. Pack closely in a clean, scalded stone or glass jar. If you wish to eat it this way, pour salted water over, or use the pickling spice recipe following.

PICKLING SPICE

MAKES ABOUT 1 QUART (ENOUGH FOR 4 PIG'S FEET)

Enough vinegar to cover the feet
1/2 cup sugar
Pepper to taste
Ground cloves to taste

1. Cook enough vinegar to cover the feet (about 1 quart) with the sugar over medium heat for about 5 minutes. Add the pepper and cloves to taste.

2. Drain the salt water (from the preceding recipe) off the pig's feet, put them in a jar, then pour the boiling pickling water over the feet. Place a plate over the jar and weight it down or the feet will come to the top and raise the plate. Keep in a cool place.

LUTEFISK

Lutefisk and *lefse* are an old Scandinavian meal, and one that's common here after the weather turns cold. People eat it between October and January, and it's on almost everyone's table at Christmas. It's a codfish, dried in Norway and sent to Minneapolis in hard sheets. It looks like stiff boards, like cord wood. Near the end of September, the distributors start soaking it in lye to soften it up. The first fish comes out of Minneapolis in the beginning of October. If you know fish, when you feel it, you can tell whether it's good fish or not. But it's tricky. A good fish has gotta be firm—firm but not rigid—some of it gets very soft and mushy; you don't want that. When you get it, it's never rinsed out enough of the lye, so I usually change its water about three times a day for two days. I put a lot of salt in there each time I soak it to draw out the lye. Then I pour that off and the third day I put on clear, cold water (no salt) three times during the day to get it rinsed off. If you don't soak the lye out this way, the fish gets slimy. If you go somewhere to eat, and the *lutefisk* isn't good, it's usually because the cook hasn't spent enough time properly soaking it. That's why it's a seasonal food. We don't have it when it's warm because *lutefisk* has to be kept cold, and you don't want it in the refrigerator because it would ruin everything with its strong, fishy smell. I keep it outside in tubs, then, at night I bring it in and stick it in the cold back room because it's expensive, and I wouldn't want it to disappear.

For many, many years—long before Garrison Keillor thought to tell the world about *lutefisk*—at our high-school football and basketball games when the opponents' cheerleaders chanted "Go team—go," Osseo's young girls have answered *"Lutefisk, lefse, tak skal du ha* (thank you very much), Osseo, Osseo, ya, ya, ya."

(For Fish or Lutefisk Chowder, see page 34.)

SERVES 6
(IF GOOD LUTEFISK EATERS)

½ lutefisk
¾ pound (3 sticks) butter, melted

1. Soak the *lutefisk* for 2 days in salt water to get the lye out. On the third day, change to clear water (change 3 times).

2. Preheat the oven to 350° F. Lay the fish in a granite or stainless steel roaster. (Don't use cheap aluminum because the lye will blacken the metal and take on a taste.)

3. Do not put water, salt, or anything on the fish. Just lay it in a single layer in the roaster and bake for about 45 minutes. The water will bake out and you'll have a nice flaky fish. The only thing you have to do is see that it's heated through. (I usually stick my finger in there and if it's cold in the center, it's gotta be longer; when it's hot through, it's done.)

4. Place the fish on a platter, pull the skin off, and discard it. Leave the flaked fish on a platter and pick out the bones. Serve with melted butter and *lefse*.

LEFSE

Lefse's a cold-weather food, too, because years ago you had to have it cool for it to keep. Electric lights didn't shine in these valleys until 1936, and then it was a couple more years before we got a refrigerator. Women would boil and save potatoes, then get together and make huge batches of *lefse,* and store it in the cellar or someplace cool. Before Thanksgiving, my mother and I would make about 150 *lefse* a day on the wood stove. I'd roll and my mother would bake. It was always better than the *lefse* we make now on the electric grill. There's something about the wood heat that really baked it better. Electricity has a tendency to dry it out. Nowadays, *lefse* from the grill is barely any bigger than pancakes. On the wood stove, we could make it five times as big. Some would even stretch it over the firebox so it got longer than a yardstick, only big and round.

If you're not Scandinavian, you may have a little trouble with the *lefse.* When you first see it, you may think it should be used for napkins, but you'd like it better if it were buttered and rolled up.

MAKES A DOZEN *LEFSE*

8 large Russet potatoes

1 cup flour

3 tablespoons butter, melted

3 tablespoons half-and-half

1. Peel the potatoes and boil them in salted water. Press through a ricer or mash real fine with a wooden masher.

2. Combine the potatoes, flour, and melted butter, and mix, using your hands.

3. Divide into 11 to 13 balls and on a floured table, roll out thin with a *lefse* rolling pin (page 262). Roll it up on a *lefse* stick and carry it to the stove or grill. Unroll and bake. (The first time I made *lefse,* I ripped it right through the middle while carrying it to the stove, so be patient.)

4. Bake on a *lefse* grill, or on top of a wood-burning cookstove (see Note). If neither is handy, use a large cast-iron skillet on a stove burner on medium heat. (Cheap aluminum will not work. Cheap aluminum is not the thing for cooking; it's the thing for burning.) Leave it on the grill until it begins to bubble (about 1 minute or so), then turn it over, and do the same till lightly browned.

5. Butter it, and roll it up. Enjoy with *lutefisk,* meatballs, or just as is. (Some like to sprinkle sugar over the butter.)

NOTE: The surface you bake this on will determine the time it takes to lightly brown. A wood stove will take less time than the grill. Use common sense.

FISKEKAKER
(FISH BALLS)

The amount of fish you wish to make

The bones and skin (remove scales)

Salt and pepper to taste (depending on amount of fish)

Dash of ground nutmeg

Enough cream to make the right consistency for balls

Enough butter to fry balls

1. Fillet the fish (any type), remove the scales, and save the bones and skin. Boil the bones and skin in a small amount of water. Discard the bones and skin, save the liquid, and strain it.

2. Grind the fillets very fine. Season with salt, pepper, and nutmeg. Mash well with a wooden potato masher, adding a little sweet cream at a time while beating, until the mixture is the right consistency to form into balls the size of a pullet egg. (You can use an electric mixer.)

3. Boil the balls 20 minutes in the liquid from the bones and skin. Then remove them from the kettle, and fry in a fry pan in butter until brown. Make a medium-thick cream sauce (page 73), pour it over the fish balls, and serve.

POTET PØLSA
(POTATO SAUSAGE)

MAKES 2 (1-POUND) RINGS

6 raw potatoes

1 medium onion

2 1/2 pounds ground pork sausage

1/2 pound ground beef

1 teaspoon ground ginger

1 teaspoon pepper

4 tablespoons salt

1 cup scalded milk

2 (1-pound) casings

1. Grind the potatoes and the onion, and mix them with the ground meat. Add the ginger, pepper, salt, and milk, and mix thoroughly.

2. Stuff the mixture into the casings (as for Home-Ground Bologna, page 54) but not too tightly; allow space for expansion, so they won't break while cooking (see Note). Make this the size of a ring of bologna, and tie the ends together.

3. Cook slowly for 1 hour in a large kettle of water. When done, remove from the water, slice into 3-inch pieces, and serve while hot.

NOTE: If you're unfamiliar with stuffing casings, look at the recipe for Home-Ground Bologna.

POTET KLUB
(POTATO DUMPLINGS)

MAKES ABOUT 18 DUMPLINGS

1 *ham shank*

4 *raw potatoes*

2 *boiled potatoes*

1 *cup whole wheat flour or graham flour*

1 *cup white flour*

1/4 *teaspoon baking powder*

Salt and pepper

1. Boil the shank until done (when the meat loosens from the bone). Remove it from the liquid, and let cool. Save the liquid.

2. Remove the meat and some of the fatty part from the bone and put it through a grinder with the potatoes. Add the flours, baking powder, and salt and pepper, making sure there's enough flour to make a stiff dough.

3. Using your hands, roll into dumplings, drop into the ham liquid, and cook at a slow boil until done (about 1 hour). Serve the dumplings with butter on top.

POTET KAGE
(POTATO PANCAKES)

MAKES ABOUT 6 LARGE CAKES

6 *large raw potatoes*

1 *tablespoon minced onion*

3 *eggs, unbeaten*

6 *tablespoons flour*

2 *teaspoons salt*

Dash of pepper

3 *tablespoons shortening (Butter Flavor Crisco is best for these)*

1. Peel and grate the potatoes very fine, and put into a large bowl.

2. Add the onion, eggs, flour, salt, and pepper and mix real well.

3. Melt the shortening in a large cast-iron skillet. Drop the potato mixture by large serving spoonfuls into the skillet, and spread the batter out with the back of the spoon to make a large cake.

4. Brown, then turn over with a large pancake turner, and brown the other side. Serve with butter on top. (Some like butter and homemade syrup, or peach syrup, page 82).

COTTAGE CHEESE

❈

Years ago we made our own cottage cheese, *gamle ost,* and *primost.* However, it is no longer considered safe and healthful to do it this way today. So while I've included our precious, old-time methods here for your interest, you should by no means proceed this way these days, but instead contact your county extension office for the updated procedure.

3 CUPS OF MILK SHOULD YIELD 2½ CUPS COTTAGE CHEESE

As much fresh cow's milk as you want to use, or the buttermilk that is left after churning cream for butter (see Note)

Salt and pepper to taste

Caraway seed (or not)

A little cream (or not)

1. Place a pan of water under a kettle of milk, place it on a burner on low, and let it set until soured (a couple of hours). (You cannot use store-bought sour milk for this, but you can sour fresh cow's milk faster by adding 1 tablespoon of vinegar to 1 quart of milk.) The temperature of the heated milk should be about 98° F for good cottage cheese. If too warm, the curds get stiff and tough.

2. When the milk has curdled, put it into either a cheesecloth bag or a strainer, and let the whey drip off. When the whey has stopped dripping, put the dry cheese curds into a bowl or crock. Season with salt and pepper to taste. Caraway seed may also be added if desired.

3. Cool and eat, or store in a covered container in the refrigerator.

GAMLE OST: Use the Cottage Cheese recipe, but put the dry curds into a crock, season it with salt and pepper, and let it set out in room temperature until it gets old and sticky and stinks like the dickens. (Note: When making your own cottage cheese, *gamle ost,* or *primost* today, do not follow these methods, but contact your county extension office.) Be sure you keep the cover on tightly at all times. This tastes a lot better than it smells. The minister and his wife I worked for had to have this for breakfast. She called it *"apateet ost"* (appetite cheese). If you like limburger cheese, you'll like this. Usually what happens is one or two people in a family like it and the others can't stand it. There was one woman up the road who loved the stuff, but no one else in the house did. She'd try to hide it in her lap under her apron when she sat at the table, but it rarely happened one of the young ones didn't smell it. As soon as they came in the room they'd say, "Oh, Ma, now you got it again!"

PRIMOST: Use the whey that is left after you take the curds for Gamle Ost. Add a little sugar and boil and boil and boil until it is thick. Remove from heat, and put in a dish or jar and eat it soft. (Don't worry, this turns brown when you are boiling it down.) If this stands too long in the air (a week or so) and gets hard, put it in a kettle, add a little cream to it, and stir it over low heat so it melts and gets runny again.

BRØM
(BROWN CHEESE)

MAKES ABOUT 1 QUART

2 quarts buttermilk

4 tablespoons flour

1/2 cup packed brown sugar

1. In a heavy saucepan, cook the buttermilk over medium heat until it begins to curdle. Then add the flour slowly to thicken it, stirring constantly.

2. Add the brown sugar, and cook until as brown and as thick as peanut butter. Stir once in a while. Put it into a dish or a jar to keep it soft. (This is much like Primost.) Store in the refrigerator.

ROMMEGRØT

Dis takes a lot of milking if yur making a few batches. Ve had a cow wid tree long teats and vun short vun. Ve used our full hand for da long vuns and tew fingers for da short vun. By golly, ve pulled so hard she vas almost a tree titter.

MAKES A 2-QUART DISH

1 quart thick cream

1 1/4 cups flour

1 pint milk

1 cup sugar

1 tablespoon ground cinnamon

1. Pour the cream into a heavy saucepan, and heat until it starts to boil. Then sift in 3/4 cup of the flour as you whip with a wire whisk.

2. Keep beating after the 3/4 cup of flour is all in, until the butter starts to come out of the cream. Then remove from the heat. The butter should continue to seep out of this mixture. Take a ladle and take off the butter, and put it in another bowl. Keep stirring once in a while until all of the butter comes out.

3. Put the milk in another kettle, and heat to boiling.

4. Sift 1/2 cup of the flour into the milk while beating. Continue beating until thick like pudding. Remove it from the heat, add it to the cream mixture, and beat with a wire whisk until smooth and well blended.

5. Pour into a 2-quart baking dish. Smooth out the top with a licker, and sprinkle the sugar and cinnamon on top. Then pour the butter you saved onto the top. Serve warm. (Just a little goes a long way.)

GRANDMA'S RISK RISINGRØT

When I was a little girl, this was made only as Christmas Eve's dessert. It was prepared in the afternoon and took at least two hours (but of course the batch was several times larger than the one here). When Grandma made this, I had to go out to the barn after dinner and milk the cow that gave the richest milk. I'd trudge in with the pail, then she would pour out the amount needed, and start her *grøt*. No matter how much anyone ate, there was always a little room left for this rich, creamy rice and raisin pudding that set in a huge bowl in the center of the table. The recipe has been handed down from generation to generation, yet I'm the only one in my generation to know the exact contents, so I'm glad to share it with you.

SERVES ABOUT 20

1 quart and 1 cup whole milk

1 pint half-and-half

1 pint whipping cream

1/2 cup raisins

4 cups water

1 cup rice

1/2 teaspoon and later 1 more teaspoon salt

1/2 cup flour

1/4 cup sugar

1. In a heavy 3-quart kettle, combine 1 quart milk, the half-and-half, and cream, and place on medium heat.

2. In a separate kettle, cook the raisins in 1 cup of the water until plump.

3. In yet another kettle, cook the rice in 3 cups of the water and 1/2 teaspoon salt until tender. Drain both the rice and the raisins and set aside.

4. Stir the milk and cream mixture slowly but constantly with the rounded tip of a wooden spoon (be sure to stir the bottom). When the milk is showing signs of steam, add the rice. Continue heating and stirring until just to the point of boiling.

5. In a small bowl, combine the flour, 1 cup of milk, and 1 teaspoon of salt, and mix well. Add this thickening to the milk and cream mixture, and keep stirring until it shows signs of thickening. Add the raisins and the sugar. Remove it from the heat, and serve either lukewarm or cold. *Gladlig Jul.*

SØDT SUPPE (SWEET SOUP)

This is a sweet soup, so you can add different juices and experiment with different brandies and wines until it suits your taste. I like to use J. Bavet Brandy, because it's mellow. Ven making da Sødt Suppe-a yoy to make-wid da spoon in vun hand and da boddle in da udder vun. A liddle for da suppe and a liddle for me. A liddle more for da suppe, a liddle bit more for me. Aw, to heck wid da suppe.

SERVES ABOUT 20

1 cup large pearl tapioca or Sago

1 1/2 quarts water

1 cup prunes

1 cup raisins

1 stick cinnamon

About 1 cup each of pineapple juice, grape juice, cranberry juice, and apple juice

Sugar to taste (about 1 cup)

About 1/4 cup brandy

About 1/2 cup wine (whatever you have on hand)

1. Cook the tapioca in the water until almost transparent. (I call them fish eyes, but they are good.)

2. In a large pot, cook the prunes, raisins, and cinnamon stick in water enough to cover until fruit is soft.

3. Add the tapioca and cooked fruit with the juices and the sugar. Then top it off with a little brandy and the wine.

KNAECKEBRØD (NORWEGIAN HARD TACK)

MAKES ABOUT 2 DOZEN

3 cups potato water

3 ounces caked yeast and 1 teaspoon sugar dissolved in 1/4 cup lukewarm water

4 cups flour (approximately)

1 cup shortening, melted (see Note)

1/2 cup sweet cream

1 egg yolk

1 tablespoon salt

Enough cornmeal to roll balls (about 1 cup)

1. In a large mixing bowl, combine the potato water, yeast mixture, and about 2 cups of the flour to make a soft sponge. Throw a cloth over the bowl and let raise overnight at room temperature.

2. The next morning, add the shortening, cream, egg yolk, salt, and enough flour to make a soft dough (about 2 cups).

3. Knead down, and let raise.

4. Make into balls the size of a whole unshelled walnut, and let raise again 1 1/2 to 2 hours.

5. Preheat the oven to 375° F. Roll each ball as thin as possible in the cornmeal, using a corrugated or *lefse* rolling pin. Roll until about the size of a pie plate. Place on a cookie sheet, and bake about 15 minutes, until brown on both sides, turning often.

NOTE: I use Butter Flavor Crisco for this.

OLD HOME TENDER FLATBRØD

**MAKES ABOUT 20
(16-INCH ROUND) PIECES**

2 cups Quaker oats

1/4 cup sugar

1 teaspoon baking soda

1/2 teaspoon salt

3/4 cup melted butter

1 1/2 cups buttermilk

*2 1/2 cups flour (or 1/2 cup more if necessary
    for rolling; see Note)*

1. Preheat the oven to 350° F. Mix the oats, sugar, baking soda, and salt together in a large bowl. Add the melted butter, and mix.

2. Add the buttermilk and the flour. (You may need another 1/2 cup of flour for rolling.)

3. Take up dough about the size of an egg, and roll it out very thin (paper-thin) using a grooved rolling pin.

4. Bake on an ungreased cookie sheet for about 10 minutes, until firm and slightly browned.

NOTE: For a sharper *flatbrød,* do as I often do. Replace 1 cup of flour with 1 cup of whole wheat flour. It gets a little darker.

JULEKAKE

This is a pretty fruit bread we always served at Ladies' Aid at Christmastime.

MAKES 2 LOAVES

2 cups milk

1 cup butter

1 cup sugar

1 teaspoon salt

1 cup raisins

3 ounces caked yeast

2 tablespoons sugar

1/4 cup warm water

6 cups flour

1 cup citron (if desired)

1 teaspoon ground cardamom

1. In a heavy large saucepan, heat the milk, and mix in the butter, 1 cup of sugar, the salt, and raisins. Set aside and cool to lukewarm.

2. Dissolve the yeast and 2 tablespoons of sugar in 1/4 cup warm (but not hot) water; add to the cooled milk when the yeast is foamy.

3. Add the flour, citron (if desired), and cardamom now. Knead slightly, and let raise about 1 hour, until light and almost double in size.

4. Divide the dough into 2 loaves, and put it into the buttered loaf pans, or make round loaves and put them into buttered pie tins. Preheat the oven to 350° F. Let raise again until almost double in size, then bake 30 to 45 minutes, until almost double in size.

KRISTIANA KRINGLE

This is a sweet, light, flaky treat, almost like pie crust. Another delight that melts in your mouth.

MAKES 2 KRINGLES
(EACH SLICED INTO 12 PIECES)

CRUST

1 cup flour

1/2 scant cup butter

1/4 teaspoon salt

3 tablespoons cold water

TOP

1 cup water

1/2 cup butter

1 cup flour

Dash of salt

3 eggs

1/2 teaspoon almond extract

Enough Basic Powdered Sugar Frosting (page 193) with a few drops of almond extract mixed in to drizzle over

1. *To prepare the crust:* Preheat the oven to 375° F. Combine the flour, butter, and salt together in a bowl, and mix, using your fingers, as you would pie crust. Add the cold water, and mix together, using your fingers.

2. Form the dough into 2 long strips about 3 inches wide, place them on a cookie sheet, and set aside.

3. *To prepare the top:* In a medium kettle, combine the water and butter. Let it come to a boil, and remove from heat.

4. Add the flour and salt, stirring quickly with a kitchen fork until smooth.

5. Add the eggs one at a time, beating well after each, using a wooden spoon.

6. Add the almond extract, mix, and spread it over the two strips of crust. Lay it on thick.

7. Bake for 45 minutes. They will be high when removed from the oven, but they will fall; that's okay. Drizzle a little Basic Powdered Sugar Frosting over when slightly cool. Cut horizontally into 2-inch strips. Eat while fresh.

JULETIDE CRANBERRY BREAD

MAKES 1 LOAF

2 cups flour

1 cup sugar

½ teaspoon baking powder

½ teaspoon baking soda

1 teaspoon salt

1 cup cranberries, sliced in half

1 cup chopped nuts

Juice and grated rind of 2 oranges

2 tablespoons shortening

½ cup boiling water

1 egg, beaten

1. Preheat the oven to 350° F. Sift the flour, sugar, baking powder, baking soda, and salt together. Add the cranberries and the nuts.

2. Combine the juice, rind, shortening, and water. Add the egg to the juice, and blend into the cranberry mixture.

3. Pour into a buttered loaf pan, and bake 1 hour, until a toothpick comes out dry.

SANDBAKKELS (SAND TARTS)

These are delightful, tasty little butter cups that resemble tart shells, but they are very fragile. They melt in your mouth.

MAKES ABOUT 96

2 cups butter

1½ cups sugar

2 eggs

1 teaspoon vanilla extract

5 cups flour (approximately)

Dash of salt

1. Preheat the oven to 350° F. Mix the butter and sugar together well in a large bowl. Add the eggs and vanilla, and mix.

2. Add the flour and salt, and mix well, using your fingers. (I usually don't put more than 5 cups of flour in to start with, then I add more if needed, but don't exceed 6 cups.)

3. Press thinly into *bakkel* tins, place the tins on cookie sheets, and bake for 25 to 30 minutes, until golden brown.

LILLIHAMAR CREAM MELTS

MAKES ABOUT 90 COOKIES

3¾ cups flour

½ cup plus 2 tablespoons sour cream

2 cups butter

Basic Powdered Sugar Frosting (page 193), or not

1. Preheat oven to 375°F.

2. In a large bowl mix together all the ingredients real good, and chill.

3. Roll out the dough to ⅛ inch thick and cut with a doughnut cutter (see Note).

4. Bake until light brown, about 12 minutes.

5. Cool and frost with Powdered Sugar Frosting, if desired, and decorate as you like as wreaths for Christmas.

NOTE: For a chewier cookie, roll the dough to ¼ inch thick.

ROSETTES

These are dainty, fragile, sugared stars or wheels made from a very light and thin deep-fried batter. You will need a rosette iron for these (page 262).

MAKES ABOUT 40

2 eggs

2 teaspoons sugar

¼ teaspoon salt

1 cup milk

1 cup flour

    Enough peanut oil to fill a heavy 3-quart kettle three-quarters full

1 cup sugar

1. Beat the eggs slightly with 2 teaspoons of sugar and the salt. (I use a hand egg beater.)

2. Add the milk and the flour, and beat until smooth.

3. Heat the oil in a heavy 3-quart kettle until a dry crust of bread, when dropped in, turns brown (see Note).

4. Heat the rosette iron in the oil for a few minutes, then remove, shake off the excess grease, and dip the iron in the batter (but do not let the batter cover the top of the iron).

5. Dip the iron in hot oil (submerge the iron completely) and cook until a light golden brown. Remove from the oil, shake off the excess grease, and carefully loosen the rosette from the iron, using a fork or a very thin dishcloth. Remove from the iron, and lay on paper toweling.

6. Put the 1 cup sugar in a shallow bowl, and when the rosette has cooled, dip it in the sugar. (You can color the sugar for the season, or not.)

NOTE: Rosettes are tricky, and if you haven't made them before, you'll have to experiment with the temperature of your grease and the thickness of your batter. If the batter is too thin (or the grease too hot), it'll fall away from the iron when dipped in. If the batter's too thick, the rosettes aren't as good. If your grease is too hot, the outside of the rosette will fry too fast, and the middle will be soggy. If the grease isn't hot enough, the whole rosette'll be soggy.

A deep-fryer can also be used here.

FATTIGMAND
(POOR-MAN'S CAKE)

A fun thing we did during the holidays was Julebukking (Christmas Fooling). We would dress up crazy with some kind of mask over our faces so no one would recognize us; we'd go from farm to farm at night after chores when it was pitch dark. We'd leave the car down the road and walk the long driveways to the houses. Usually wine with *fattigmand* was served to try to get us to unmask, then we'd all have a laugh and try to convince our hosts and hostesses to join in and go along on to the next place. It could get to be kind of a merry affair.

MAKES ABOUT 75, DEPENDING ON HOW BIG YOU CUT THEM

4 eggs

4 tablespoons sugar

4 tablespoons cream

Pinch of salt

Enough flour to make a stiff dough

Enough oil to fill a heavy frying pan three-quarters full

Sugar for sprinkling

1. Whip the eggs until mixed, stir in 4 tablespoons of sugar, the cream, and salt, and mix well.

2. Add enough flour to make a stiff dough.

3. Roll out thin and cut into 3 × 5-inch triangles or diamond shapes with a slit in the middle of each. Heat the oil in a heavy frying pan. Fry these in the hot oil until light brown on each side. (Turn with 2 forks.) Watch closely because they brown fast.

4. Remove from the oil, and lay out on a paper towel. When cool, if you like, sprinkle a little sugar over the top.

5. Store in airtight containers.

KRUMKAKA

A lot of people mistakenly call *krumkaka, goro,* but it's entirely different. *Goro* is flat and thin, with a lacy design. *Krumkaka* is thin and fragile, too, but is rolled up like a hollow cigar. One Christmas I spent a whole day making *krumkaka* and I stored it in tins for weeks in a bedroom upstairs. Coming down the stairs, I tripped, and broke every one all to pieces. I cried.

This is a large batch so it will take a while, but it's worth it. You'll need a *krumkaka* iron (page 262). I use my greatgrandma's iron. These days they have electric, but this recipe will work for both, so just forget the stove if you're using an electric iron. But when eating *krumkaka,* handle with care or it'll break all to pieces before you even have a chance to eat it.

MAKES ABOUT 50 TO 60

½ cup (1 stick) butter

1 cup sugar

2 eggs

1 cup milk

1½ cups flour

1 teaspoon vanilla extract

1. In a bowl, cream the butter and sugar together, add the eggs, and mix, using a wooden spoon.

2. Add the milk, flour, and vanilla, and mix well.

3. Heat the *krumkaka* iron on medium heat on the stove until hot, then put a teaspoon of batter on the bottom iron and press the top and bottom iron together. When brown on one side, turn over and brown again. Remove from the iron and roll up around a stick or a cone-shaped piece of wood. Remove, and repeat with the next one.

SPRITS

During the days of Christmas, kids would sneak and fill up so full on cookies and baking like this, they never wanted to eat their meals, so we used to tell 'em they'd soon get so weak when a good wind came it'd blow 'em right on out to North Dakota. (North Dakota used to seem like a long ways off back then.) In fact, there's a joke—Scandinavians love to tell "Ole and Lena jokes," the restaurant hums with them—anyway, this one goes something like this: Ole and Lena had their wedding, and on their honeymoon trip, they were almost to Minneapolis when Ole put his hand on Lena's knee. Lena giggled, and said, "Ole, you can go farther if you vant to." So Ole drove all the way to North Dakota.

MAKES ABOUT 60

$1/2$ pound (2 sticks) butter

$2/3$ cup sugar

3 egg yolks

$2 1/2$ cups flour

1 teaspoon almond extract

1 teaspoon vanilla extract

1. Preheat the oven to 350° F. Cream the butter and the sugar together in a medium bowl.

2. Add the egg yolks, and mix.

3. Add the flour and almond and vanilla extracts.

4. Mix, and press the dough through a cookie press onto a cookie sheet (see Note). Bake about 10 minutes, until lightly brown.

5. Store in an airtight container.

NOTE: For this recipe you will need a cookie press.

These are so small you can put about 4 in your mouth at once. You can make different designs, or whatever comes with your press.

KRANSERKAKER (WREATH PASTRY)

MAKES 3 TO 4 DOZEN

2 hard-cooked egg yolks, mashed

2 raw egg yolks

1/2 pound (2 sticks) butter (must be room temperature)

1/2 cup sugar

3 1/2 cups flour

2 egg whites, slightly beaten

Crushed sugar lumps (see Note)

Crushed nutmeats (or not)

1. Preheat the oven to 350° F. Combine the mashed egg yolks and the raw yolks in a large bowl. Add the butter and sugar, and mix real well, using a wooden spoon.

2. Add the flour, and mix, using your hands (it will be quite firm).

3. Take a teaspoonful of dough, and roll it in your hands to form a narrow roll about 4 inches long, then form it into a circle like a wreath.

4. Dip the top in slightly beaten egg whites, then into the crushed sugar. Scatter the nutmeats on top if you like.

5. Place on cookie sheets, and bake for 15 minutes, until light brown. Store in tightly covered containers when cool.

NOTE: To crush sugar lumps, place between 2 pieces of stiff paper or cloth, and pound with a hammer. Regular sugar sprinkled over will not work; it's so fine it disappears.

KRINGLA (SWEDISH TEA CAKES)

FOR MEDIUM OR SMALL TINS

1/3 cup butter

1/4 cup sugar

1 cup flour

PASTE

1/3 cup chopped almonds

1/4 cup sugar

2 tablespoons butter

1 1/2 tablespoons sweet cream

2 tablespoons flour

1. Preheat the oven to 350° F. Cream the butter and sugar together in a medium bowl.

2. Add the flour, and mix.

3. Press into *sandbakkel* tins and partially bake, about 15 minutes.

4. Mix the paste ingredients together, and cook over low heat, stirring constantly until it boils.

5. Remove from heat and set in a pan of hot water to keep it from getting hard.

6. Put a small amount of this mixture into each partially baked *sandbakkel*, then return the *bakkels* to the oven, and bake about 10 minutes more, until light brown.

HOME-RENDERED LARD

1 pig skin with the fat left on

1. When butchering a pig, slice off the fat with the skin.

2. Put the skin in a roasting pan in a 325° F oven until the fat melts and the skin gets crisp and crunchy. This is called krot (perfect for Krot Cookies, page 203).

3. If not butchering, go to a good meat market or a locker plant and ask for a fatted pig skin. (Nowadays, they may have ground fat that will render more quickly. Put this in the oven and when the fat melts, little balls, krot, will remain.)

4. Place the melted fat in clean metal containers. You have lard when it hardens.

HOMEMADE SOAP

This is the way we made soap years ago; it really gets the clothes clean. It's also good for pots and pans and dishes. It's especially good for soaking overused feet.

> *10 cups hot water*
> *9 cups melted fat or drippings, strained*
> *1/2 cup ammonia*
> *3 tablespoons borax*
> *1 (12-ounce) can lye (see Note)*

1. Pour the hot water, fat, and ammonia into a large earthenware crock, and then add the borax.

2. Sprinkle the lye on top, and stir slowly, using a wooden broom handle. After 20 minutes, the mixture will be like whipped cream.

3. Line wooden boxes (peach crates are good if not slatted) with cloth, and pour in the soap. When firm, cut into bars.

NOTE: Always be careful and follow the manufacturer's instructions when handling hazardous materials.

GOOD KITCHEN TOOLS

TOOLS

and

MAIL-ORDER PRODUCTS

There's an old saying on the farm, "You can't hoe with a stick, so take care of your blessings." It's sad how in these hard times when people get weary and money is short, you see machines broken down and even patched together with baling wire. But for the most part, farmers have always taken pride in their tools and the old names they can trust. The same is true in the kitchen. Oh, on some things you don't have to be so fussy—and when it is possible to improvise I say so. But I found through the years that it's best to scrimp and save and buy quality rather than quantity: Who wants a kitchen full of junk?

For quite some time, I've been getting calls and letters from people wanting to know what products I use, and the truth is that a lot of what I use, because it was good to start with, has lasted long enough to be outdated—or it's unavailable in certain areas—so I've gone about trying different products and I've come up with the following thoughts:

• *Cast-Iron Skillets:* I always reach first for cast-iron skillets. There are some very fine old ones around here you can pick up cheap at thrift sales and farm auctions, but if you're in the city and would like something a little fancier and can afford it, Le Creuset makes a beautiful, complete line of very sturdy, prime-quality cast-iron cookware. Also, not to be forgotten, General House Wares Corp. makes Wagner's 1891 Original Cast Iron, good old-fashioned cast-iron pans in three sizes (but you must remember to season them properly).

• *Stainless Steel:* I swear by stainless steel kettles and bowls. And I wouldn't have anything but stainless measuring cups and spoons. In fact, I like just about any tool that's a good-quality stainless. But as far as cookware, Magnilite Professional Stainless has a first-rate product with a hundred-year warranty; Revere/Corning, these two old reliable companies that are together now, also makes a gem of a set in Revere-Pro Line that has a lifetime warranty. Cuisinart Professional Stainless Steel is also top-notch. It's absolutely beautiful both in performance and to look at.

• *Ovenware:* Revere Ware has beautiful, high-quality stainless steel roasters, cookie sheets, cake and pie pans, and loaf tins. Kaiser Bakeware also makes a wonderful product in heavy-gauge aluminum.

• *Pressure Cookers:* I've been using Presto for years. The company's home base is just twenty miles up the road here. Innova makes a product that is also very good, although usually a bit more expensive.

• *Mixers:* KitchenAid has been my choice in the restaurant, hands down. I love that machine. But if you're not in the kitchen as much as I am, and don't want to make the investment, Bosch has a very good Universal mixer that is lightweight yet can handle large batches of dough, and Hamilton Beach you can always count on.

• *Blenders:* You can't beat the old trusted names of Waring and Hamilton Beach.

• *Meat Grinders and Food Processors:* The old-fashioned metal meat grinders you can sometimes find at thrift sales or auctions, but if you're city folks, White Mountain still makes a real good metal hand grinder. If you're a little lazy and like things electric, Cuisinart is king for food processing and grinding, even juicing. Also, KitchenAid and Bosch both have excellent slicing, shredding, meat-grinder, and sausage-stuffer attachments. And Hamilton Beach makes a Deluxe Meat Grinder and stuffer that would have made my grandmother dance.

• *Knives:* There's no better friend in the kitchen than a good sharp knife—especially one made of high-carbon steel. In fact, J. A. Henckels Zwillingswerk, Inc., and Wüsthof Trident both make knives that are so good they can change your life in the kitchen. Gerber Legendary Blades also makes a beautiful and very fine set right here in Wisconsin. They also make very good scissors under the name Fiskars. Chicago Cutlery, The Walnut Tradition can't be forgotten either; they make a gem of a knife (sets as well) that will last you many, many years.

• *Ice Cream Makers:* There are a lot of them out there now, but this is what I think: If you want quick and easy, and a small quantity, Donvier

has revolutionized ice cream making with a terrific, high-quality, little-effort, hand-crank freezer that requires neither ice nor salt, and it's easy enough for kids to use. If you want the old-time feeling—either just for your family or if you're feeding the whole valley—White Mountain makes a variety of machines and has made a lot of effort to keep with tradition. I like their electric because it doesn't make your arms fall off, but if you want to do as we used to, they also make a high-quality, hand-crank freezer. Salton is also a good modern-day choice.

• *Toasters:* It used to be a shame to have to slice plump fresh loaves of homemade bread thin enough to fit in a toaster and then have to go fishing with a fork for the pieces that didn't pop up. But no more. Today there're many good, new, wide-slot machines: Proctor-Silex and Bosch are my choices. (Proctor-Silex's toaster/oven broiler is also wonderful for this as well as broiling.)

• *Electric Roasters:* These are great for the roasts and gravies in this book. Both Hamilton Beach and Nesco (a dandy which is made right here in Wisconsin) will do a job that makes your mouth water.

• *Scandinavian Necessities:* See the mail-order list on page 262.

Mail-Order

Names and Addresses

If you have no *krumkaka* iron, rosette iron, *lefse* rolling pin, stick, or grill, or no *sandbakkel* tins, send away for a Maid of Scandinavia catalog to Maid of Scandinavia, 3244 Raleigh Avenue, Minneapolis, MN 55416. (Also Vitantanio makes a real nice *krumkaka* iron that's available in a lot of good department stores, as well as from the Maid of Scandinavia catalog.)

• For White Mountain products (ice-cream maker, meat grinder, and cherry pitter), write White Mountain, P.O. Box 459, Winchenden, MA 01475.

• If you're interested in prize-winning smoked meats, stop by or write Pat's Country Meat Market, Intersection of Highways 93 and 95, Arcadia, WI 54612. UPS shipping is available. For a catalog, order, or information: Call 608-323-2131 (Fax 608-323-7314). (Fresh meat shipped with dry ice by special-order only.)

• Falls Meat Service is another good, though smaller, butcher shop that readers might be interested in: Box 37, Pigeon Falls, WI 54760. Call: 715-983-2211.

• Hasty-Bake is the smoker I recommended in the section on meats and bolognas that will smoke your homemade sausages for you. Write: Box 471285, Tulsa, OK 74147-1285. Call 1-800-4ANOVEN. This company also has an all-natural hickory charcoal with that old flavor that's hard to find.

INDEX